MEN'S STORIES FOR A CHANGE

Ageing Men Remember

The Older Men's Memory Work Group:
Randy Barber, Vic Blake, Jeff Hearn, David Jackson,
Richard Johnson, Zbyszek Luczynski, and Dan McEwan

MEN'S STORIES FOR A CHANGE

Ageing Men Remember

The Older Men's Memory Work Group:
Randy Barber, Vic Blake, Jeff Hearn, David Jackson,
Richard Johnson, Zbyszek Luczynski, and Dan McEwan

COMMON GROUND PUBLISHING 2016

First published in 2016
as part of the Aging & Society Book Imprint

Common Ground Publishing
2001 S. 1st St., Suite 202
University of Illinois Research Park
Champaign, IL
61821

Copyright © Randy Barber, Vic Blake, Jeff Hearn, David Jackson,
Richard Johnson, Zbyszek Luczynski, and Dan McEwan 2016

All rights reserved. Apart from fair dealing for the purposes of study, research, criticism or review as permitted under the applicable copyright legislation, no part of this book may be reproduced by any process without written permission from the publisher.

Library of Congress Cataloging-in-Publication Data

Names: Barber, Randy, 1949- author.
Title: Men's stories for a change : ageing men remember / The Older Men's
 Memory Work Group: Randy Barber, Vic Blake, Jeff Hearn, David Jackson,
 Richard Johnson, Zbyszek Luczynski, and Dan McEwan.
Description: Champaign, IL : Common Ground Publishing, 2016. | Includes
 bibliographical references and index.
Identifiers: LCCN 2016008172 (print) | LCCN 2016018120 (ebook) | ISBN
 9781612298580 (hbk : alk. paper) | ISBN 9781612298597 (pbk : alk. paper) |
 ISBN 9781612298603 (pdf)
Subjects: LCSH: Older men--Attitudes. | Aging. | Interpersonal relations. |
 Older men--Health and hygiene.
Classification: LCC HQ1090 .B37 2016 (print) | LCC HQ1090 (ebook) | DDC
 305.26/1--dc23
LC record available at https://lccn.loc.gov/2016008172

Cover Photo Credit: Phillip Kalantzis-Cope

Table of Contents

About the Authors ... xiv
Acknowledgements ... xvii
Introduction ... xviii
    Who We Are and Why We Are Doing This ... xviii
    How the Group Started ... xx
    How the Group Developed ... xxi
    What is Memory Work? ... xxii
    Method and the Process ... xxiv
    Where Does Our Work Fit? ... xxvii
    Finally… ... xxix
    References ... xxx

The Stories

Chapter 1
Ageing   1
    Vic Blake
    Introduction ... 1
    Going Underground ... 3
    Lots of Losses ... 4
    Remembering Grandfather ... 5
    Nan's Bible ... 6
    Growing Older and, Hopefully, A Little Wiser ... 7
    Edgeworthia Chrysantha ... 8

Chapter 2
Hair   10
    David Jackson
    Introduction ... 10
    An Hairy Man—Or Not ... 13
    My Hair, My Body, My Face ... 14

An Embarrassing Story 15
Changing My Hairstyle 15
The Fiftieth Birthday Party 16
I Want My Hair To Be Like a Breaking Wave 17
Pub(l)ic Inspections 19
The Vascectomy, A Very Intimate Haircut 20
Get Your Hair Cut 20
The Electric Shaver 21
Time to Get Smart 22
One Hairy Lovable Son 23

Chapter 3
Clothes   24
   Jeff Hearn
   Introduction 24
   Wearing Your Best 27
   Clothes—A Difficult History 28
   Men and Suits 29
   The Big Black Coat 30
   Stuck in the Drawer 31
   What Clothes? 33

Chapter 4
Peeing   35
   David Jackson
   Introduction 35
   Taking Drink Like a Man and the Problems of Holding On 37
   Peeing, Young and Old 38
   It was Now Called Weeing 39
   Pissing Myself 40
   Peeing in Solidarity 41
   Peeing ... and/in My Pants 42
   The Inconsistent Dribbling of My Penis 42
   The Medical Me 43
   A History of Embarrassing Pees 43
   Peeing Again—Ten Years On 45

Chapter 5
School and Schooling   46
Dan McEwan

Introduction 46
Meeting the Boy Again 47
The Strange Boy, Lucy 49
School Daze 49
Travelling through Girls and Boys 50
A Tingly Feeling 52
The Homeless House 53
First Time? 54
Playing Fair 56

Chapter 6
Disruptive Bodily Changes   58
Vic Blake

Introduction 58
A Nasty Accident 62
My Shoulder, My Back And My Stomach 63
Proud Legs and Thighs 64
Well-being 65

Chapter 7
Sport   67
Zbyszek Luczynski

Introduction 67
Sport (Especially Football) Viewed by an Entirely Non-sporty Man 68
Two Times When Sport Had a Major Impact on My Life 69
Two Sporting Incidents 71
Not the Sporting Hero 72
My Sporting Life 73

Chapter 8
Sisters   75
Zbyszek Luczynski

Introduction 75
Getting By 76

Heavy Action Down the Mine 77
Sisters, A Moment of Trust 77
Sentimental Stories 78
A Strong Bond and the Last Blood Tie 79
Big Sister... 80

Chapter 9
Food 82
Randy Barber

Introduction 82
The Most Dangerous Room in the House... 83
Scraps from the Table 84
Food: my life story.. 85
Food of Love My Mother Gave Me 86
On Food and Fads, A Very Emotive Subject..................................... 87
A Very Fast Cook 88
No Picnic... 90

Chapter 10
Intimacy with Men 91
Randy Barber

Introduction 91
My History of Challenging Relationships with Men........................... 92
Some Very Close Relationships... 93
The Challenge of Intimacy of Men and Men 95
Intimacy—Intimately told 96
Challenges, Intimacy, Men 97

Chapter 11
Love 99
Jeff Hearn

Introduction 99
Love: the Wrong Subject... 101
Love: A Ten-Thousand-Letter Word.. 102
"Is this love?" 104
Love in My Life: Homily 104
Loving Peter 105

Chapter 12
Saying Goodbye to Mothers   108
Dan McEwan
Introduction 108
Separating from My Mother 110
Always Saying Goodbye 111
Saying That Long Slow Goodbye to My Mother 112
Trusting Me 113
A Deep Sea Diver 113
Being with Mum, Not Being with Mum 115
I Never Said Goodbye Properly 116
Anger and Love 117

Chapter 13
Political Moments   119
Richard Johnson
Introduction 119
An Important Part of My Politicisation 122
Becoming a Socialist about Ten 125
Challenged to be Politically Active 126
'Doing Something about It' – Getting 'Political' Again Post-11 September 2001 127
A Political Awakening 129
Thanks J for That Slap! 129
Being Active Abroad 130

Chapter 14
Power   133
Richard Johnson
Introduction 133
Power—Not Always What It Seems 135
'Don't Funk It, Boy!' 137
Navigator Extraordinaire 139
Not the ARTIST? Father and Son Story (1959?) 140
Some Kinds of Power 141
The Sting (2007) 143

Chapter 15
Violence   144
Zbyszek Luczynski
Introduction 144
Hits.. 145
Not Totally Out-of-Control... 146
Violence, A Nasty Business.. 147
'She's Only Six'... 148
Learning Not to Counter Punch 149
My Experience of Violence 151
Violence at Some Remove.. 152

Chapter 16
Fathers and Fathering   154
Randy Barber
Introduction 154
Oedipus Vexed—A Fathering Story 155
Fathering: The Second Chance 156
Too Late To Be A Father?.. 158
A Father Story Becoming More Gentle.................................... 159
A World of Fathers 160
How Slowly the Heart Reveals Itself 161

Chapter 17
Work   164
Zbyszek Luczynski
Introduction 164
On the Subject of Domesticity.. 165
Disappearing in Part.. 167
Working Hard at Being a Man.. 168
'Retirement'... 170
On Work, Ageing and Me 172

Chapter 18
Sexuality and Relationships   174
Vic Blake
Introduction 174

Sexuality, Always a Complicated Subject 176
Wondering about Sex 177
Towards a Non-phallic Tenderness and Intimacy between Ageing
Husband and Wife.. 179
Loving Sex for Ever 180
How I Started and Hope to Continue.. 181
Masturbation 182
My Changing Sexuality 183

Chapter 19
Ending the Group 185
Am I Ageing? Am I Changing?.. 185
Reflections on My Time in the Group 186
Being "M" and Saying Goodbye 187

Chapter 20
Reflections: Opening Out on Ageing, Politics and Men 189
Vic Blake and David Jackson
Setting Our Work into a Background of Gender and Sexual Politics 190
Misconceptions about Ageing Men 192
Awakening to Gendered Differences.. 193
Developing an Awareness of Gender Equality and Respect 195
Developing an Awareness of Gender Equality and Respect for Women..... 195
Understanding the Past and Imagining   the
Future Differently.. 197
Critical Exposure and Political Change 199
References.. 204

About the Authors

Randy Barber is 69, Canadian by birth. He moved to Australia in 1972 and except for a two year break to travel and return briefly to his home town, Randy lived in that country until 2003. Since then he has been residing in the UK. As well as his obvious love of travel and new experiences, Randy has followed a varied work history as an agricultural economist, radio presenter and administrator, student union manager, bakery proprietor, and, most recently, massage and Bowen therapist and teacher. Semi-retired now, he devotes his spare time to hill walking, volunteer roles with Prostate Cancer UK and the Ramblers, reading, going to the cinema and, of course, participation in local men's groups.

Vic Blake was born in London soon after the end of the war. His family moved to Hertfordshire when he was 12 and after leaving his secondary modern school, aged fifteen, he worked in a number of unskilled and semi-skilled jobs which included a spell in the army. From his mid-twenties he taught sociology and then, twenty years later, he became a psychodynamic counsellor specialising in working with men. He was forced to retire in 1998 for health reasons but in his retirement he keeps up an active interest in research and writing on men and masculinity issues. He has contributed to a number of publications around this area, and is currently working on a book on the subject.

Jeff Hearn is originally from London, spent over 20 years in Bradford, Yorkshire, and since the late 1990s has lived in Finland. He became involved since the late 1970s in men's anti-sexist, profeminist politics, and critical studies on men and masculinities in research and publishing. He has recently become formally retired as a professor in Hanken School of Economics, Finland, meanwhile working part-time at Örebro University, Sweden, and University of Huddersfield, UK. He has published a lot, most recently, *Men of the World: Genders, Globalizations, Transnational Times* (2015), *Opening Up New Opportunities for Gender Equality Work* (2015), with Anna-Maija Lämsä and colleagues, and *Rethinking Transnational Men* (2013), co-edited with Marina Blagojević and Katherine Harrison. He is a co-founder of *profeministimiehet* (Profeminist men), an activist group in Finland.

About the Authors   xv

David Jackson is a retired, pensioner activist and writer. Born into a working-class family in 1940 he became fascinated by viewpoints from below. He taught as a Comprehensive, mixed ability, English teacher for almost 20 years. Later he became an educational anthologist often featuring marginalised voices. He has been involved in men and masculinity issues for about 30 years. His books include *Unmasking Masculinity: A Critical Autobiography* (1990) and, with Jonathan Salisbury, *Challenging Macho Values: Practical ways of Working with Adolescent Boy*s (1996). He has just published in 2016 the book *Exploring Aging Masculinities: The Body, Sexuality and Social Lives*. Over the last 15 years he has focused on ageing men's issues; and setting up ageing men's groups. He is particularly interested in investigating the lived, bodily experiences of socially vulnerable and disabled men of lesser power. For the last ten years, he has been a committee member of the Nottingham Pensioners' Action Group.

Richard Johnson taught history and cultural studies at the University of Birmingham from 1966 to 1993. After the death of his first wife and his father in 1992, he and his mother went to live in a complex household in Leicester where he remarried and worked at Nottingham Trent University till 2004. He helped set up postgraduate programmes in the Humanities Faculty influenced by his experience of the University of Birmingham Centre for Contemporary Cultural Studies (CCCS). This often involved resisting neo-liberal forms of management. Today he is interested in the political legacies of CCCS. These include forms of group organisation which challenge masculine and other hierarchies, and the splitting of theory and practice. He continues to hope that Left politics will be refigured by taking culture seriously. He is proud of both his children and step- children and delights in all the grandchildren.

Zbyszek Luczynski is a member of the Ageing Men's group based in the East Midlands UK, the father of two sons, and a second generation immigrant of Polish extraction. He has retired from being a local government officer, having spent 35 years in Community Development supporting community groups and participation. He has also been active in trade unionist politics and left of Labour campaigns, as well as profeminist political and male awareness groups.

Dan McEwan was brought up in a working-class Catholic family in Paisley, Scotland. His background, strong identification with intellectual work, and educational successes led him to study for the priesthood in Louvain in the 1960s, an exciting time both personally and politically. Partly because of its views of sexuality and his own doubts, he decided not to become a priest, left the church and got married. A man of deep loyalties, however, he kept close to his class, his family and to religion, becoming a Religious Education teacher in a progressive secondary school in Leicestershire. From there he applied for postgraduate study at the University of Birmingham Centre for Contemporary Cultural Studies (CCCS) and was involved in its research projects on education. He continued researching, writing and giving talks mainly on theological topics after retirement, but suffered from periodic ill-health, dying very suddenly in 2014. Our Ageing Men's group accompanied him, his wife, three children and family on a last adventure at the remembrance ceremony in a Quaker Meeting House. We miss him terribly, especially for his gentleness and his commitment to 'understanding'.

Acknowledgements

We especially acknowledge the written contributions of Jean-Pierre Boulé, David Morgan, Rob Pattman, and Linn Sandberg, and the presence of Harry Ferguson and Ray Marshall in the group. Jeff Hearn warmly thanks David Jackson and Brenda Mould for their friendly hospitality over many years, Sharon Wray for collaboration and encouragement, Ian Holk for managing the production and publishing of our text, and Zorana Antonijević for editorial advice. We also thank Common Ground and the anonymous review for having faith in our project.

Introduction

It's time to write about being ageing gendered men. What do older men make of the situation we find ourselves in? How do ageing men tell stories? How do men turn ourselves into and out of being men, and into and out of being manly?

WHO WE ARE AND WHY WE ARE DOING THIS

This book results from our long-term memory work group of older men. For thirteen years we have met twice a year to focus on our memories of age and ageing, gender and gendering, along with other social divisions and experiences. Drawing on our own memories and dialogues, or perhaps more accurately 'polylogues', we have been especially interested in exploring, individually but mainly collectively, the gendered ageing of men or, if you prefer, the aged gendering of men.

The first meeting was in April 2002 when seven of us gathered, and the group continued to meet about twice a year until February 2015, meeting altogether on 26 occasions. Though we didn't all know each other beforehand, everyone knew at least one other member. We came together specifically to do reflective memory work on ageing, gender, men and masculinity. We have written the memories and this book for one another and for others interested in the construction of older men in terms of age and gender. In doing this, we aim to recognise how we are located in the gender order and how our masculine subjectivities have been constructed, as well as the impact of wider social conditions and social divisions.

We have a shared agenda in seeing the personal as political, and developing ways of writing, thinking and doing that are more than just telling stories. We are interested in how we became the men we are, but not simply as a personal issue, but as a more general political project of change to a more equal and just society.

Inevitably we have had diverse histories, before meeting in the group, but we share in all being older men, ranging in age from 43 to 62 at the start of the group, and from 68 to 76 by the end of the group. Several of us have significant health problems or disabilities, and our ageing bodies have been an increasingly prominent theme in our meetings and writings.

Our own individual histories also need to be placed into a broader and historical canvas. All of us grew up in the 1940s, 1950s and 1960s, and, as such, we have been influenced by what may seem to some rather far-off times. The experience of (the Second World) wartime, with its social disruptions, its class, gender and ethnic mixing, and of course the violence, loss and trauma, certainly affected our upbringing, for some in very direct ways, for others indirectly through our parents, families and neighbours. Growing up in the Second World War the 1940s was traumatic for many, with childhood experiences of ghostly appearances and sudden disappearances, as well as the enforced encountering of strangers. Post-war austerity (Kynaston, 2007) and the return of women to the nuclear family (Riley, 1983) were familiar for some of us in childhood, sometimes along with adults' own memories of lost family and friends. All this was complicated by the coming end of Empire, the founding of the welfare state, economic rebuilding, and various migrations and resettlements.

This combination of major socio-economic changes provided the backcloth for opportunities for us, as boys and young men, in terms of secondary and tertiary education available to far fewer pre-war. The 1950s were a period of both clearly defined gender divisions. As an indication of this, in the UK the probability of women under 50 marrying rose to 94.6 percent in 1951-55, and 96 percent in 1956-60 (Titmuss, 1958; Kynaston, 2009). Following the relative gender stability of the 1950s came the relative social change of the 1960s, at least the late 60s. Times were beginning to change. In the UK conscription for young men ended with the last recruitment in 1960, and in 1967 male homosexual acts in private for men over 21 were decriminalised. Feminist, gay, anti-war, anti-nuclear, green, anarchist, new left and other social movements grew, as well as new patterns of consumption and culture. These politics and lifestyles of the 1960s have influenced us all, albeit sometimes in convoluted and contradictory ways.

However, to put this in perspective, gender relations did not change abruptly. For example, the first demand of the British National Women's Liberation (WLM) Conference in 1971 was for equal pay, at a time when women's average gross weekly earnings were just 54.5% of men's (Coote and Campbell, 1987). The seventh demand of the WLM from the 1978 National Conference was: freedom for all women from intimidation by the threat or use of violence or sexual coercion regardless of marital status; and an end to the laws, assumptions and institutions which perpetuate male dominance and aggression to women. This followed the formation in 1974 of the Women's Aid Federation against men's violence to women and children, and the 1976 Domestic Violence and Matrimonial Proceedings Act, giving new powers of injunction and arrest. Yet even with further legal reforms in the 1980s, women's freedom from men's violence remained fundamentally neglected in state policy. Indeed earlier stability and subsequent change in gender relations should not be overstated. The rise of the feminist movement in the 1970s challenged many of us to support women's fight for equality and against domestic violence. That is when some of us began to form men's consciousness raising groups, and read feminist and profeminist literature, and in some cases also began to write for such anti-sexist and profeminist magazines as *Achilles' Heel*, *Men Against Sexism Newsletter (M.A.N.)*, *Lone/Low Plains Drifter*, and *Men for Change*.

Another important contextual question concerns place. Most, but not all, of us live either in the Nottingham or Leicester in the East Midlands in the UK. All but one of us in the core group are British citizens, originally from different parts of the UK, and with different social backgrounds. Several of us have had experience of living in, working in or strong personal or family connections with other countries. In fact, amongst the full group if we include the seven others who have come to some meetings, we find significant family or living connections with Australia, Belgium, Canada, Finland, France, Ireland, Italy, Poland, South Africa, Sweden, and Zimbabwe. This may at times have meant some awareness of relative place and space, and the peculiarities of our base in the UK. We, in the core group, are white, with very different ethnic backgrounds amongst us, and different gender and sexual identities. We have gone through different educational pathways but have had higher education, and several of us have been involved with writing and publishing.

In short, we are a relatively privileged group, even with our vastly different class origins and experiences. Importantly, we have also all been involved in some kinds or aspects of men's anti-sexist, profeminist politics and/or men's personal development work, along with other personal and political activism in various other arenas – such as anti-nuclear, anti-racism, green, left, socialist, peace politics – over the years.

There have inevitably been some tensions and differences of emphasis in the group. Our major differences are perhaps more about our different ways of understanding, different emphases of politics and personal development, along with different geographical locations. This has meant we have to handle difference, often by accepting those differences, rather than trying to convince others they are "wrong".

How the Group Started

There are also differences in how to trace how this group begun, or how the pre-story is remembered. Some of us, David, Jeff and Zbyszek, had been involved together in Men and Socialism (Men, Masculinities and Socialism Group, 1990)

Introduction xxi

events in the 1980s; some had been together in the Men For Change groups and network; several, Jean-Pierre Boulé, Dan, David, Richard, Vic and Zbyszek have been in the Ageing Men group in Leicester and Nottingham that was formed in the late 1990s. In addition, writing men's critical politically informed auto/biography had also influenced us.

Richard, Jeff and Dan had had previous experience of doing or facilitating memory work. David and Jeff, along with Tony Jefferson, had some initial discussions in the early 1990s on setting up a men's memory work group along the lines of that made known by Frigga Haug (1987) and colleagues in the book, *Female Sexualization*; so it was just ten years later when the idea became a reality.

HOW THE GROUP DEVELOPED

The first meeting was convened on 11th April 2002 by David, Richard and Jean-Pierre, with the title 'Memory Work and Changing Men' ... 'A practical writing workshop with a group sharing and collective analysis, in the light of a masculinities-aware frame of interpretation'. It was held in a room in Nottingham Trent University, with three pre-circulated short reading extracts from longer texts (Haug, 1987; Clare and Johnson, 2000; Pease, 2000), and, in the meeting, a short introduction to the method from Richard. The initial attendees were Dan, David Jackson, David Morgan, Jean-Pierre, Jeff, Richard, and Zbyszek. Five of these seven continued throughout. At least five other men who we thought might be interested were invited initially but didn't come.

Then there is the question of the leavings and the stayings in the group. The membership of the group changed significantly over this period, with various comings and goings: one man (David Morgan) leaving after two sessions, another leaving after several meetings (Jean-Pierre), one new member coming for just one meeting and then being unable for practical reasons to come again (Ray Marshall), a fourth joining and leaving after a few meetings (Harry Ferguson), another joining and then moving country, being unable to attend in person, but continuing as a member at a distance (Rob Pattman), and a sixth joining after some years, and staying for many meetings until the end (Randy Barber). Tragically, Dan died suddenly in 2014, in the very final stages of the group, and was only absent for the last few meetings. So, all in all, there have been thirteen of us. In addition, for one meeting we were joined by a woman (Linn Sandberg) who was conducting doctoral research on older men, bodies and sexuality (Sandberg, 2011), and another woman, a film maker, approached us and was welcomed but in the end didn't take up the offer. The final group comprised David, Jeff, Randy, Richard, Vic, and Zbyszek, plus Dan in spirit.

WHAT IS MEMORY WORK?

Memory work is work on memories of and about some agreed focused issue(s), in our case: the making and unmaking of men through age, ageing, gender, gendering, and other intersections. Within this broad overall area of interest, topics or themes that are important, and perhaps emotive, are chosen and, in group work, agreed for writing memories. Then participants chose individually for themselves an episode or episodes in their lives relevant to that topic on which to write. It is important to work hard on actually remembering the episode and, in representing it in writing, to be specific and concrete, and not too 'detached'. These written pieces are then discussed in the group. This means writing in certain definite ways and within certain limits, which can then be critically and reflexively interrogated, in many different possible ways, usually by the writers themselves. Sometimes the emphasis is on the social conditions and sources of that writing and knowledge, for others the direction more towards the construction of identity change. There is now a rather large literature using memory work, much of it directed towards collective memory work but also some conducted by individuals alone, or in some composite ways (e.g. Haug, 1987; Radstone, 2000; Pease, 2000; Hyle et al., 2008; Livholts and Tamboukou, 2015). Memory work can be used in a variety of contexts, including research and theory development, experimental writing, personal development, politics, and teaching and learning (Petö and Waaldijk, 2006; Livholts and Tamboukou, 2015).

Group Memory Work of the kind used in this book developed from several different sources: from feminist consciousness-raising, collective study and auto/biography, from the Worker Writer movement, from oral and community history and most generally perhaps from the need to reach beneath the public narratives to subjective feelings about everyday life experience. For feminist activists and researchers the method had a particular salience, for women's experience was often in tension with the preferred masculine forms of public knowledge. Memory work gained additional impetus from the growth of interest in all forms of memory, commemoration and forgetting from the 1980s onwards. Here the emphasis shifted from memory and oral history to recover hidden facts and subordinated experiences to the stories themselves as a way of forming subjective identities and anchoring personal change. In the academy, it has become a burgeoning area of interdisciplinary study, often dealing with traumatic events that have sharp political implications. (e.g. Passerini, 1987;

Friedlander, 1993; Winter, 1995; Ashplant, Dawson and Roper, 2000; Dawson, 2007).

In the next section of this Introduction we discuss in detail the group's own history. But a few general points can be made here about the appropriateness of the method for our purposes. There are several differences with both auto/biography and oral history interviewing. The short written pieces are produced on the spot, and can therefore be read and analysed more immediately and intensively than a long written personal narrative, a long transcript, or indeed a literary work. The public-ness of the story is immediately present in the room. Indeed its agenda and expectations have already helped to form the story. Feedback is also immediate (though may be more prolonged afterwards). The experience of writing and reception can therefore be very formative. The meaning of the story for its author can change, sometimes with implications for behaviour or identity. Unlike interviewing or ethnography, however, there is no formal split between 'source' and analyst: everyone is a source, everyone comments. Everyone (with some division of labour at the end) becomes an author. The collective nature of the process is very important because it maximizes opportunities for reflection, comparison, even challenge. As Frigga Haug puts it:

> Experiences are both the quicksand on which we cannot build and the material with which we do build. We cannot therefore simply rest content with collecting experiences and claiming that these are women's socialization ... . A method has to be found that makes it possible to *work on experiences*, and to *learn from them*. (Haug, 2000, p. 156, our emphases)

A method of this kind was especially important given the shared interests of our own group. Our overarching issue lent itself to this form of inquiry. The marked silences around both men and masculinity, and ageing, could best be broken by careful co-operative group work with men who had come to trust each other, not to compete with, nor criticise each other destructively for instance. Since we were all in different ways searching for new ways of inhabiting contradictory gender and age relations, the changeful, self-reflective nature of the method, and also the support it gave, was appropriate and welcome. The method gave opportunities for expressing individual points of view on an issue of common concern. In our case, selecting topics or themes has been a careful and sometimes extended process, in which each of us chose for themselves and without discussion an episode or episodes on that sub-theme to write on. The group early on developed rules of confidentiality and feelings of trust that made this both a safe and an invigorating space to work in. Whatever the hesitation, you just had to write on this topic, but, then, what would the others think of it and what in addition might you learn?[1]

METHOD AND THE PROCESS

The meetings were almost always away from our homes, usually in a 'neutral space' in rooms or halls in the community. We generally began at half past nine or ten o'clock with greetings, tea and coffee, and then a round of usually fairly quick updates, catching up on what had happened to each of us since the last meeting. We then went on to agree and choose a theme or topic for each of us to write on separately, but in the same or nearby space, a memory on the topic. In practice, there have been many different ways of establishing a theme and agreeing a topic, sometimes this was agreed at one meeting for the next meeting, sometimes through email discussions, and sometimes there was more than one option on the table and a disagreement resolved by compromise, and on at least one occasion by voting, and on another by each person choosing their own topic.

The very powerful talk in discussing themes in and between meetings has often been a key motivation in the writing that followed. Writing, by hand, rather than via a keyboard, has been done at some speed, for between 40 and 60 minutes, before reading, discussion and analysis. First person writing has been the main method, but some of us have also used the third person at times. These written memories were then read out by each of us, without comment from the rest of us. After lunch, we read the memories out again, and then discussed them, and what they were saying, what they were telling us or not. At times, some of us have had to take rest breaks during the day or have shortened meetings for health reasons. After the meetings we typed up the memories and circulated them to each other. Sometimes we discussed and analysed, in writing and/or in discussion, the written memories from the previous or earlier meetings. There has also been extensive email discussion and analysis, in part on possible interpretations of the stories. We also experimented with other modes, such as use of photographs from an earlier lives on one occasion.

Our memory work has involved memories, stories, and diverse forms of writing, some factual, some more descriptive, some autobiographical in tone, some more as story-telling, some more literary in style. Thus there are differences in how these memories are conceived, framed, and expressed. The writings varied from fragments, shards, of memory to well-formed and written out stories, from recollections from long ago to contemporary experiences. Importantly, the stories

Introduction xxv

were not written with the aim or assumption that they would be published years later, and in that sense they are more or less "raw".

In general, there has been more attention to memories of childhood and growing up, on one hand, and recent ageing, on the other, rather than the in-between periods of adulthood. In a few instances, for example, where one of us was absent from the original meeting, their stories were written later. Moreover, the way the writing was done also brought up memories and things forgotten, not fully worked out and not consciously planned in advance, even when the topic of the day was known. And to repeat, they were written over the extended period of thirteen years, and thus with our own significant ageing.

The main topic themes we have written memories on are listed here, along with the year when we started writing on them. As noted, the original themes were chosen as we proceeded with the group, meeting to meeting. In some cases the original themes overlapped and have been combined for present purposes, and some themes were returned to and written on again later:

- Ageing (2002)
- Hair (2002)
- Clothes (2003)
- Peeing (2004)
- School and schooling (2007)
- Disruptive bodily changes (2005)
- Sport (2009)
- Sisters (2006)
- Food (2006)
- Intimacy with men (2007)
- Love (2009)
- Saying goodbye to mothers (2008)
- Political moments (2003)
- Power (2008)
- Violence (2013)
- Fathers and fathering (2011)
- Work (2014)
- Sexuality and relationships (2014)
- Ending the group (2010)

The way we have organised the themes here in this book is slightly different from how we originally decided the writing topics, so that now the topics of the 26 meetings are consolidated to 18 main themes, covering the anonymised stories themselves, plus a short theme on ending the group. Sometimes we have had to consider or reconsider what exactly is the theme about: what kind of theme is it? How specific should it be? How lifelong? How much talked about or not talked about, for example, peeing? How and why it is talked about so much, for example, sport? There are also what might be considered missing, obvious or even avoided themes. Perhaps significantly, the themes of sexuality, violence, and work were addressed explicitly towards the end of the group. In addition to the themes often overlapping, certain meta-themes, such as masculinities, loss, sexuality and of course ageing, figured across and within other themes. For example, a memory on peeing might also be about ageing; or another on ageing might also be about sexuality. The order of the consolidated themes presented here is loosely chronological, but also seeks to recreate some of the complex, and at times somewhat capricious, nature of the group process, sometimes moving between very different kinds of themes in successive meetings, sometimes maintaining clear continuity.

The individual and collective reflective process in and of the group has been very important, and has interconnected with the content of the memory work. Highlights include the developing group feeling and trust, and our affection for each other. The mode was care and critique, not therapy. The process whereby we ageing men supported each other in reflecting on how our lives where steered by our ever changing masculinities has sustained our friendships and helped us resolve conflicts in our lives, our personal and family relations, and political awareness and activity.

These personal writings can be seen as explorations. Listening to others' written stories has been a central part of the process, as has the feedback and comments given to each other. We have developed some shared analysis, but this has been quite difficult at times, not least because of differences of approach amongst us, and at some points we downplayed the attempt at a common analysis. Towards the end of the group an e-archive of the memories was established by Vic, and this helped to identify missing stories and so on; as such, this became crucial in the production and editing of this book.

This Introduction has been written collectively, and the final reflection has been written by Vic and David. The mini-introductions to the theme sections are authored by different individuals with different styles, concepts, and even purposes. We decided to keep and accept this diversity rather than pretend that we had a common voice. Selected quotes, short and long, and unattributed, are also included here in some of these mini-introductions to illustrate some of the more

Introduction xxvii

general themes and sub-themes. The first full version of the manuscript was assembled by Vic, and then the general editing of the book was done collectively, and then in more detail by Jeff.

WHERE DOES OUR WORK FIT?

We would like to comment on where our work may fit. One of the fascinating things about doing memory work is that it is very hard to categorise and put in a single box. It makes the writers into both subjects and objects, and cuts across that division too. Rather similarly, this written production, albeit tidied up to some extent, can be located in various ways and traditions, and forms of writing. Most obviously it is collective memory work (Haug, 1987; Pease, 2000). This immediately raises the question of how do such memories relate to what happened in the past, how we and others experienced them then, to what extent these memories can be said to be accurate, and indeed whether accuracy is the most appropriate way to think of these writings.

But there are many other ways of seeing all this. It could also be located more directly as political, reflective profeminist writing on men by men (Hearn, 1983; Jackson, 1990; Seidler, 1991, 1992), within the more academic, profeminist writing (Porter, 1992; Digby, 1998; Schacht and Ewing, 1998), or alongside studies of anti-sexist and profeminist men and men's politics (Pease, 1990; Christian, 1994; Goldrick-Jones, 2002; Ashe, 2007). It can be seen as a form of oral history (Seldon and Pappworth, 1983; Thomson, 2007), or perhaps writing on reminiscences, reminiscence therapy, and life story work (Gibson, 2011) more generally. Then there is another set of the framings in terms of group work, whether self-help, more or less political engaged therapy, or consciousness-raising (Bradley, 1971). However, in its method and content this book is very different indeed from simply being an edited version of discussions in a men's group,

This work can also be placed within more academic contexts, most obviously, memory studies (as in the journal of that name, 2008-) and critical studies on men and masculinities (Kimmel, Hearn and Connell, 2005). Much, perhaps most, previous research, even critical research, on men and masculinities has largely ignored ageing and older men (*pace* Thompson, 1994; Hearn, 1995; Arber, Davidson and Ginn, 2003; Fennel and Davidson, 2003; Calasanti, 2004; Sandberg, 2011; Jackson, 2016). This book represents an attempt to fill in the gaps in our knowledges about ageing men's embodied and lived experiences. It can also be seen in terms of studies on constructions of subjectivity, and studies on age, gender and intersectionality (Calasanti and Slevin, 2001), cultural gerontology (Twigg and Martin, 2015), and critical autobiography that disrupts the tradition of the heroic male (Jackson, 1990), including reflecting on the relations of ageing, autobiography and writing (Jackson, 2001, 2003).

The approach used can also be related to more methodological concerns, for example, accounts of past actions (Scott and Lyman, 1968), participatory action research (Kindon, Pain and Kesby, 2007), story-telling, restorying, narrative inquiry, and creative writing, with their own varieties of genres and styles (Livholts and Tamboukou, 2015), or even as autoethnography (Muncey, 2010; Holman Jones, Adams and Ellis, 2013). However, these are retrospective connections, so, for example, the project was not conceived as autoethnography, is not specifically understood by us as autoethnography, and is different from most approaches to that method.

Most importantly, neither the group process nor the product, the book, have been designed as a research project or a 'test' of previous empirical research. The whole collective project has taken a different shape and purpose, or shapes and purposes, often with differences between us in how we see it, as it has developed over the years of meeting and writing. Put simply, the book is not easy to categorise, and does not fit easily into existing academic definitions. It is perhaps best seen simply as a record of some time-limited and unedited personal-political writings of a specific group of relatively similar men, at a certain historical time. It is also an example and a product of a kind of "slow research" into and on our own lives that can now be interrogated, analysed, and critiqued by others. Arguably, the detailed interrogation of ageing men's lives has subversive potential to change men, masculinities, and gender relations more generally (Jackson, 2016).

Beyond this, we are aware that our work is situated within a broader and rapidly changing social, political, cultural and economic context. In much of the world, and notably in the UK and similar countries, this context may be defined as being neoliberal and is generally characterised by a 'freeing-up' of economic and market practices combined with a rolling back of the state (though not everywhere – China for example) (Harvey, 2005). The title of this volume, *Men's Stories for a Change*, therefore raises certain questions as to what kind of change might be envisaged and how – indeed *whether* this fits in with this current context.

Within this context social policy tends to be preoccupied with reducing reliance upon the state, and to some extent this is reflected in the huge explosion of books on *self*-help and *self*-improvement, and the growth of an entire industry dedicated to these ends. However, our collective memory work spanning thirteen years has taken us in a very different direction from this trend. Insofar as this project has been concerned with the raising of consciousness, this has been a collaborative and, at times, deeply critical venture with little, if any, thought given to issues such as self-reliance, independence, and increased performativity. Nonetheless, we hope this project will help, if only in some small way, in opening up these issues, freeing up in a profeminist direction the voices of other men individually or collectively, ageing or otherwise. We are aware that many men are not so good at this, and that this can have an impact upon violence, suicide, health, amongst other questions. But, more importantly, men, or at least some men, are also the gatekeepers to change (Connell, 2011), especially gender change, and it is within this context that this project should be read.

FINALLY...

There have been recurring analytical cross-cutting issues and meta-themes within and across the 26 topic themes we have written on, for example, ageing, bodies, class, ethnicity, gender, health, masculinities, sexualities, and some of these are returned to later in the book. The ordering of the themes partly reflects the changing progression of topics we addressed over time in the group, and partly the editing process in the final stages. A few of the individual stories have been edited very lightly indeed, for reasons of, for example, anonymity or clarity of meaning, involving various micro-decisions on presentation. At times, we have wondered if some writing is simply too obscure and of no interest to others, and here we have erred on inclusion. A handful of stories have not been included as not fitting with the main topics; only one of all the written stories has been specifically omitted on ethical grounds. We have not edited to avoid embarrassment. Almost all are as originally written, in the heat of the rapid writing, as described. In a few instances two overlapping memories have been combined into one text; in a very few others the writing has been rearranged. Although we have talked a lot about the analysis of the memories, and also written quite a lot on this too, we decided not to make extensive written analysis or evaluation of what we have done – in part as we would probably not agree, in part simply that to do that would take much more time still, and partly as this would be difficult with our ageing bodily energies. The importance of knowing limits should not be under-estimated. Others may do that, if they wish.

This is a project that is both finished and unfinished.

NOTE

1. The memory work practice adopted in the group had a particular provenance. In the early 1980s a group of women from Berlin who were working on women and sexuality visited the Centre for Contemporary Cultural Studies (CCCS), at the University of Birmingham. They talked about how they each wrote short stories about their lives and feelings, then critically discussed them together (see Haug, 1987). This was of particular interest to a group in CCCS who were working on war and nationalism in the wake of the Falklands/Malvinas conflict. Here at last was a way to get below the nationalistic narratives, dominated, interestingly, by Mrs. Thatcher's own voice. Why not seek to articulate, then to discuss, our own experiences of these and allied experiences, recognising the salience of gender, as well as class and national identity? The Popular Memory Group did not produce a collective book, but its work resonated through the research, and teaching practices of its individual members, till finally arriving at the meetings of the 'Memory Men' from 2002 (see below and for instance, Dawson, 1994; Johnson et al., 2004, especially Chapters 3, 4 and 12; Clare and Johnson, 2000

REFERENCES

Arber, Sara, Davidson, Kate, and Ginn, Jay (1995) *Gender and Ageing: Changing Roles and Relationships*, Maidenhead: Open University Press.

Ashe, Fidelma (2007) *The New Politics of Masculinity*, London: Routledge.

Ashplant, Tim, Dawson, Graham and Roper, Michael (eds.) (2000) *The Politics of War Memory and Commemoration,* London: Routledge.

Bradley, Michael (1971) *Unbecoming Men: A Men's Consciousness-raising Group Writes on Oppression & Themselves*, Albion, CA: Times Change Press.

Calasanti, Toni (2004) Feminist gerontology and old men, *Journal of Gerontology*, 598: 305-314.

Calasanti, Toni M. and Slevin, Kathleen F. (eds.) (2001) *Gender, Social Inequalities, and Aging*, New York: AltaMira Press.

Christian, Harry (1994) *The Making of Anti-Sexist Men*, London: Routledge.

Clare, Mariette and Johnson, Richard (2000) Method in our madness: identity and power in a memory work method, in Susannah Radstone (ed.) *Memory and Methodology*, Oxford: Berg, pp. 197-224.

Connell, Raewyn (2011) *Confronting Equality: Gender, Knowledge and Global Change*, Cambridge: Polity.

Coote, Anna and Campbell, Beatrix (1987) *Sweet Freedom: The Struggle for Women's Liberation*, Oxford: Blackwell.

Dawson, Graham (1994) *Soldier Heroes: British Adventure, Empire and the Imagining of Heroes* London: Routledge.

Dawson, Graham (2007) *Making Peace with the Past: Memory, Trauma and the Irish Troubles* Manchester: Manchester University Press.

Digby, (ed.) (1998) *Men Doing Feminism*, New York: Routledge.

Fennel, Graham and Davidson, Kate (2003) "The invisible man?" Older men in modern society, *Aging International*, 28(4), 315-325.

Friedlander, Saul (1993) *Memory, History and the Extermination of the Jews in Europe*, Bloomington: Indianapolis.

Gibson, Faith (2011) *Reminiscence and Life Story Work: A Practice Guide*, 4th edition, London: Jessica Kingsley.

Goldrick-Jones, Amanda (2002) *Men who Believe in Feminism*, Westport, CT: Praeger.

Harvey, David (2005) *A Brief History of Neoliberalism*, Oxford: Oxford University Press.

Haug, Frigga (ed.) (1987) *Female Sexualization*, London: Verso.

Haug, Frigga, (2000) 'Memory Work: The Key to Women's Anxiety', in Susannah Radstone (ed.) *Memory and Methodology*, Oxford: Berg, pp. 155-179.

Hearn, Jeff (1983) *Birth and Afterbirth: A Materialist Account*, London: Achilles' Heel.

Hearn, Jeff (1995) Imaging the aging of men, in Mike Featherstone and Andrew Wernick (eds.) *Images of Aging: Cultural Representations of Later Life*, London: Routledge, pp. 97-115.

Holman Jones, Stacy, Adams, Tony E. and Ellis, Carolyn (eds.) (2013) *Handbook of Autoethnography*, Walnut Creek, CA: Left Coast Press.

Hyle, Adrienne E., Ewing, Margaret S., Montgomery, Diane, and Kaufman, Judith S. (eds.) (2008) *Dissecting the Mundane: International Perspectives on Memory-Work*, Lanham, MD: University Press of America.

Jackson, David (1990) *Unmasking Masculinity: A Critical Autobiography*, London: Unwin Hyman/Routledge.

Jackson, David (2001) Masculinity challenges to an ageing man's embodied selves: struggles, collusions and resistances, *Auto/Biography*, 9(1 & 2): 107-115.

Jackson, David (2003) Beyond one-dimensional models of masculinity: a life-course perspective on the processes of becoming masculine, *Auto/Biography*, 11(1 & 2): 71-87.

Jackson, David (2016) *Exploring Aging Masculinities*, Houndmills: Palgrave Macmillan.

Johnson, Richard, Chambers, Deborah, Raghuram, Parvati and.Ticknell, Estella (2004) *The Practice of Cultural Studies*, London: Sage.

Kimmel, Michael, Hearn, Jeff and Connell, Raewyn (eds.) (2005) *The Handbook of Studies of Men and Masculinities*, Thousand Oaks, CA: Sage.

Kindon, Sara, Pain, Rachel and Kesby, Mike (2007) *Participatory Action Research Approaches and Methods*, London: Routledge.

Kynaston, David (2007) *Austerity Britain, 1945–51*, London: Bloomsbury.

Kynaston, David (2009) *Family Britain 1951-57*, London: Bloomsbury.

Livholts, Mona and Tamboukou, Maria (2015) *Discourse and Narrative Methods*, London: Sage.

Memory Studies (2008-) (journal) London: Sage.

Men, Masculinities and Socialism Group (1990) Changing men, changing politics, *Achilles' Heel*, 10: 17-21.

Muncey, Tessa (2010) *Creating Autoethnographies*, London: Sage.

Passerini, Luisa (1987) *Fascism in Popular Memory*, Cambridge: Cambridge University Press.

Pease, Bob (2000) *Recreating Men: Postmodern Masculinity Politics*, London: Sage.

Petö, Andrea and Waaldijk, Berteke (eds.) (2006) *Teaching with Memories: European Women's Histories in International and Interdisciplinary Classrooms*, Galway: National University of Ireland, Galway.

Porter, David (ed.) (1992) *Between Men and Feminism*, London: Routledge.

Radstone, Susannah (ed.) 2000) *Memory and Methodology*, Oxford: Berg.

Riley, Denise (1983) *War in the Nursery*, London: Virago.

Sandberg, Linn (2011) *Getting Intimate: A Feminist Analysis of Old Age, Masculinity and Sexuality*, Linköping: Linköping University Electronic Press.

Schacht, Steven and Ewing, Dorothy (eds.) (1998) *Feminism and Men*, New York: New York University Press.

Scott, Marvin B. and Lyman, Stanford (1968) Accounts, *American Sociological Review*, 33(1): 46-62.

Seidler, Victor J. (ed.) (1991) *The Achilles' Heel Reader: Men, Sexual Politics and Socialism*, London: Routledge.

Seidler, Victor J. (ed.) (1992) *Men, Sex and Relationships: Writings from Achilles' Heel*, London: Routledge.

Seldon, Antony and Pappworth, Joanna (1983) *By Word of Mouth*, London: Metheun.

Thompson, Edward H. (ed.) (1994) *Older Men's Lives*, Thousand Oaks, CA: Sage.

Thomson, Alistair (2007) Four paradigmatic transformations in oral history, *Oral History Review*, 34(1): 49-70.

Titmuss, Richard (1958) *Essays of the 'Welfare State'*, London: Allen & Unwin.

Twigg, Julia and Martin, Wendy (eds.) *The Routledge Handbook of Cultural Gerontology*, London: Routledge.

Winter, Jay (1995) *Sites of Memory, Sites of Mourning The Great War in European Cultural History* Cambridge: Cambridge University Press.

The Stories

CHAPTER 1

Ageing

Vic Blake

INTRODUCTION

Ageing has been a constant backdrop for this group from the start so, taken as a specific theme, it becomes one of key significance for the group. This is also down to the fact that many of our members also belong to a local ageing men's group. Much of what has been written by us on a variety of themes might, therefore, also be read I suppose through this prism of ageing. And along with ageing, of course, comes a range of related and often difficult issues to do with health, bodily change, formative experience, life-change, and loss, all of which have been talked through and critiqued through the eyes of a group of anti-sexist men who are collectively committed to change for the better.

One of our members begins by associating ageing with deterioration, failing capacity and loss, and describes these changes as tedious:

> These are things that tend not to get better so you live with constant medication. They become a constant part of your life – and the rest of your life. The expectation that they will be 'cured' has gone. This makes me feel like an older person too.

He sees these changes as being not only difficult in themselves but also as emasculating in the ways they increasingly restrict his capacity for doing those things which previously helped to define him as masculine. Another member makes a similar point in his account of being unable to move a heavy pot plant and his wife calling upon a younger, fitter man to do the job for her - or even his daughters:

> But we have to wait for somebody younger and fitter than me, with a fully functioning left hand and arm, to help her carry the pot outside. So I wait, reluctantly, for our friend to come again so that we can ask him,

or we have to wait for my daughters, to take the other side of the pot. I wait in silence but I don't like it.

But all is not negative; there are also more positive reflections on ageing among the stories. One member also writes of the benefits of experience coupled with an increased self-reflexivity – something which has helped to enrich his life even though it brings with it certain regrets:

> Life seems to me to be completely the wrong way round. I needed all this 'maturity' and 'wisdom' and 'integrity' (such as it is) all those years ago when it really counted, when others counted on me.

As a group I believe we have tried to view ageing very much as a positive process but while always trying to remain realistic, given that some of its consequences can sometimes be extremely difficult to bear. The alternatives - the bemoaning of lost youth and vigour or the retreat into denial, we have seen as both self-defeating and unrealistic. Being able to talk about ageing in this way, and in an environment which is both supportive and critical, has certainly drawn us closer, made us more trusting, more open and more positive about ourselves. As such our work together has enriched our ageing lives in ways that might have been difficult to imagine at the start.

This more positive approach might be seen by some as a direct affront to the current celebration of youth which is such a powerful driving force in the modern world. It is certainly clear to us that the process of ageing is not just about bodily decline and loss of faculty. It is every bit as much about our social relationships generally, about dominant cultural values and harsh economic need. In other words, our ageing is not only about us and how we are changing; it is every bit as much about politics - about others, how we treat them and how they value and treat us.

This is a theme which emerges out of two of the stories in particular. Note, for example, this writer's reflections on his early experiences:

> The reproaches and the self-reproaches crowded in. Grandad said nothing, but Dad and (more gently) Mum had much to say: I had just shown that I could not be trusted; I was not responsible; even at my age I was obviously too young to have the key to the house.

In a more positive way, it is also a theme in another writer's recollections:

> Honour was satisfied all round. I learnt that I was near to but not quite yet a man, that my parents & in this case my father could sort things out, though I came later to disagree with him on most things, perhaps apart from his occasional critical directness. I much later realised that I did admire him (& his protection). I also learnt then the importance of words (in the adult world).

These two very different stories reflect upon the negative and the positive elements in the gradual formation of our adult masculine selves. It is implicit in the very nature of our group, however, that the process does not stop there. One group of stories gives voice to a lifetime's honing and re-working of our adult masculinities. For sure a significant part of this will have to do with loss but for us ageing matters are not *only* about loss but also about the gradual movement towards something more positive. The fact of bodily (and, I suppose, I should add *mental*) decline and creeping decrepitude, and their implications for our personal sense of masculinity, are only part of a story which is every bit as much about our extensive personal life courses and the many different experiences that we have had along the way.

We know that this experience – be it good or bad – can often be extremely rich. But it is enriched not only by the telling of the stories themselves but also, and in some ways more importantly, from our candid reflections upon them as a group. It is the individual and collective working through of the past (and the present) in this way – always with at least one eye to the future - which has helped to define us as an Ageing (rather than 'Old') Men's Memory Work Group.

And so now we turn to the stories themselves.

***

GOING UNDERGROUND

I was on a London underground train at least ten, possibly more, years ago. The train was crowded and I was standing. A young Jewish boy (how do I remember him as Jewish? –presumably he was wearing a skull-cap) got up and offered me his seat. Smiling, I refused his offer but I did not feel insulted. I think that this was the first time anything like this had happened to me and it worried me since usually other people have imagined me to be younger than my actual age. I continued to puzzle about it. At the time I had a long, rather untidy, beard, and I wondered whether the young man thought that I was some Jewish elder. I was reminded of a usually suppressed part of my background, namely Jewishness. My mother's maiden name was Goodchild and her father – or grandfather? – was Jewish. I have some practising Jewish relatives in South Africa although contact with them has been highly infrequent. In the past other people have thought that I 'looked Jewish' (a landlady in Manchester, my present partner's sister) although I feel no particularly strong affinity with this part of my inheritance just as I feel little identification with the Welshness on my father's side and reflected in my name.

Having written this I realise that it says nothing about masculinity although this is implied in my reference to my beard and possibly why I did not accept the offer of a seat. This one episode (which lasted barely a minute) encouraged thoughts about age and ethnicity but only later masculinity.

Shortly after I shaved my beard off and people thought I looked a lot younger.

Lots of Losses

Lots of losses make me who I am. Being left alone. A scary place to be. First it was being left in school at the age of five, not speaking English, not even knowing how to ask how to go to the toilet - so I had to pee myself. That's how I broke out of the cocoon of my family. Then it was going to get the slipper from the headmaster. Then it was losing a best mate over a fight, alone again till the next best mate, and then the next fight. That's how I learned to keep a friend.

Being left in my first year at university, knowing no one, alone. Not having a friend. Then not having a girlfriend. Having a girlfriend who I loved leave me for her precious boyfriend, left me shattered by love.

These losses are how I learned to cope with life and relationships. Going through the loss of trust, breaking into new scary situations, coping, becoming stronger, prepared me for the next loss of my father, then of my mother. The pain was unbearable at every new loss but each one has paid off in some ways in resilience. That ability to survive loss of close and dear relationships has hurt but also given me greater self-healing powers. I feel a stronger man today for those experiences with a willingness to accept the process of ageing, the loss of some physical abilities, an acceptance of slowing down. Loss of work, retirement.

My ageing involves the accumulated loss of little losses of power in the workplace, over children's lives, over my body's sporting abilities, and energy left for involvements in political struggles. I am welcoming this slowing down, accepting the loss involved as opportunities to become less driven, more caring for myself, my mind and body. Relaxation and meditation through yoga has become a very important coping mechanism for me.

In a life of hustle my time being semi-retired has been a revelation to me. I must admit I was scared of giving up work. This semi-retirement process has helped to put mindless work in proportion, has given me time to be more objective and reflective, to be more human and it's more fun.

REMEMBERING GRANDFATHER

I guess I must have been in my teens. Mum, Dad, my two younger sisters and I went for a day to the seaside. Does that mean my brother, twelve years my junior, had not been born? I can't remember. As we walked home along Lennox Terrace at the end of the day, my dad went a few paces ahead to open the door. He turned in horror. Somebody was in the house. How could this be? How could this have happened? Who had been last to leave the house? Whose fault was it? Oh no! I had borrowed the key to go back for something I had forgotten. I had left the door unlocked all day.

Relief! The man at the stop of the stairs inside the house was my grandfather, Big Tommy. In generations of little men broad shoulders had made my grandfather "Big Tommy" although he was probably only five-foot-nine.

He never came to visit us like that, but somehow the good weather had made him feel like a walk; and he found our front door open.

The reproaches and the self-reproaches crowded in. Grandad said nothing, but Dad and (more gently) Mum had much to say: I had just shown that I could not be trusted; I was not responsible; even at my age I was obviously too young to have the key to the house.

I think I also discovered (though I am not sure if I knew at the time) that my dad, himself also the eldest son, felt safe when his dad was there. The big carpet weaver whose skill and hard work provided for a large family; but only just, for my father had had to leave school at the earliest chance and start earning. He could not even do an apprenticeship like his two younger brothers.

The only other time I knew of my grandfather visiting us, although Dad and I used to visit Grandma and him nearly every Sunday, was before I was born. When my mother died in hospital, alone for my father could not go there when the nurse rang because I was out ... so again it was my fault. When my mother died, Dad was carried back twenty-nine years in memory to the death of two-year old Thomas, their first born, the big brother I never had. Grandad, I learned, had sat there in silent grief with his hand in the empty cot.

NAN'S BIBLE

(I didn't really want to write this ...) So why did I select it? The episode that keeps coming to mind is one that happened when I was about 11 or 12, I think, but it might have been slightly younger. It centrally involves my great grandmother, Granna, a Victorian figure, who always wore black, who was incredibly thin, energetic, strict, disciplined, somewhat terrifying & Christian. She was by this time in her mid-late 80s. She was an avid reader of the Bible. She also thought a lot of me, her oldest great grandson, perhaps because I had previously spent time with her doing jigsaws, and so on. I admired her. One day when I was visiting her on my own to my surprise she told me she was going to give me one of her favourite Bibles – it had a particular significance to her – I can't remember what – but that I had to agree to read it every day (as part of the deal). I was very confused, as it wasn't important to me at all to have the thing (though it was good to be recognised by her as worthy of one of her prized possessions). I agreed to the *condition* (reading it every day), though I had no intention of doing so. I lied to her. I had this terrible sinking feeling in my stomach. However, I remember thinking and calculating that this was less of a difficulty (or a sin) than disappointing her and her plan to give this before she died. She thought I was now *old enough* for the responsibility of this kind – a child but almost or soon to become a man.

I told about this deal to my parents who were worried about all this forced imposing of conditions, unrealistic conditions, on me. Then to my further surprise, slight embarrassment, and confusion, and very *unusually* my father intervened on the next time she visited our house, and said to her, calling her name (which he didn't usually) do), 'Nan ... You can't make the boy do this' – 'but you can give it to him if hasn't got to read it *every day*.' My father was probably a kind of believer but <u>ardently</u> and (to my pleasure now) enthusiastically anti-organised religion and 'stupid religion', which he saw as feminine, judging by the make-up of the local congregation.

Honour was satisfied all round. I learnt that I was near to but not quite yet a man, that my parents and in this case my father could sort things out, though I came later to disagree with him on most things, perhaps apart from his occasional critical directness. I much later realised that I did admire him (and his protection). I also learnt *then* the importance of words (in the adult world).

GROWING OLDER AND, HOPEFULLY, A LITTLE WISER

I write this story a long time after the others as I wasn't at that meeting. Since then a lot has happened and I feel that I have aged a lot – even though I am far from sure what that means exactly.

I suppose several things impact most obviously on my sense of ageing, post-middle age. The first of these is my health. For a large part of my life health issues had no real impact on how old I felt. But there passes a point where these issues begin to say something about where you are on that measure of things. A good example is my hearing. I have been hard of hearing since I was about twenty and have had to wear a hearing aid for most of that time. For many years people would ask me why I was deaf, what was wrong with my hearing, had I always been like that. But then there came a point in my life where people stopped asking. It was as though they were just presuming that I was 'elderly' and that 'elderly people' tended often to be hard of hearing. The exact same is true of my limp, the result of an accident many years ago.

Other health matters are tedious: a slightly enlarged prostate, recurring respiratory problems; a hiatus hernia which causes reflux problems; various injuries, dry skin, and so on. These are things that tend not to get better so you live with constant medication. They become a constant part of your life – and the rest of your life. The expectation that they will be 'cured' has gone. This makes me feel like an older person too.

Then there are the health problems and issues that prevent me *doing* things. This brings me on to the second impact on my sense of ageing.

Doing things; doing particular things, doing them in a particular way and to a particular standard, all these have helped define me as a male for many years and a reasonable sense of health and fitness has been crucial to these. But as I have become older I have become less fit and can no longer do most of these things. Various health issues add to this considerably so that certain things become painful, or affect my health negatively, or else they just make me very tired.

Thus my sense of being older (in the sense of being and *'older person'*) is very much defined by these changes and deteriorations in my body and in my general state of health.

A third aspect of feeling older concerns my view of my life so far, as I have more to reflect back on. I see my mistakes and the things I have done wrong so much more clearly now and feel the regrets much more painfully. Getting older has meant having to live with these, especially the regrets that I have not been able to address or work through with the others affected; those where there is no possible sense of closure. This is like permanent indigestion. One way that I deal with these issues is to be far more open about them with others.

This brings me to my final aspect, which is far more positive and which, in many ways, depends so much on what has already been said. Put simply – I know and understand so much more now, and experience (including, and *especially* the experiences that I regret) adds tremendously to this, and is helped by my ability to be critically reflexive. This has to be done carefully though as it would be very easy to become broody and depressed. Talking to others about these things helps so much.

Life seems to be me to be completely the wrong way round. I needed all this 'maturity' and 'wisdom' and 'integrity' (such as it is) all those years ago when it really counted, when others counted on me. As I said in these first two verses of a poem that I wrote:

> Shit happens,
> Nose hair grows,
> The sun comes up then down she goes,
> That's just the way the story goes
> And no use in complaining.
>
> We're young too early, wise too late,
> Hair deserts the balding pate,
> But grows like weeds on your best mate.
> It's always bloody raining.

Edgeworthia Chrysantha

There is a conservatory built on to the side and front of our kitchen, in which my partner grows semi-topical plants and shrubs. One of these plants, shadowing a major part of the conservatory doorway, is called an Edgeworthia Chrysantha.

For at least half the year we keep the plant outside and it seems to cope well. But the plant is half-tender so during the late Winter months, when the night frosts are wrecking plants and shrubs, the Edgeworthia is brought in to the comparative shelter of the conservatory.

The plant is beginning to grow extremely tall and it's now planted in a huge pot with a weighty amount of compost and soil covering its root system. It's now far too heavy for me to help in the lifting of it, even with my partner taking the other side of the pot. This complicates matters for us in the movement of potted shrubs around the garden. She has manoeuvred the plant into the conservatory by asking a male friend to help her in the lifting.

I now struggle to accept my physical limitations. My pacemaker is implanted under my left armpit and my plastic heart valve is on that side of my body as well. So now I rarely lift anything with my left hand. I now look at the Edgeworthia: half of me suggests that I could do the shared lifting with my right hand working alone, protecting myself against any left side of my body exertion. But my partner recommends that I don't try. 'It's too risky,' she says. One part of me agrees. The other half looks repeatedly at the plant blocking the conservatory doorway. It needs to go out. It's flowered inside. But we have to wait for somebody younger and fitter than me, with a fully functioning left hand and arm, to help her carry the pot outside.

So I wait, reluctantly, for our friend to come again so that we can ask him, or we have to wait for my daughters, to take the other side of the pot.

I wait in silence but I don't like it.

CHAPTER 2

Hair

David Jackson

INTRODUCTION

Men and hair may at first seem a trivial theme but on closer consideration this subject often reveals a more serious concern and anxiety in ageing men's lives about unresolved dilemmas and contradictory desires.

Gender

From a gendered perspective, hair can be seen as a powerful symbol of men's virility and strength, as in the story of Samson. Conventionally, 'real' men are perceived as hairy men. Beards, moustaches and displays of chest, facial and pubic hair are usually associated with dominant manhood in western societies.

The most common and perhaps the most intense reaction in the group's writing was fear and shame of hairlessness and a linked anxiety about not measuring up to the cultural and bodily ideals of being a 'proper' man:

> I used to despair at not shaving and at my voice not changing. People used to mistake me for a girl on the phone and I hated it. As for my hair, it used to cover my ears (I had a complex about my ears sticking out, and so did other school friends so we used to cover them.) Often in the morning, your hair was stuck up from the night and if you wet it above your ears used to end up with what we called 'rat tails'.

And:

> From the back I was mistaken for a girl. I used to be whistled at regularly by boys on mopeds and when I turned around you could see their faces registering, 'Hell, it's a bloke!'

A Sense of Masculine Inadequacy

Closely tied in to this shame of hairlessness is a recurring sense of masculine inadequacy, as in talk about being 'deeply insecure, confused and frightened' as a younger man, and failure to grow a 'real' beard:

> I have had a go at growing a chinstrap beard à la Manfred Mann – and a friend's older and very macho brother, with a slightly malicious twinkle in his eye, is gently taking the piss out of me, saying that when you put a comb in it and it stays put, then you have a real beard. He demonstrates and says that mine is not and I 'should shave the fucking thing off!

Gendered Ambivalence

One way of fighting back against this insecurity and humiliation was through a more complicated position of gendered ambivalence. Hair was sometimes seen as a rebellious feature that could express 'repressed longings to be softer, more flowing, more sensual':

> ... blond curls were more sexy and alive than straight hair ...

And again,

> perhaps a contempt for the neat parting and Brylcreemed hair of the 1950s bank clerk in Britain?

Also the experience of preparing for a vasectomy with the cutting off of his pubic hair gives rise to the possibility of a creative, new beginning in his life:

> ... my vasectomy's hairlessness begat my middle-aged, non-child bearing years. The start of a new kind of creative phase in my life. One based on developing my senses and feelings of a less hairy man.

Changing Perceptions of Hair as Men Grow Older

Changes in time, space and location as men grow older bring with them changes in the meanings of masculinity. One man in his early years grew a moustache to make himself 'look older, more experienced, more powerful than I actually felt.' Looking back twenty-five years later. He reflects that:

> I felt the time had come in my life when I didn't need to hide anymore behind bristle and hair on my face. I wanted to accept my face as it was, perhaps soft and vulnerable but my own. And I didn't want to go on pretending I was more mature and manly than I actually was.

This coming to terms with the emotional and physical realities of his life is mirrored by the comments that 'I think I have learned to accept my face and to love it.' Also another writer's adolescent life was haunted by a combination of a secrecy culture at boarding school and a fear of peer group ridicule. A minor skin condition was exaggerated by his fearful imaginings. It was only much later in his life that he was able to risk 'public hairlessness' and opt for medical examination. Now, not so driven by his anxieties, he is able to integrate his bodily worries into a more open sharing with other men he is able to trust rather than becoming a target for the peer group's vicious tongues:

> I am reconciled to my hairless pubis by now and TCP keeps the spots and itches away. I am really fond of it in fact-but public showers, like those at school-hmmm-never! Well anyway, I'd need a different relation to the other men involved for sure.

Responding to Women

Perhaps not surprisingly, women's responses to our hairstyles were crucial to our choices and decisions about how to present ourselves. This was particularly relevant in one account where reference to three, separate women who influenced his hairstyles was made. This is how he explains his decisions:

> I had my quiff cut off. I was influenced in this decision by my desire to impress the lovely L who I lusted for and who lived nearby.

> I also realised that another woman whom I had fallen in love with didn't seem particularly keen on it [his beard]. So the beard went.

> Advice from a male friend about how I needed to smarten up my hair if I was to make a better impression on a third woman.

Institutional Regulations and Length of Hair

Sometimes the institutional contexts that we find ourselves in through our lives shape our decisions about hairstyles and length of hair, for example, story illustrates these choices and dilemmas. He is preparing for a university interview and feeling anxious about his 'untidiness'. He is also wondering whether he should get his hair cut especially for the occasion. But a woman friend advises him to go as he is and he gets the job.

Other institutional contexts influence us about our decisions about hair. Some examples are military contexts, school regulations, and university environments. Although most of us have memories of being disciplined about hairstyle and length it's also important to notice that these institutional sites can become sites of occasional defiance, rebellion and non-conformity through our lifetimes as well.

***

AN HAIRY MAN—OR NOT

This incident happens when I am about seventeen years old. I am deeply concerned about my masculinity. Feeling deeply insecure, confused and frightened but having to get by so I am trying my best to act the part. Sexual frustration is a big part of my life and I feel that if only I can have sex with a girl then somehow it will all be alright. Deep down, though, I am actually frightened of everyone – other males because so often I had been bullied and humiliated by them in the past and females because they constantly remind me of my sense of inadequacy.

Straight hair is the thing to have these days but of course mine is fairly curly. A good haircut mostly overcomes this 'failing'. Sideburns, another must, are more of a problem. Unlike my friend whose sideburns were dark, thick and wide, mine were narrow, fair and wispy.

I have cut myself shaving and quite like having to put a small piece of cigarette paper over the nick. I have had a go at growing a chinstrap beard à la Manfred Mann – and a friend's older and very macho brother, with a slightly malicious twinkle in his eye, is gently taking the piss out of me, saying that when you put a comb in it and it stays put, then you have a real beard. He demonstrates and says that mine is not and I *'should shave the fucking thing off!'*

I was delighted when, three years later, I grew a goatee type beard and it looked like a real beard at last. It also happens that, at around that time, I first had full sex with a girl.

I now have a full, grey beard and have no thoughts of shaving it off. My hair is thinning very slowly and has been for at least thirty years. I don't like going bald as I feel it makes me look older – not just in the way that being grey does but in a sense of being 'over the hill', as though the loss of hair means the loss of my desirability as a man, a visible sign of deterioration. I envy those men (and women for that matter) with a 'good head of hair'. It has the potential quality somehow of the 'body-as-sculpture or art' which now seems denied to me. In spite of all this I have often been told by women that I am attractive, which I am happy but very puzzled about as, quite honestly, I still don't see it.

My Hair, My Body, My Face

As a teenager I was a year ahead in school until the age of 13. Since you could repeat a year in a class, I was 13 with most boys being 14 and some boys who were 15 and even one or two who were 16 and not very bright but real bruisers.

I used to despair at not shaving and at my voice not changing. People used to mistake me for a girl on the phone and I hated it. As for my hair, it used to cover my ears (I had a complex about my ears sticking out, and so did other school friends so we used to cover them). Often in the morning, your hair was stuck up from the night and if you wet it above your ears you used to end up with what we called 'rat tails'. My hair was a little long and one's masculinity was judged on how one got the upper hand on dominating his parents in not getting one's haircut. I was struck by D's remark: on reflection I too believed that my hair was not part of me but a nuisance that had been invented to create daily misery for me.

From the back, I was mistaken for a girl. I used to be whistled at regularly by boys on mopeds and when I turned round you could see their face registering: 'Hell, it's a bloke!' I hated it. The amount of times people swore they saw friends of mine in a car with a girl, when it was me was incredible.

I believed that as soon as my voice would break and I would have to shave, all would change. So I started to have a wet shave every day, in the hope that it would accelerate the process of me having to shave. As I remember, we always used to talk about shaving in the school play area. I used to go to bed at night willing that I would wake up with a full beard, believing in the paranormal.

When I met my present partner (I was nineteen) I remember how relieved I was when she told me that she loved my body because it was not hairy and that men with hair on their back gave her the creeps.

A few years ago, I decided to have a number two haircut. I have since kept my hair very short. Most people around me do not like it as short as that, but I feel really liberated. My hair is so easy to manage! I have grown so used to seeing my ears and to accept them as part of myself that I don't need to hide anymore. In fact, they are not as stuck out as that. But in the early seventies, it is something schoolboys used to focus on.

I think I have learned to accept my face and to love it.

An Embarrassing Story

This is an embarrassing story about hair. The first time I learned that women had pubic hair I was about seventeen years old. I was studying Greek (Classical) for the Scottish Higher Leaving Certificate. We had been struggling through the translating of a Greek comedy, Aristophanes' *The Clouds* if I remember rightly. In it I met a word which translated as the (for me) new word "depilated".[1] Good conformist pupil that I was, I then looked that word up in the English dictionary. Its meaning released in me a process of wondering and solitary reflection. This terrible new information connected in my head with a detail I had picked up from *The Miller's Tale*. Whether I had previously read Chaucer's tale or did so subsequently I cannot now recall. In any case two fragments of knowledge collided in my head to produce new and really useful knowledge. Perhaps this is the seed from which grew my later concerns about identities constructed around individual academic subjects ("I'm a theologian") and my professional commitment to Integrated Humanities and interdisciplinary work.

Changing My Hairstyle

I have only changed my hairstyle a few times in my life. My hairstyle is a *part* of who I am at the time that I want to like.

The first time was when I moved from having a boy's neat flat hair that was parted on the side and brushed across the top of my head. I had that in my school photographs until at about 11 when I went to grammar school. I was encouraged by my father to use *brylcreem* (the word brings back the sickly creamy smell), so that I could then comb my hair back into a *quiff*, a mini-Elvis style on top. My dad had always in my memory used brylcreem to brush (very vigorously) his hair flat back – though I have seen a few photos of him with a quiff when he was young, late teenage I think. (So was I being recreated as him?)

I had the quiff style throughout most of young teenage years, except when I went to France on an exchange stay of several weeks when I was 13, and they had no brylcreem so there are photos of me with my hair again combed to the side (*sans quiff*). Apart from that the quiff was my trademark as a teenager.

Then at 17, I got my place at university, and on the day or so after the confirmation of the offer of the place, I had my quiff cut off. I was influenced in

---

[1] deprived of or removed of hair, plucked

this decision by my desire to impress the lovely L who I lusted for and who lived nearby, and who happened to be a friend of one of the boys at my school who had a similar non-quiff, shorter hair, vaguely mod-ish, student look. So this was the appropriate style for becoming a student.

At university I kept the same style except that I grew it much longer especially at the back, and then grew sideburns. I had the experience of walking out in the middle of a haircut at university; the male hairdresser started moaning about long hair and long hair being dirty. And then on a postgraduate course grew a moustache and rather briefly a beard. The beard was an experiment I didn't really like, and I also realised that another woman whom I had fallen in love with didn't seem particularly keen on it. So the beard went. The Crosby, Stills & Nash moustache stayed, as did the sideburns, when I started working, and I had to defend against my boss's antagonistic comments on the length of my hair. I think I compromised, made a gesture by removing the moustache rather than shortening the back.

Though the fashions changed and my hair got shorter at the back – that is, I got it cut shorter – my hairstyle stayed more or less the same until 1979. I was in a men's group and my best friend there gave me a mini-lecture in the Turkish bath how I needed to smarten up my hair if I was to make a better impression on a third woman whom I had fallen in love with. My old sideburns had to go completely and my hair should be brushed back no parting more or less as it is now.

My hairstyle hasn't changed since – except that who cuts it has – my ex-partner, did it for some years, sometimes rather reluctantly, then a man who was a friend of one of my closest friends and who used to come and cut it in my house, which was real luxury, and now at a black women's hairdressers. Going there is the best thing, and Roberta, an Indian Jamaican, is the friendliest most welcoming person, along with Mi and Fi. The 'salon' was recommended by my best friend, who used to go there, but doesn't now, as his hair is shaved so short. And that was where we rendezvoused this week, as his first social visit to the salon for a year – a kind of return of the prodigal son.

THE FIFTIETH BIRTHDAY PARTY

It was a time for balloons and a multi-coloured frieze. It was my fiftieth birthday party that was planned from 12.00 till 8 in the evening. I was newly retired (two years ago) and the party offered me the possibility of entering a different phase of my life, of life without paid employment and a new sense of masculine self that might go with these changes. I decided that I wanted to celebrate my growing sense of fresh possibilities by shaving off my moustache.

Originally, I'd grown my moustache at a time of great anxiety and insecurity in my life. Back in 1968 (22 years before) I had become a Head of the English department in a small, Lancashire comprehensive school, taking mainly white, working class kids from a large council estate nearby. In 1968 I was very young and innocent looking for my age, and I was extremely worried about my ability to keep discipline in my classroom, especially when dealing with the boys. So I started to grow a moustache in the Summer holidays before I started at this new school. I wanted to make myself look older, more experienced, more powerful than I actually felt. I wanted to speak with a manly authority and to present my face as a face that should be listened to.

My first attempts at growing hairs on my upper lip were messy. My moustache hairs were wispy, straggly and erratic. The hairs wouldn't grow as fast as I wanted them to, and I worried that I would be laughed at. I'd always been a late developer in terms of my need to shave regularly and I was very aware now that I wasn't producing stiff bristle on my upper lip but something softer and more downy. But I persevered. I don't know exactly why and over the months grew more used to my ginger hairs sprouting on my upper lip.

Until now at fifty. That morning of my birthday party I took up the razor and shaved all my moustache off. I felt the time had come in my life when I didn't need to hide anymore behind bristle and hair on my face. I wanted to accept my face as it was, perhaps soft and vulnerable but my own. And I didn't want to go on pretending I was more mature and manly than I actually was.

So I slowly scraped off my moustache of 22 years standing. I nicked myself in several places and there were small cuts and spots of blood on my face. And bits of tissue paper. And then I looked in a mirror and saw what I had done. I had revealed a naked, puckered upper lip. I called down to my partner, 'What do you think of this?' She came up and laughed out loud. She couldn't stand my pallid, under-a-stone upper lip. So after a few days and a lot of talking I grew my moustache back again and it's still with me now.

I Want My Hair To Be Like a Breaking Wave

I want my hair to be like a breaking wave. I carry a great deal of my sex in my hair. I imagine that it might be a seductive charge to some women. I also carry my repressed longings to be softer, more flowing, more sensual in my hair. And there's some defiance there as well. Perhaps a contempt for the neat parting and Brylcreemed hair of the 1950's bank clerk in Britain? I'm not sure.

I think I must have picked up the idea from my childhood that blond curls were more sexy and alive than straight hair. In the 1940's my mother told me to 'Eat up all your crusts or you won't have curly hair'. I think she favoured me against my sisters and that showed in the contrast she made between the straight hair of my sisters and the more prized (at least in our family), curly hair of myself as a very young boy. There's some ambivalence in me about my curly hair. On one hand I heard my mother praising it and on the other I heard these other strange voices murmuring around me: 'Blond curls are wasted on a boy.' And the other day a railway ticket collector in London called me 'Madam' without any hint of irony.

As an ageing man of nearly 63, my full head of hair seems to keep me desirable, at least in my dreams. I'm proud of the fact that, so far, I've kept myself at a distance from baldness and thinning hair. I like to feel my hair frothing around the sides of my head, even though it's going grey. I like to run my splayed fingers through my hair covering my forehead and feel my quiff springy and resilient. Often before I go out to meet the eyes of the world, I rearrange my curls in front of the mirror. I still want my hair to be seen as wild, vigorous and attractive.

My fear is of losing my curls, of my hair becoming flat. One particular episode from my personal history reminds me of my fears. In 1986 I was in hospital for 16 weeks fighting endocarditis, a bacterial infection in my heart that might have grown out of the detritus left by my leaking heart-valve. I was full of despair and my body reflected that draining away of energy in me. I had just come out of the intensive care unit, after major, heart surgery, and my curls were crushed. My hair was flattened with sweat and dirt and was matted close to my scalp. I just sank back into my pillows and didn't want to move. I was disappearing into a drowsy slur.

Until a nurse shook me out of it. She was the one nurse on the ward whom I really disliked. She was bossy, arrogant and usually biting in what she had to say. But this one morning she approached my bed and said: 'This morning we're going to wash your hair.' I groaned inwardly. I didn't want to be disturbed out of my torpor. But later that morning she got me up, clutching my portable heart-battery and, helped by two other nurses, got me into a wheelchair. She wheeled me around to the wash basins.

I can remember those wash basins. They were wide, shallow basins, with chipped and cracked ceramic. The basins were still greasy from other patients' morning swills. The nurse encouraged me to slowly stand up and lower my head down into the filled sink. Then she shampooed, dunked, shampooed, dunked my hair and got out of my hair all the dirt of the last few weeks. She then refreshed the water and washed the shampoo out. She did it firmly and briskly, not buttering me up but just getting on with the job.

She was the last person on the ward that I would have trusted. And yet her actions made a difference to me. She didn't change her attitude to me or me to her. She was still the bossy, loud-mouthed one on the ward but she did put some of the spring back into my hair and into some of my life.

PUB(L)IC INSPECTIONS

You shouldn't always go by appearances in matters of the hair. Having it on top may not tell the whole story. So here goes.

It was a curious ritual at my second boarding school, happening once a year or was it twice? We all lined up - 'juniors' first, outside the study of the house master, a room with certain disciplinary connotations, though it was only boys who did the beating in our house. Then you went one by one into a darkened room, curtains drawn. I remember walking uncertainly towards the elderly gentleman, crouched in a chair at the far side of the room. He had a torch in his hand. "Trousers down", he said - I think - and then, for sure, shone his torch and peered at my crotch, rather intently. He said nothing but I knew he'd finished. So pulled up my trousers and went out, none the wiser, and what this was all about but both shaky and relieved. I could make any sense of the ominous joking of the older boys.

I never learned what the school doctor was looking for. And can only speculate today. At the time, however, inspections were full of fearful meanings.

Would the dreadful disease I had contracted from certain boys hands in rituals of initiation be discovered? Did my desire for other boys or my masturbatory tendencies show in some way? Was I hairy enough down there?

Actually I had a relatively minor skin condition that remained untreated for many years. Maybe my fear of showering in public had something to do with it. The main symptoms were itchiness and hair loss; I was losing my pubic hair soon after gaining it. It would have been an easy matter, wouldn't it, to say to the school doctor ...? But I never did, filling this silent ritual with much worse horrors of my own. I dreaded discovery, exposure and blame (for what exactly?) each time, congratulating myself after every inspection but also holding onto and feeding my fear in secrecy, part of a bigger secret I'd always kept from everyone at home.

It was only much later, after I married J., that I broke this secret, apparently so small, but also so dominant 'inside'. Fearful of infecting her, I sought treatment for a condition that proved life-long. As late as the mid-1980s I was still attending the Skin Hospital with a consultant who liked to introduce me to his students as 'one of his professional patients'. By then I was publicly hairless, the odd fringe apart, while growing an incongruously hairy middle-aged tummy, It turned out I had most minor skin conditions going, all non-contagious, and especially a form of dermatitis of the sweat glands, 'common in adolescence'.

I am reconciled to my hairless pubis by now and TCP keeps the spots and itches away. I am rather fond of it in fact - but public showers, like those at school - hmmm - never! Well anyway, I'd need a different relation to the other men involved for sure.

THE VASCECTOMY, A VERY INTIMATE HAIRCUT

I've never felt as hairy since I cut my pubic hair clean for the vasectomy.

I was cutting clumps out with scissors and feeling colder and colder.

Tremulous at the prospect of my manhood being cut open and stitched up.

Lying on the operating table the nurse said, "you've made a very clean job of shaving yourself"

I didn't know whether to feel proud or humiliated.

Had I overdone the cutting?

I felt exposed vulnerable and apprehensive but her comment distracted the fear.

In a strange way it humanised what felt like a deflowering operation.

They never grew back as thick.

As well as being a sexually liberating process whereby I no longer needed to worry about contraception, my vasectomy's hairlessness begat my middle-aged non-childbearing years.

The start of a new kind of creative phase in my life. One based on developing of senses and feelings of a less hairy man.

GET YOUR HAIR CUT

For the first twenty plus years of my life people told me to get my hair cut. "People" meant, firstly, my parents who, it seemed, carefully monitored the length of my hair and regularly initiated the battle of wills which led, ultimately, to my going reluctantly to the barbers'. With National Service, of course, getting your hair cut was one of several unpleasant rituals that one had to submit to along with parades and inspections. Once I started at university the cries of disapproval became less frequent, confined to vacations, and less effective. When long hair for men became more acceptable, I felt more at ease although never quite managing anything shoulder length.

In my more mature years I used to dread the conversation which began with "Got the day off, then Sir?" which forced me to develop a slightly apologetic stance and almost inevitably led to my having to explain what Sociology was. Now I am in the happy state of going to a barber – or stylist – who does not expect or have a great deal of conversation.

Why did I dislike my childhood trips to the barber? There are several possible answers to this question but part of it reflects my overall relation to my hair. This was one of indifference. I didn't want to be bald but I did not have any sense of how I wanted my hair to look, no role models. I did however dislike the part of my hair which refused to grow in the proper direction (and still does) and which I assumed would be an immediate turn-off for any girl I might have been interested in. Even generous applications of Brylcreem (which then seemed to be part of the natural order of things) failed to keep it down. Hair represented an unnecessary chore rather than part of me or part of being a man. The same also applied to bodily hair and I cannot remember ever being the slightest bit interested in how much hair I had on my chest or between my legs – or anywhere else.

Shaving was only slightly different as I do remember discussions with my peers about beginning shaving and the transition from a dry shave to a wet one. I also remember being vaguely proud of the odd cuts on my face which I took with me to school. But I saw no particular virtue in being clean-shaven. In my thirties, while camping in the mountains in 1968, I grew a beard or, to be more accurate, I stopped shaving. Now, beardless, I quite enjoy the sensuous pleasure of shaving, especially the warm water on my face after having removed the beard.

When my son was in his teens he discovered my bald patch and took great pleasure in rubbing it as if it were an apple on a greengrocer's stall. I found this slightly disquieting but didn't want either to reverse or accelerate the process.

THE ELECTRIC SHAVER

I remember trying to use an electric shaver when I was a teenager. It never really worked properly. I always felt slightly unshaved – it was not close enough. The electric shaver, I guess it was a Ronson or a Philips, I was given when I was about 16 just sat in my wardrobe even when I was into my 40s.

I could easily have given it away or thrown it away but I decided to keep it, as it said that I had positively chosen to use a wet shaver, Shaving with a wet shaver is now a _real_ pleasure, especially with these new aloe shaving cream mixtures. Not shaving in the morning is a disaster. I feel totally unclean.

TIME TO GET SMART

This is a story about hair and also quite a hairy story. It happened about a month ago. I had got an interview for a research post and a colleague who's quite a lot senior to me and who's incredibly warm and friendly asked me to phone her for some advice about how to prepare myself. I phoned and we chatted away and suddenly when there was a slight pause in the conversation she said 'right' in a more sombre tone as if we had got on to the main point of the phone call. She said there were two pieces of advice she wanted to give me. The first was not to be so self-deprecating and to convey that I was more clued up than I normally did and that I wasn't crap at anything to do with numbers, and the second was to smarten myself up. George Bush looks smart and look at him. But that's not what I thought. I thought shit what does she mean, why is she saying this. I wear a shirt and trousers and shoes, maybe it's my trainers, but other people wear trainers as well. And I thought it's got to be my hair as it's always been my hair that people have mainly complained about when they've said I'm untidy in the past. Like my mum who used to go on and on at me and when my brother got married pleaded I got just a trim and promised it would be really easy as she would get her hairdresser to do the job in the comfort of our home and I would look so handsome with my face unveiled. But now my hair's stopped growing long and though it sort of bushes out a little it's not really my central feature. I wanted my colleague on the phone to say what it was which made me untidy but it felt quite difficult and she wasn't at all specific as if she expected me to realise what the problem was and maybe was too embarrassed to spell it out. She made me feel I exuded untidiness, like a tree which grows it as its leaves. I fished around for bits of advice. I asked her if she thought a tie would help, something in fact I hadn't until then dreamt of wearing for the interview, and she seemed really non-committal saying 'depends how you feel', 'only wear one if you feel comfortable.' It felt like she was trying to offer me friendly advice without being judgmental, which was impossible. I just wanted her to say what was fucking wrong with me but I was embarrassed about embarrassing her and especially as she's so nice and offering me friendly advice. I was sure though if it wasn't my hair, my hair had a lot to do with it and later I asked another friend if she thought I should get it cut for the interview but she said don't bother as it wasn't long. I didn't get it cut but I wore a tie and got the job. So maybe it wasn't my hair but why did she say I looked untidy if it wasn't for my hair.

One Hairy Loveable Son

He came into the house crying like a lost baby
He stuck his face in my cheek
One hairy loveable son.
The short bristles scratched my soft shaven skin
And proved a stark contrast to the intimate embrace we were having.

I held him to me strongly but gently, trying to relax his body
As he continued to cry with the happiness he felt in being home with us.
Away from that impersonal environment he was struggling in at university
In that ageing corridor of cells with its smelly kitchen and mouldy shower.

As I remember this my memories of school boy showers came back.
The furtive looks comparing colours of pubic hair, levels of growth and ridicule in the absence of any.

This layered with comparisons of dick size still vivid after forty years.
Competitions for supposed levels of each boy at the end of each P.E. lesson.

CHAPTER 3

Clothes

Jeff Hearn

INTRODUCTION

The writings on clothes include much detailed description and reference to specific clothes and uses of clothes, often in a rather explicitly gendered way. So let us begin with gender ....

Gender

Clothes are easily understood as a mark of being masculine, or not, and men's relationship to clothes can be deeply linked to masculinity in very many ways: "Where else can we show our own creativity and personality to others, define restrictions, show feelings and trace our life history so easily?" This includes references to gender, sex, masculinity and sexuality. Sometimes this is about using clothes to affirm masculine power and authority, sometimes to undermine or subvert that.

Perhaps for these reasons clothes are often represented here as a long-lasting problem, perhaps unresolved, through feelings of discomfort, even to the extent of not feeling "entirely comfortable with any choice" of clothes, or somehow never learning "to create a style". From this, with biographical changes their meaning can even progress to their being "an absolute statement of what I no longer am! Even when I am being scruffy it is a considered and thought about scruffiness". The impression of not caring about clothes may be presented but this may obscure being "really concerned about what I look like in clothes, and especially clothes which I wouldn't be seen dead in".

These complications and difficulties can extend to the very act of shopping for and buying of clothes: "(s)hopping for clothes is a nightmare, usually done superfast, without pleasure, so I often buy what I don't like or doesn't fit". This antagonism may be rooted in a boyhood antipathy to spending time buying clothes constructed from an early age as feminine.

Class and Politics

These gendered experiences may be overlain by class experiences. Class, gendered class, also bears on clothes. Early year class-based experiences, as recalled through clothes, are, for some, spoken of as formative. Childhood poverty may engender feelings of gendered inadequacy, as when being obliged as a boy to wear sister's cast-offs to school, leading to jeering and calling of girls' names there.

The class dimension may figure in a different way in wanting to use suits to appear not working class but a cooler, more elegant and more middle class man. Alternatively, class positioning may also be part of a more rebellious masculinity as a personal political protest against mainstream institutions, and an attempt not to seem middle class, through being against the wearing of suits. At times and more subtly, an inappropriately class-(or gender-) coded piece of clothing can be made acceptable by addition, an accessory, such as a long scarf.

Sexuality

Sexual meanings of clothes are hard to avoid. Clothes can provide a superficial assessment of relative beauty and handsomeness. Dominant meanings may involve men's clothes as, firstly, dull and drab and yet, secondly, some modes seemingly making men smarter and more mature, and so holding out the fantasy of making men more sexually desirable, and thus the thrilling promise of sex. Even seeing particular garments associated with sexual encounters may bring back their memory.

Meanwhile clothes may lead in other less dominant directions, as towards experience and engagement with gay camp, disapproval from older people for their erotic potential or experimentation with women's clothes as the feminine/erotic. For example, "I tried on women's underwear when I was in my 20s and I was completely amazed by the fact that clothes could feel so erotic." "I look round the women's shops full of wonder and envy at the colour, the style and the erotic and expressive potential of it all."

Uniforms and Events

Clothes, perhaps most clothes, can be seen as a uniform of some kind. This can be traced back to the very British and odd phenomenon of the school uniform, often leaving a deep and ambivalent mark. Indeed a special word needs to be said on uniforms, especially but not only, in relation to schooling, but also other similar contexts, such as the military or events, rituals, ceremonies, specifying and demanding particular formal mods of dress. Social events specifying smart dress could be a trial and a test, at times overlain by racialisation. Some similar feelings were reported around religion and dress, and sometimes religion and schooling, with priests maintaining "an aura of the supernatural". The dressing of the religious leaders might be complemented by the competitive "wearing your best" at church service.

In later years such gendered relations to clothes and uniforms were sometimes apparently transferred to the man's so masculine suit. Thus for some suits brought power, authority and solidity, whilst again often accompanied by uneasinesses about wearing suits, as stuffy and stifling. This ties in very much with class locations and feelings: personal rebellion against the conformity of the formal suit. Together, these feelings may make for ambivalence towards suits, sometimes having their pleasurable even sexual uses.

Pleasure

Finally, clothes bring pleasure, as with liking to look smart and fashionable, and seeking means of self-expression more generally. This may be very conscious or only incipiently recognised through others' valuing and admiration of men's clothes. These are direct possibilities of pleasure from clothes – either direct recognition of looking good oneself or others saying so, so bringing pleasure from that. Clothes can be kept for ages, taken-for-granted, can be prized, even treasured: "Even today I will buy some new jacket or trousers and keep it in the wardrobe for weeks or maybe a month until the occasion warrants "my Sunday best" to be worn. This deeply ingrained status defining function of clothing persists despite my espousal of an egalitarian socialist philosophy and commitment." With ageing, attention to appropriateness of clothes may be complicated by the tension between what style is liked and possible ridiculousness of how that might look. As one man put it: the 1960s hippy years were best.

These issues of – gender, class, sexuality, uniformity or not, and pleasure or not – all interconnect with, and often reinforce, each other in the stories that follow.

***

WEARING YOUR BEST

Clothing is very important to me. I like to look smart and a bit fashionable. So I will look through M&S, House of Fraser, and Debenhams for cut and style: influenced by my father's military tastes and mother's love of being beautiful and showing off.

This was nurtured by the rituals of each week wearing your best, competing with the other families at the end of mass at the church service at the Cathedral. I remember it had a courtyard at the back into which the congregation would spill out, after one and a half hours of soaring emotional voices, incense filled praying, and intense inspection of what the girls in the pews opposite were wearing. Clothes provided a superficial assessment of their relative beauty and my competing handsomeness. What a veritable post religious fashion parade.

Even today I will buy some new jacket or trousers and keep it in the wardrobe for weeks or maybe a month until the occasion warrants "my Sunday best" to be worn. This deeply ingrained status defining function of clothing persists despite my espousal of an egalitarian socialist philosophy and commitment. I find echoes of this among young people today who express their identity and sense of belonging through their clothing.

School uniform did a similar thing for me. At primary school the Sisters of Mercy, their habits floating along the ground like giant penguins, used their uniforms as part of a powerful tool to control our behaviour and morals. As did my uncle, on his visit, in his Dominican monk's cassock.

So together with the Augustinian priests at my secondary school maintaining an aura of the supernatural, these clothing based spells and rituals, kept me relatively supplicant for twenty three years.

The feeling of nakedness, being naked without clothes was rare in those formative years, and part of jettisoning the restrictions of religion in my mid-twenties involved peeling off the layers of rituals and an intellectual undressing of beliefs. At the same time putting on the new clothes of Marxism and socialism, as I developed a new sense of myself, what I believed. Though I would never lose that touch of the "Sunday best" style of dressing from my life.

My image remains important to me and though fashion designers provide ever new uniforms, I no longer feel in competition with anyone about the clothes I am wearing. The clothes I wear are still an expression of my personality, a small space for exploring who I am and meeting my need to be noticed and admired I learnt at church.

Where else can we show our own creativity and personality to others, define restrictions, show feelings and trace our life history so easily?

CLOTHES—A DIFFICULT HISTORY

My relationship to clothes is deeply linked to my masculinity in so many ways. My early experiences are very formative and reflected my poverty and inadequacy and helplessness as a poor and 'delicate' boy.

Age about eight years: For some reason I have no clothes to wear to school and I am put into my elder sister's blouse and jeans. She is four years older than me so they are way too big and have to be rolled up a long way and pulled tight with an elastic snake belt. They are big in the bum, waisted and tight at the ankle – and worst of all, they have a zip up the side. I want to crawl into a hole but I am made to go to school. Children laughing, pointing, jeering – calling me girls' names. Worst point is when I go to the (outside) loos in the playground. At the urinal I have to loosen the belt to pull the jeans round so that I can piss out of the zip. I hate my parents for subjecting me to this humiliation and I hate being poor even though I am not especially aware of the fact – I just hate my life.

My first memory of expressing myself though clothing was when I got my first pair of jeans – probably aged about 10-11 years. They were off-white and NOT BAGGY – i.e. fashionable and for the first time gave me a sense of pride in my body. I also got some baseball boots which made me feel both fashionable and agile.

Now I am 13/14 and at secondary school. We have moved away from London and there is a school uniform but I don't even remember being in it – just occasionally a tie. My clothes are grubby, ill-fitting. Cardigans knitted by my dad. I really stick out and feel constantly humiliated and scared.

A teacher (geography) tells me to stand up in class. All the kids are silent and looking at me expectantly. 'Come out here...... Stand there....... Do you ALWAYS come to school like THIS!!!!'

I mumble something inane; 'My good jeans are in the wash.' I am utterly humiliated and don't choose geography in my upper school options. A kindly caretaker gives me some P.E. kit from lost property and I feel a bit better.

Clothes now are an absolute statement of what I no longer am! Even when I am being scruffy it is a considered and thought about scruffiness. I mostly don't choose to be SMART (i.e. suits and the like) because they don't feel like me. They make me feel like I am acting a part.

But I also like to express myself and indulge myself in clothing up to a point, though I find most men's clothes (at least the affordable stuff) to be completely uninspiring, drab, and as stating something with which I just cannot connect – especially the logos and the awful colours (though they are now getting better).

I tried on women's underwear when I was in my 20s and I was completely amazed by the fact that clothes could feel *so erotic*. This was something completely unknown to me and increasingly since then I have sought to wear clothes that <u>felt</u> good as well as look good. I find now that I envy women enormously. I look at the awful drab colours of men's clothes in the shops, the horrible or dull styles, the constricting designs – the sheer drabness and lack of imagination – and I look round the women's shops full of wonder and envy at the colour, the style, the soft textures and the erotic and expressive potential of it all.

As I get older and my shape changes I find myself more constrained by the incongruity between what I would like to wear on the one hand and the sense of how ridiculous it might make me look on the other.

I have interfaced powerfully through clothes and it has always been an issue for me because of my childhood experiences. The hippy years of the 60s were the best.

MEN AND SUITS

I've always been uneasy about wearing suits. There's something stuffy and stifling about them for me. At one level, that's about my own personal rebellion against the conformity of having to wear a formal suit to fit in. But, in fact, I'm much more ambivalent about suits than I'm making out. Indeed, in my life history, suits have had their uses.

I remember a charcoal-grey suit that I borrowed from my cousin to gain entry into the 'hottest' dance hall in town: 'The Casino'. It was the late 1950's in South Devon. I was 17 and I didn't have anything to wear that would get me in to the dance hall on the sea front. The dance hall operated a strict dress code on Saturday nights and I yearned to be a part of the highly sexed atmosphere of the place.

That charcoal-grey suit offered me the fantasy possibilities of being more desirable to the women I danced with. Although the suit was slightly too big for me, I liked the feeling of sexual grown-up-ness that I experienced when I walked down the hill towards the 'Casino'. At that time I still had a quality of fresh-faced innocence and youthfulness and I suppose I wanted to appear more mature like the lounging, movie star Cary Grant. To seem more mature held out the thrilling promise of brushing suggestively against women's bodies, park seat groping's, of French kisses and fondling bare breasts. Also I think there might have been a class dimension in all this as well. I think I wanted to use my cousin's suit to transform myself in my own imagination from a working class scruff to that of a cooler, more elegant man.

The other main memory about suits, that surfaces in me now, is my midnight-blue pinstripe suit with matching waistcoat that I bought for myself in the late 1970's when I was head of the English department in a comprehensive school. I'm not sure whether I bought the suit for an interview, a funeral or a conference performance but I do remember the most significant moment when I actually wore the suit.

This pinstripe suit had very wide lapels, flares and padded shoulders and I hoped that it made me more sophisticated than my usual, casual and sometimes wild presentation of self. At that time I had recently come back from a holiday in Morocco where I had bought a goat hide jacket. I used to wear this goat jacket while teaching and I think I wanted, generally, to create the impression of a wild, raffish, rebellious self. That self wanted to protest about the institutional norms of schooling.

My main memory of wearing this pinstripe suit was associated with a heads of department meeting with the senior management team in the school. I wanted a suit that would make me feel more solid, more elegantly mature instead of coming to that meeting wearing cheese cloth, my goat jacket and with tumbling hair. I think I wore the suit to be taken more seriously by the other heads of department, particularly the head of math's who was always making ironic, sniping comments about the English department.

Temporarily, while wearing that suit, I felt associated with a powerful authority and power. I felt I could crush my enemies with one steely gaze and my suit reassured me and, briefly, normalised me in that group of senior teachers. That late afternoon, after school, I felt more coherent and focused in what I said. As I was about to leave the meeting, the head teacher sidled up to me with a sneaky grin and said, 'You should wear that suit more often to these meetings'.

The Big Black Coat

Clothes are a problem. I can never feel entirely comfortable with any choice I make, anything I wear, or so it seems. Shopping for clothes is a nightmare, usually done superfast, without pleasure, so I often buy what I don't like or doesn't fit. It's like all clothes are a uniform of some kind, like the green cap and blazer and grey shorts of early school days. Somehow I never learned to create a style.

My big black coat is a good example. When my niece got married, my partner and I decided to go to the wedding. It was to be in a chapel in the hills overlooking their valley. It was early Spring. The chapel was unheated and my sister said it would be very cold and my niece asked me to read one of the lessons. And it was going to be small but posh. I imagined my rich relatives all looking extremely elegant. How was I going to look smart, even smart casual, but remain something like myself - that is, not a 'clothee' really and usually trying not to look too middle-class.

My partner, I think, suggested a long black coat. It was a bit the thing then, popularised by the Matrix hero. In my city, though, you couldn't get a long black coat outside Rackhams, the poshest store, though it had a sale on.

Once bought, I hated it. Also be-suited, with black shoes, I looked and felt not just middle class but posh and rich. The performance in Church reminded me of a self, aligned to older middle class men reading lessons in Anglican churches, especially since I clearly had had practice and could project rather than mumble. So I was a posh man with a big voice – what's new? Getting the damn thing there and back meant wearing it through the airport routines - posh there and back. So, once home, it stayed firmly closeted, for the summer months, perhaps for a whole year or more.

I don't remember when and why I got it out again, perhaps an especially cold spell. I started to wear it at work where I had some notoriety, and, with the red trainers, it started to be a hallmark of some kind. When I retired I wore it down the long corridor there, to say - what? 'I'm still here?' Somehow it went with the image of someone who confronted the new VC and took the side of students and younger staff. I'm not sure when I started to wear it with the long scarf. But after this, people kept saying, friends and in the street, I looked like Dr Who. I sort of liked this. The Doctor? A Time Lord? Powerful but also a bit spooky and fey and capable of silly mistakes? What kind of man *is* he?

Anyway I wore it plus scarf when I met a party leader I admired a lot off the train at Leicester – 'I'll be one in the long black coat' I said, and also when I met my closest woman friend off the plane at the local airport in January. I must have worn it a lot because both pockets have worn holes in them, so mobile phone, gloves, wallet and keys have to be fished for from the lining. Will it last another season? Is it really me? Unresolved entirely. But I am changing too. But then, perhaps, it all depends on contexts.

STUCK IN THE DRAWER

They have always been a problem for me. I do buy them but not that often and most of my clothes I've had for ages and I can't remember how I got them, I think quite a few as presents.

When I was a kid I remember showing how pissed off I was being taken into a big departmental store by my mum to get clothes and trying them on and refusing to say whether I liked or disliked them, and my mum explaining 'he's a boy' and the male assistant who must have hated me, smiling. I was definitely trying to show how boyish I was hating buying clothes with my mum, but also, I didn't like having my middle classness rubbed into me, which being the centre of adult attention, with a well groomed, obsequiously polite male assistant, in the smart boys' clothes section in a departmental store, did. While I have always given the impression of not giving a toss about clothes, I am really concerned about what I look like in clothes, and especially clothes which I wouldn't be seen dead in which my brother and sister in law used to give me at Xmas, like jerseys with high throttling necks which I stuck in a bottom drawer in my room with the wrapping paper still on.

Some years ago, my brother and sister in law discovered them still stuck in the drawer when they were helping my dad move house, and were really hurt and said that's the last time he's ever going to get clothes from us. Now they just give me peanuts and raisins at Xmas. I get criticized for wearing the same boring things all the time by students I'm currently teaching. But I like the interest they show in me and my clothes, it feels friendly. Though I'm amazed how much more they know about what clothes and colours I've got than I do. Just recently when I was over in London for a few days, I bought some clothes at Selfridges. I hadn't planned to, but I was in Selfridges getting my computer seen to, and I passed all these trendy clothes on racks, and it was quiet and there was lots of space so I just started looking around and got carried away and was there for hours carrying as much stuff as I could into the fitting rooms and looking at myself in the mirror and usually it looked horrible but sometimes I thought it looked pretty good and I just bought it even if it wasn't a bargain, like some white trousers which felt really comfortable and looked, I think, quite cool on me, and cost 70 pounds which is something I wouldn't dream of paying for clothes (except running shoes if running shoes are clothes) and when I got back to Durban I wore them and loads of my students, mainly women, and some men said they looked nice and were surprised, as did a few women members of staff, and I was pretty pleased.

I wasn't so pleased though when I got a recent invitation for a party specifying 'smart dress.' I hate going to things where that's stipulated and never usually go, and this was for a party at the running club I've recently joined to celebrate Comrades, a 55 mile ultra-marathon which has become an institution in South Africa and is run on a public holiday commemorating the Sharpeville massacre. I ran in Comrades, and as I had one of the fastest times I was going to be awarded a prize, and I was glad I was in London at the time, as it would have been a hard decision to go. There were about 150 runners from our club doing

Comrades and most of them (and the best ones) were black, but I'm sure not many blacks would turn up for the party, especially with it specifying 'smart dress'

WHAT CLOTHES?

I. When he was/is quite young, maybe six or seven, he had/has a cap, his "bobby dazzler" – the very mention of the words made and makes him feel proud, but largely because the adults around, especially his mother, was/are overwhelmingly so proud of it, and (would) refer to it and to him and to other adults – "Have you got your bobby dazzler? You look really good in it." It was/is a school-type cap, mainly bluey-green, with a shiny, satiny, glossy bluey gold insignia at the front that had itself no particular connection with him. Wearing his bobby dazzler, he was and became a bobby dazzler, if only one removed.

II. When he was 10 he got a place at Grammar School. On the summer before going at 11, he went with his family on holiday to Plymouth (of all places). His father had for no special reason always supported the football club all his life. His parents, especially his mother, encouraged him to wear his virginal school uniform (that is, before he had started at the school) on the train journey to the holiday camp, which was heralded as being especially long (he remembers 6 hours). He felt ambivalent about this, both proud and unsure if this was such a good idea. The train journey passed, all six hours of it, an achievement in itself. Outside Plymouth Station, whilst waiting for the bus connection to the holiday place, a smoothly dressed man came up and said "Hallo, Boff's Grammar School". This was true recognition. So it was a good idea to wear it after all.

III. It was time to get some hipsters, and where better to go than Carnaby Street. He felt very nervous, but was determined to buy some. The accompanying companion is blurred. Eventually a pair of dark green wool textured with black strip seemed to fit the bill. The camp young sales assistant said "I won't say that they suit you, but what are you doing tonight?" The hipsters were successful, though really a bit, or actually rather, tight on the crotch. His girlfriend Cheryl's father, some kind of self-employed building industry businessman was particularly disapproving when they sat together on the sofa. But at least she was a good kisser.

IV. Since leaving university he had bought very wide flared trousers with turnips, matching very long coat, and flowery pink tie to go along with his longish hair and walrus moustache. When he was back to visit, one of the lecturers remarked how smart and fashion-conscious he had become.

V. It was important to look the part. He wanted to look familiar, ready to brave cold winters. So he went to buy a really good quality, <u>long</u>-length black coat – the most ex(t/p)ensive he'd ever bought - £300 plus a particularly attractive multi-coloured scarf. He felt at home, secure in it. He arranged to meet her, for the first proper time, at the station. She arrived, walking in the slightly uneven way she does, also in a long black coat, of course, and they continued as partners. The scarf was probably lost a few years later when it was lent and never returned, and that was that! The coat is now nearly 10 years old and is getting near to needing replacing.

CHAPTER 4

Peeing

David Jackson

INTRODUCTION

Changing Age Relations

Changing age relations, particularly 'Then' and 'Now', structure our experiences of boys and ageing men peeing. When we were boys playing pissing games our stories revel in the triumphant virility and force of our peeing: "I used to pee with the force of a geyser."

Some of our early physical sensations of peeing were about establishing a competitive hierarchy amongst boys ("Who could pee the highest?") and also that our "streams of piss" seemed like an uninterrupted, 'natural' gush that was valued as some irrepressible torrent that we could barely control or discipline.

But much later, ageing often brings anxiety and tension to our peeing. From "an unstoppable urge to pee" when younger, one of the men developed a sense of bodily difference with increasing age: "Yet my body is no longer the one I was in my 40s. I am ageing which is more difficult to realise."

Ageing men's bodies and our peeing habits change rapidly because of sudden, bodily accident and physical deterioration and functional incapacity. As a result, peeing in ageing men has to deal with a 'restricted flow' and a more hesitant and inconsistent 'pee-flow in age.'

Shame, Humiliation and Peeing

The experiences of a life-time of peeing are often closely linked to early incidents of humiliation and shame. Peeing our pants as young boys often stays with us in our memory hoard. One member of the group can remember a very early experience of classroom peeing: "... a puddle of pee there on the shiny black bitumen classroom floor". Also in our memories of peeing, there is some self-disgust expressed particularly connected to the smell of peeing. Several of our group responded negatively to the stink of pee. Another recalls "that mossy, stinky cavern, the boys' urinals at Primary school." And a third explored a more adult and personal moment :

> ... my underpants were a little soggy and then I realised that a part of the front of my jeans was not only a bit damp but was actually smelly-or at least I could smell it! I feared that colleagues would immediately be passing by and smelling me.

It is both the intimate discovery of being smelly and the imagined, public shame of being sniffed as stinky by a passing colleague that frightens.
the public and social context of peeingMMO4 also deals with the occasional anxiety and frozen pee-flows associated with trying to pee in public urinals:

> But thinking, remembering, back, one of the old difficulties was going to the public toilet, the stand up loos or pub toilets, and not being able to pee – through feeling anxious because of the other "fellow" pee-ers – as they seemed threatening, intimidating, or quick pee-ers or wanting to pick me up. One of the few solutions then is to count very quickly over & again several times to get the peeing going.

It seems here that the fear of possible masculine inadequacy publicly exposed to other male pee-ers in a public urinal, paralyses his pee-flow. As also does his possibly, fantasised fear projected onto other pee-ers imagined as 'threatening, intimidating'. Perhaps the other men are threatening, in a real and imagined way, who might show him up or might turn out to want 'to pick me up.'

Self-regulation and Self-surveillance

Age often brings more explicit, conscious awareness of physical functioning, including peeing – "Older, I now have to think of peeing" – rather than peeing being an inconspicuous, indivisible part of who I was as a young boy. This more explicit, conscious awareness in ageing men may become more of an anxious, watchful self-surveillance :

> But my urine, the nurse said, showed signs of blood and protein. It would have to go to the lab. So of course I began to worry about cystitis and prostate, starting to test myself in all kinds of ways. How long could

I hold it? How often did I go especially at night. When is 'urgency' (a term used in manuals)? What's pain or 'a stinging feeling'?

What is most striking in this quotation is the emphasis on "starting to test myself in all kinds of ways." The reader senses the beginning of a self-regulating, disciplinary, bodily regime in this man's life. As he comments later about this tendency: "I'm still an avidly, anxiously watchful pee-er."

Gendered Ambivalence

Occasionally in the stories it was possible to come across more positive, contradictory aspects of peeing rather than it continuing to be a segregated preserve of traditional masculinities. This may entail the pleasures of sitting down to pee as a man: "Sitting down particularly at night and first thing in the morning is so much more relaxed and womanly." Here there is a blurring of the rigid boundaries between masculine and feminine behaviours and an enjoyment of androgynous choices, partly female and partly masculine.

***

TAKING DRINK LIKE A MAN AND THE PROBLEMS OF HOLDING ON

The embarrassing humiliation of holding on when you desperately want to pee is a frequent part of our experiences of peeing. As one man put it with openness and honesty about the problems of holding on: "Holding on has always been an issue for me." He recounts a story of being driven in a flashy sports car after a drinking session with a friend and, "I hadn't the guts to ask him to stop to let me pee. That might have shown me up as not being able to take my drink."

The shame of not measuring up to the cultural ideals of heroic, performance masculinities being driven in a red sports car prevents him from admitting that he has a fallible, human body with urgent needs. So he opts for wetting himself still seated in the car: "Then finally giving up the struggle I gushed out over the leather seat, my trousers soaking down to my knees." The two men never discussed what happened and they just drifted apart after this embarrassing moment.

Peeing, Young and Old

I remember that when I was a kid I used to play pissing games with the other boys in the urinals at school. We used to try to piss as high as we could up the urinal, pinching the end until our penises until it felt as though they were going to burst and then letting it go with an explosive gush up the wall. Peeing games like this were just a part of being young boys together, bonding if you like, involving collective games and rituals with mysterious and unspeakable bodily parts and functions. Other games would include trying to wet the entire surface of the urinal so that no dry patches remained, and – of course – flushing any little piece of debris (or unfortunate fly) along the urinal with our streams of piss until they disappeared down the drain at the end. Somehow this seemed like such an achievement.

More adult versions of the same game involved pissing on discarded cigarette ends in the urinals in pubs until they entirely disintegrated and were flushed away. The trick was to try to complete the task before you actually ran out of supply.

My next thoughts on the subject involve the days after an accident in 1985 when, among other bodily interventions, I had to be catheterised because I could not pee. This was a dreadful feeling; actually (and almost literally) bursting for a piss to the point where it was physically extremely painful and then the bizarre but blissful relief of a doctor shoving a quite wide, clear plastic tube right up your penis to the point where suddenly I felt the pressure beginning to subside. I almost filled the bottle which was quite alarming really. After several subsequent operations I found the same situation and I presume that something about the process sends my urinary system into shock or something.

A few years after my accident, and maybe related to being catheterised so often, I developed a persistent urinary infection. But it was not like infections that I had heard other people talking about. This infection made me incredibly ill and only then did I begin to get the usual symptoms of burning and so on. This kept coming back for about three years and nothing seemed to shift it until a friend of mine who had been a nurse said, 'Oh, you need to drink lots of Robinsons Lemon Barley Water. That will sort it out.' And it did. And it never came back.

Now I have reached the prostate years. Peeing is sometimes not a problem at all but at other times the flow is restricted and I have to resort again to pinching the end of my penis so that the pressure builds up. I imagine this pressure also widens the aperture of the prostate a little – but I don't really know. Anyway it seems to do the trick more or less.

Then there are the drips to contend with. I had noticed a while ago that 'afterdrips' were wetting the front of my pants. I was familiar with this because after being catheterised it would take me some time to regain proper bladder control. Now, therefore, I have to be careful to wiggle and shake and otherwise cajole my penis into giving up its last before I feel safe enough to leave and go about my business.

It Was Now Called Weeing

When I was a young boy it was called "weeing". It was later I discovered "pissing" and then the more neutral "peeing". When I was a child we had an outside toilet, so night-time meant using the pot under the bed. There was a strange languid pleasure in seeing in the morning what it looked like, how much there was and what colour and consistency it had, sometimes still slightly warm. I noticed my fathers' had more and it was darker - - heavier stuff! At the same time or era peeing in the outside loo was not all bad, the occasional slight cold wind from outside refreshed a little, just as it does now in the outside toilet on holidays.

It is quite difficult, or very difficult, to remember specific memories of *ordinary peeing* – apart from peeing in my pants, or peeing when bursting or when drunk, or in the sink in a hotel or somewhere else, because the shared toilet was occupied. Ordinary peeing is perhaps more interesting – why?

—One of the great achievements of my adult life is discovering the pleasures of sitting down to pee (not to shit). I don't know when I discovered this, but it was when living in a house of three (adult?) women and a very strong taboo on *missing* the bowl (I remember going to a neighbour with two sons and the toilet smelling of missed piss). Sitting down particularly at night and first thing in the morning is so much more relaxed and womanly.

Another pleasure is the relief even following the slight pain of wanting to but not being able to pee. Sitting down is also better for that. Then there's coordinating the end of the flush so that it coincides with the finishing of the peeing.

But thinking, remembering, back, one of the old difficulties was going to the public toilet, the stand up loos of pub toilets, and not being able to pee – through feeling anxious because of the other "fellow" pee-ers – as they seemed threatening, intimidating, or quick pee-ers or wanting to pick me up. One of the few solutions then is to count very quickly over and again several times to get the peeing going.

PISSING MYSELF

I have been up since five o'clock, awoken by my asthmatic chest and so catching up with some writing in the early morning light - a mug of tea by my side, as I often do these days. Then it comes back to me. Why have I never told this story to the group before, even having written two stories already on the subject of peeing?

I am about fourteen and I have just joined the local scout group. I like outdoor and practical activities anyway and this is meant to be a good opportunity for me to meet new friends in the bargain. My father is immensely proud of me, in his usual pompous and self-gratifying way.

I think it is my second meeting. It is also the Queen's birthday, a point lost on me at first. At the first meeting I had already began to learn some useful things, like the names and configurations of certain basic knots and how to tell which way is north on a cloudy day from the mossy side of a tree (not very reliable). We continued with these kinds of activities at the beginning of our second meeting and then, half way through, we were told to take a break and go out and play on the field.

I guess I must have been absorbed in play because I suddenly became aware of how badly I needed to go to the loo. Almost at that moment the orders were barked urgently from the door of the scout hut, *line up, hurry up about it, come on ... come ON, where do you think YOU'RE going* (directed at me)! We were all made to line up in ranks and then 'left-righted' back into the hut were we were ordered to 'left-turn' so that the three lines now faced the front, one behind the other. I was now standing in the rear line, fidgeting and desperate to go to the loo. I tried putting my hand up but it was waved away dismissively by the scout master.

And there I stood for as long as I could, fidgeting like mad, almost crying with desperation, too frightened to disobey orders and break ranks. I have no recollection of what else was going on at the time and eventually, unable to hold it in any longer, I pissed myself. Hot relief coupled with hot-faced embarrassment, I stood there and just let it happen, wanting the world to open up and swallow me. And still the hot piss ran down the left leg of my trousers, filling an ever-expanding puddle at my feet.

Then it was over; first the pissing episode and then the parade. *Right turn! Dismiss!*

As the other boys broke ranks and wandered about the hall my only concern was to get away from the incriminating evidence. I could only hope in my desperation that no-one would actually look down and see the long black, wet streak down the leg of my trousers. But the puddle was to be an even greater problem. It was HUGE, right there in the middle of the hall for everyone to see, and the more I tried to get away from it so the more the wet footprints followed me wherever I went, away from its centre and all around the room.

'*WHO DID THAT!*' someone demanded from the front. He seemed to go up on his toes as his stern eyes scoured the room for the culprit and, as he did so, I sought to avoid his gaze by scurrying around the room. But the incriminating evidence – the wet footprints, along with the other boys' eyes, followed me everywhere....*here he is! There he goes!*

The rest is a blur. All I remember is running home in my now cold, wet trousers, in full view of everyone who chanced to look my way, and trying my absolute hardest not to cry. It was one of the most humiliating moments of my life and it was years before I ever told anyone about it.

PEEING IN SOLIDARITY

It was perhaps fifteen years ago. Near Leicester Market I met an elderly Polish man whose son I had taught as a teenager maybe ten years earlier. 'What news of Stefan?' I asked him.

This sparked off a long sad tale about how he had failed to keep his son on the straight and narrow: 'He no longer goes to Church. He is no longer a Catholic. I no longer see him. It is a few years now.'

Suddenly an urgency added to the old man's loneliness and misery. 'I need a pee. Here, will you hold my shopping? It is difficult with my walking stick.'

He limped three paces from me and pee-ed at the side of a house.

I had his address, but I never made the effort to contact that man again.

Now aged sixty-four, I have a strange, imaginative solidarity with him. An early sign of my prostate problem was a sudden unstoppable urge to pee. I once had to take two paces off the pavement and pee against a tree in Victoria Park. I had to do it another time into somebody's hedge on Avenue Road. Fortunately it was dark – and raining. It's true that with medication things are much better now and I have had no accidents for a year or more. Yet my body is no longer the one I was in my forties. It is ageing. I am ageing, which is more difficult to realise.

What about my relationship with Bernard, my son? It certainly hasn't broken down like that of the Polish man and his son. In fact Bernard is the only person who has ever given me a gift of flowers. Yet there is some separation there. His unwillingness to talk about his work. Is it just, as he says, that when he is with me it is his leisure time? A time not to talk about work?

PEEING ... AND/IN MY PANTS

I usually think of memories in the past, the fairly distant past, but peeing is in the present. Before writing this, I had to go and pee. I pee in the present. The past has caught up with me. I am the same person/boy/man when I'm peeing.

So my main memory is from last week, I think, I was working very hard at work, accomplishing, trying to that is, lots of things, on and around the computer. I noticed that I wanted & needed to pee a lot, at one point once again after about half an hour. Is it the adrenalin that produces more pee? It wasn't just that, but the pee seemed to be seeping, so much so that my underpants were a little soggy, and then I realised that a part of the front of my jeans was not only a bit damp but was actually smelly – or at least I could smell it! I feared that colleagues would immediately be passing by and smelling me – perhaps even crouching down deliberately. That evening at home I washed just that patch of my jeans and left them to dry overnight. Next morning the jeans were dry and I was back to normal, no more seeping.

THE INCONSISTENT DRIBBLING OF MY PENIS

I used to pee with the force of a geyser, or so it seemed to me. I wanted to put out smoking log fires in the woods. I used to love aiming directly into the glowing embers with a boiling hiss. And in that mossy, stinky cavern, the boys' urinals at Primary school. I would marvel at my looping arc of piss reaching up and darkening the dry, green spaces at the top of the urinal wall.

Today things are different. The varied and inconsistent life of my penis is much closer to me. Now my pee-flow is jerky, hiccuping, interrupted. Particularly when I'm cold and in some anxious, tensed up state. Often I have to wait in the toilet, coaxing my flow to start. But sometimes it doesn't want to come. So I have to wait until a few dribbles begin. Then, getting up steam, a fuller flow emerges, then stops. So I wait, start again, look up, look down, waggle a few more dribbles of pee from the end of my penis. Then I rip some toilet tissue off the holder and wipe the wet tip of my penis. I think it's dry, put it back inside my underpants, and then, inevitably, another droplet of pee soaks into the cotton fabric of my underpants. So I have to unzip again and shake the end of my penis until I think it's properly dry this time.

Older, I now have to think of peeing, or, sometimes, where I'm going to pee. Whereas before peeing was an inconspicuous, indivisible part of who I was, often enjoying the spurt and steam of my peeing in the open air, covering a row of ants, a snail shell or a rock.

Now I'm aware of my flow and my occasional dribbles. Now I have to be more cautious about what I drink before I go to bed. If I go to bed at 11 o'clock I can usually manage until about 5 or 6 the following morning. But this is different when I drink my cup of 'Night Time' too late at night. I might go for a pee afterwards just before I turn over in bed and go to sleep. But sometimes I can't help waking up bursting for release in the middle of the night and knowing that, if I do, my pattern of sleep will be disrupted for the rest of the night.

THE MEDICAL ME

The latest episode in my long history of peeing began accidentally really. I was due for a check on my breathing problems - emphysema plus asthma – and got allocated to the wrong nurse at the surgery. I got the general-health-check routine instead of the airflow and lung capacity test. I was fine about this - ostensibly - having intended to have everything tested on retirement. But my urine, the nurse said, showed signs of blood and protein. It would have to go to the lab. So of course I began to worry about cystitis and prostate, starting to test myself in all kinds of ways. How long could I hold it? How often did I go especially at night. When is 'urgency' (a term used in manuals)? What's pain or 'a stinging feeling'? How far can I pee, in conditions of windforce 3, facing the right direction, into the bramble patch, or pathetically short of it? When is dribble symptomatic? Why do I always want to pee immediately after drinking? What's the danger point in nightly visits – one, two or three? Is my flow adequate and sustained? On long car journey's I've taken to loosening my belt and partially unzipping to ease the bladder pressure. So do I have to add my bladder, or its adjacencies, to my lengthening list of organic deficiencies and oddities, especially my lumps and blockages, in the genito-urinary region?

Sensitivity to deficiency 'there' is something of a life theme for me, from early adult infertility onwards, so - though with no news good news – from the lab, I'm still an avidly, anxiously, watchful pee-er, eager to share these stories too, I realise, with other ageing men. It would be good, as I told another group, to move from oscillating between panic and denial, to some more rationale address (and appreciation) to the state of my ageing body, and the practical ways to maintain myself.

A HISTORY OF EMBARRASSING PEES

Holding on has always been an issue for me. I never could hold my bear, it's in the genes from the Tartar in the east.

The first memory which stands out as a formative peeing in my pants is when I was in my first week at St Joseph's private primary school in 1953. My first experience of being left abandoned by parents in an English-speaking school. I had played with very few English children, because we had had a very close and intimate network of Polish immigrant families that visited each other every weekend.

It was a military battalion officer based extended family which extended to demob camps in Loughborough Leicester Derby London and all over Nottingham. So I did not speak much English at home and with the children on these visits.

So there I was in the infants class knowing no other children, when I could not hold on any longer to my urge to pee. I was too scared to ask for the toilet so I let it out through my short trousers a puddle of pee there on the shiny black bitumen classroom floor, in front of the teacher and all the children I had just met.

It was the kind caretaker Mr Holland I still remember his name, who whisked me off to his cubby hole where I finished off and got a fresh pair of pants I think.

The next peeing memory is at university following extensive drinking sessions I remember meeting some famous people in the Mountford Hall toilets. There was the time I had the honour of peeing next Brian Patten the Liverpool poet I had so admired at the readings at the O'Connor's Tavern and the Philharmonic. Drinking and listening to poetry was trendy and enjoyable in the mid to late sixties in Liverpool and rounding off the experience on this occasion at the Student Union reading peeing next to the star poet made the whole experience even more personal.

There were other peeing crises in my life that stick in my memory.

On the way to watch Liverpool play Bournemouth and Boscombe FC in 1969 with my best mate who came from there, in his red MGB2 sports car going at 120 miles per hour down the M5. I was trying desperately not to pee my pants.

Then finally giving up the struggle I gushed out over the leather seat, my trousers soaking down to my knees.

I hadn't the guts to ask him to stop to let me pee. That might have shown me up as not being able to take my drink. Looking back I wonder if he noticed how wet the seat got and the dark line on my Lee Cooper jeans betraying the peeing level I had sunk to. We never discussed it I just remember we drifted apart after that, though he never did rib me about it.

PEEING AGAIN—TEN YEARS ON

Our original Peeing stories were written in the group's early days. I write this now though – more than ten years later and in the group's closing stages, because it conveys so well the some of the changes that have occurred to me with ageing.

After a party at her house a friend of mine once remarked – in obvious exasperation, *'Why is it that men always piss all over the bathroom!'* I was turned sixty at the time and attempted to offer her some kind of explanation.

I already knew that with ageing, men's urine flow tends to become restricted and erratic but I was still quite disappointed when it happened to me. Instead of the healthy stream of fast-flowing, well-aimed pee of my younger days, what I now had was a reluctant fine spray, seemingly with a mind of its own. Oddly, as well, the more desperate I am to go to the loo, the more restricted and reluctant my flow becomes. As a result I have taken to sitting down to have a pee which, somehow, still feels like a very un-masculine thing to do but it does avoid making a mess of the place. In addition to this I also found that I was having to go more and more often as my bladder became less effective at emptying itself fully in one go. This can become extremely tedious, during the night for example, or after drinking tea, when I am liable to need to go to the loo several times in quick succession.

There is also another side effect which is associated with this but which is rarely spoken about. With this restriction of flow I discovered (and I now know that I am far from alone in this) that my urethra was also not emptying properly. Where once my healthy youthful flow meant that a good shake in the urinal afterwards was all that was needed, now I find that I need to put my hand between my legs and manipulate myself to banish the last few remaining drops and then to use a piece of loo paper to dry myself off. I am sure this can look odd to some people when I am using a public urinal, but then, as I get older, I care much less about what others think. I suspect that men's failure to take all this on board is one of the reasons why older men are so often talked about as being 'smelly' or unsavoury. I suppose if older men are determined to carry on peeing while standing, then I would imagine that these kinds of effects are almost bound to follow.

I know as well that these same issues can arise much earlier in men after prostate treatment so they are far more common than I had realised.

No more pissing all over the bathroom!

CHAPTER 5

School and Schooling

Dan McEwan

INTRODUCTION

This was the only one of our meetings where a woman took part in the session. A researcher from Sweden, she was much younger than the rest of us were in our fifties or sixties.

When I compare her story with that of the male writers, one difference stands out. She and her girlfriends discussed in the changing room the fact that the male PE teacher never gave a foul against the girls no matter how rough they played against the boys. The girls seemed to enjoy taking advantage of this but they commented on "how unfair it was that he [the teacher] thought so little of us, assuming we could never hurt somebody or intentionally play rough." On the other hand, all the stories written by men remember the author as confronting alone the challenges they faced at school. Of course, this difference may not be rooted in gender. After all, her schooling took place decades after that of the male writers and in a different country. Nevertheless it raises the question whether male solidarity and sharing tend to be different from that of females.

The stories either develop an incident that illustrates the pressures in schools which help to create our gender identity or by recalling several incidents that suggest some sort of development in gender formation. For example, one man recalls the experience of being prepared for "first confession" in a Catholic school, and another, after setting the scene, explores the legacy left by one incident of verbal bullying. On the other hand, a third sketches the development of his masculinity from entering primary school till his final year in secondary school, and another traces his story from primary school to late secondary with a glimpse forward to university.

In some stories it feels as if the author as a child is on the receiving end in the unequal relationship between teacher and pupil, or more frequently in the power relationships of the pupil pecking order. One account tells how one threatening teacher spanked him, not with the slipper or the cane, but with a piece of string: "It of course did not hurt, it was just humiliating and worrying." Another explores the lasting effects of the ridicule he received from other boys after using the words "tingly feeling" to describe his reaction to masturbation: "I had stupidly used a language of home intimacy in a fiercely institutionalised, school space."

In other stories the child finds ways to resist the pressures weighing on them. One man found that his height and his punching the older bully protected him from some of the humiliations inflicted on new boys in his boarding school; but for the most part he protected himself "by being initially quiet and good" and by escaping into a fantasy world based on his reading. Another finally responded to eleven years of teasing and bullying about being poorly dressed by an act of defiance: he decided "to stop going to school several weeks before my final exams. I swatted hard, turned up on the day and got distinctions across the board."

Several of the stories involve some sort of sexual awakening. Much, indeed for some all, of the schooling took place in an all-male context. Suddenly in a school kitchen after a rugby match, one account tells of being alone with a young woman; they kissed. It gave him the opportunity to tell his friends about "this amazingly sexy woman". The two of them even arranged to meet again, but he took along a friend from school, which led to rather awkward conversation. He was able to tell others that he had had "a fantastic time". Another memory reports wistful admiration for a young woman seen at Sunday Mass, but it was not easy to talk to girls from the convent school across the road from the all-boys school. Similarly, another tells of how with his first girlfriend "fumblings and snogging were controlled by my still-strong Catholic codes and confessions." As the writers re-construct on the page their early experiences they are perhaps exposing something of the processes that lead to most sex taking place, according to some, in the head.

***

MEETING THE BOY AGAIN

It is of course difficult for me, a man aged sixty-five, to meet once again the boy aged about seven. His name was pronounced in full to distinguish him from his father and his father's cousin.

He was still, I think, in Miss McB's class when he was being prepared for his first communion and, of course, first confession. He always felt safe when Miss McB was around. It used to be assumed in the Catholic Church that one always had to go to confession before going to communion. It was all a part of growing up. Grown-up Catholics went to confession to have their sins forgiven so that they could receive communion when they went to Mass. The Penny Catechism, which then cost sixpence, taught us that about the age of seven we reached something called 'the age of reason'.

We had to learn the Ten Commandments so that we would know if we had committed sins. Some of the commandments were easy to understand. 'Thou shalt not kill.' 'Thou shalt not steal.' 'Thou shalt not have false gods before me.' The problem was he didn't do any of those things. True, Miss McB said that 'not killing' could include not getting angry. So there might be a sin there.

Some commandments were difficult to understand: 'Thou shalt not commit adultery'; 'Thou shalt not covet thy neighbour's wife'; 'Covet' was easy. It means 'to want'. But 'adultery'? Always ready to try new words, he had made two words of it, the indefinite article and the rest. But what did 'dultery' mean?

I don't know how well Miss McB explained it, but it was all a mystery. 'Impure thoughts, words and deeds' had something to do with it. Maybe it had something to do with wanting to look up girls' skirts. But that was boring. He could see his sisters' knickers in the washing at home. No big deal! Had it something to do with playing with his willie? 'Pete', they used to call it in his family. Toy soldiers were better fun really.

The boys did talk about some of these mysteries. 'Dirty thoughts' sounded more exciting than 'impure thoughts'. But what were they?

Somewhere, I don't know when, he tried confessing 'impure thoughts' as well as 'being angry with his sisters' or 'not doing what his mother and father told him.' The priest seemed to understand and, through the veil, the young boy learned what his penance was 'Say three Hail Marys and ask God to forgive you' or something similar.

Finding out that rubbing his willie on the sheets in bed could be very exciting did not happen to him until a few years later. By then the family had moved house. He had a bed and a bedroom of his own and no longer shared a bed with his two younger sisters and cousin when he stayed over. His cousin and the twins were two years younger than he was. They still are, actually.

M., who lived nearby, used to cause him wild thoughts. She was gorgeous at Mass on Sunday in her blue coat and yellow hat. By then he was in the boys' secondary school and she was in the convent school across the road. It wasn't easy to get to talk to the girls then; except his sisters and their friends, but they were all too young really.

The Strange Boy, Lucy

The earliest memory of school was being labelled the strange boy who had a funny nickname of Bishop and shunned by cruel boys in the playground of my primary third and fourth year when I was eight or nine years old. Having a nickname was instrumental in becoming Henry, my second name, adapted for a more English identity.

There I had my first experience of a strong female. I was dragged into the girls toilets in the girls' playground for a short kissing session. I can't remember much about this but it made me feel shy around girls.

I saw some boys paring up with girls and going out together in the last year of primary and that's when I had a crush on CM, who later appeared twice more in my life, once at age 17 at ballroom dancing classes at the all-female Catholic Girls' Grammar, and then fleetingly at a gig at Liverpool University. I think it was when I was 20 years old. She no longer had the same effect on me, seeming to be far too conservative and unexcitingly normal.

At primary school I craved acceptance by the boys which I managed by being good at cricket. Respect was also gained by sometimes getting into trouble. I was the first to get slippered. This was continued in secondary school where I again got into conflict with some Polish boys who nicknamed me Lucy as I was more English than they, having been from West Bridgford, and more middle-class than they. Having a female name used as abusively as this by 14-year-old Lads in an all-boys' grammar school can cause all sorts of heartaches, which made me tougher, often getting into fights with short lived best mates to establish my position in the pecking order. This was halfway nearer to the sporty strong leaders by being in the cricket and athletics teams and away from the non-sporty, clever or weak boys at the bottom of the hierarchy.

I never got into girls again till we started the Polish Sunday youth club when I was 17 years old and had my first girlfriend. At that age platonic and fumblings and snogging were controlled by my still-strong Catholic codes and confessions. I had gathered up some courage with girls by then who I had seen mainly as friends of the family, on visits to parents' parties over these teenage years.

School Daze

I don't think any one specific memory stands out that shaped or helped shape my gender identity at school. Rather it was a difficult and rocky landscape of relationships which I had to negotiate. I never did masculinity well; I was frail, delicate, small and frightened from the start. Almost everyone and everything felt frightening and this feeling continued to the end. Many of these experiences I have already written about.

From the very beginning though I knew I was quite clever; my paintings were exhibited in local exhibitions, my writing and spelling were usually top marks and my teacher often gave me the other children's books to mark. He would even get me to sing to the class as a treat if they worked well. From this I learned that performing well in different skills and tasks was a way of feeling positive about myself. This eventually would become a major part of how I defined my masculinity, not always for the good.

Other pupils often picked on me, and bulled and teased me. My family had little money and I was mostly poorly-dressed and unkempt. Even teachers sometimes humiliated me in front of the class about this and so it was very difficult for me to feel positive about my-self as opposed to my abilities. But once I reached puberty and began to become interested in girls this took an even greater toll on me. 'Getting the girl' - or not - just became one more way of failing as a male - not just vis-à-vis other boys now but also now vis-à-vis girls. My school work started to decline as I became more and more preoccupied with my need to feel accepted and affirmed for what I was – not just what I could do.

What I learned from this is just how all-encompassing and total the male pecking order is in school. Everything seemed to reinforce this in one way or another. Everyone was constantly ranked and being tested, re-tested and re-ranked. Eleven years of this had me convinced not just that I was a crap person but that I was a crap male. Being good at school work meant next to nothing - I had to be good *as a boy* and that I constantly failed to achieve.

My piece-de-resistance was my decision to stop going to school several weeks before my final exams. I swatted hard, turned up on the day and got distinctions across the board and then I left without going back for a further optional year as originally planned. This act of defiance and subsequent success was enough to confirm something in myself that later on I would go on to develop and that would help me gain confidence. I still like to do everything well. Even the things I am rubbish at I am really, *really* rubbish at!!!

TRAVELLING THROUGH GIRLS AND BOYS

There are so many (of these memories) but the one that refuses to go away is my first Primary School. I went when I was just five and a few days – one of the youngest and stayed there until seven. Before that I lived in the woman's world/the world of women – my mother, sister, two grandmothers and a great grandmother. Then I went to school. I remember the 'first day of school' – it was all one word. Like many children I cried a bit, one girl kept on crying a lot. I was in Mrs. Pugh's class. I recall now Mrs. Pugh was slightly darker skinned than usual. (I have never thought of that until now.) My favourite activity was brick building – I can just about recall the satisfaction of constructing patterns and small towers. But most of all it was my three friends all girls I remember – not a <u>particular</u> memory but a sense of warm companionship that we were friends. The three were all different – Mavis was the loyal and less beautiful friend; Judith the most pretty, socially jolly and fun loving; and Gillian was also glamorous but in a more withdrawn and sophisticated way. I think I loved her most of all. They were my friends for the 2 years. The only boy friend I can think of is a small boy called Martin but he was secondary to the girls.

Then at seven I changed schools, as everyone did, to the all boys' school, the Junior Boys and that was naturally the *last I ever heard or saw* of them. There was no question of it being otherwise. The only remnant was that I was told by the new teacher that my green report card given from the Primary School that I was good at brick building.

From 7 to 18 I was at all boys' schools. There are so many (of these experiences) in the all boys' schools. 'Try two or three of them! Step up!!'

In the top school, the Grammar School (11-18), there were several very threatening teachers and a few who were labelled 'effeminate'. One of the threatening ones, Mr. D., the French teacher, was not the most threatening but threatening enough. He insisted on telling us boys not to funk it – at the time I was unsure if this had sexual overtones? The slipper and the cane were available though not often used. I remember one occasion when Mr. D. (who certainly had the slipper and/or cane at his disposal, if he wished) – insisted on punishing boys if they got a French verb wrong by calling them out to the front of the class. This included me on one occasion. He then spanked me but with a piece of string. I was not quite sure if the piece of string might suddenly change into a slipper or a cane – or mysteriously hurt, as if it had some secret powers. It of course did not hurt, it was just humiliating and worrying.

And then there was rugby … injuries, rugby songs, early age drinking, keeping friendly with the big brute players, especially the one who would punch you hard on the arm, a thug who was also good at his school work. The most vicious games were the inter-house competition games within the school. In my final year we, Day House, won against the all the odds, against the much stronger Lucas House. I still remember especially my crushing rather brutally a much smaller, younger boy playing for Glyn House called Martin Sage.

A TINGLY FEELING

I've often wondered why I choose to sit with my back to the wall in a far corner of the room facing the door, in pubs and public places. Perhaps it's linked to an episode in my school days that might explain a few things.

After my mother's death in 1952 I was sent away, against my wishes, to a state boarding school in Devon that was used by the education authority for asthmatics, boys with other illnesses, farmers' sons living in isolated parts of North Devon and boys like me, dislocated by family upheaval and break-up.

In this boarding school, I immediately missed warmth and softness. The awkward iron beds and single lockers made me feel ripped from the hot cocoon that I'd experienced cuddling up to my mother while my father was away in London working as a firefighter. At about 13, I think I can remember trying to comfort my freezing, grieving body in this iron bed. Surrounded by eight other beds in this brown-linoed dormitory, I was initiated into this boys' culture of jokes about masturbation ('H! What are you doing over there? Stop wanking!') sexualised banter, and young boys' fantasies of power and conquest.

Open grieving was out so I learnt, tentatively, to fondle and caress myself under the sheets, often with my legs drawn up in a foetal position. This sometimes led to a long arousal of my penis, and to my surprise, a sticky wetness smeared my thumb and fingers.

One day, the dormitory banter shifted to the subject of orgasmic coming. I don't know how it started but soon jokes were flying around the dormitory about coming and spunk. I remember my desire to be accepted as one of the lads, and I entered the conversation by saying: 'I like that tingly feeling that you get.'

The dormitory prefect, Fat R, a wobbling bear of a young man, snorted with contempt and stared at me, witheringly, saying: 'Oh listen to *Him*! He's got a 'tingly feeling'. He's got a tingly feeling.'

All the other boys collapsed in ridiculing laughter, and I was left stranded in the middle of a humiliating and lonely space. These boys continued to guffaw and chanted:

> 'He's got a tingly feeling. A TIN-GU-LAY FEELING!'

Later I recognised my mistakes-never drop your guard when in close contact with other boys who might be out to get you. I had stupidly used a language of home intimacy in a fiercely institutionalised, school space and I had made myself a figure of fun and ridicule. I decided never to trust a large group of boys or men again. I would watch myself for sneaking, unguarded mistakes of explicit 'weakness' and vulnerability. The only space that I could really trust from then on was the enclosed, one to one sharing where my fear of betrayal and disloyalty could be more closely defended against.

That brings me back, full circle, to why I choose to sit in the far corner of a pub with my back against the wall. It brings out an understanding of my defensiveness about being got at, of being sneered and laughed at with open contempt for my unguarded moments. That's why I have tried to protect myself over all these years around strangers who might turn out to be like Fat R.

THE HOMELESS HOUSE

There were signs that in the past someone had cared about the 'new boys' at the boarding house of my second school. The Common Room that was our home for two years was next to the Housemaster's study, under his living quarters and looked out into his garden. But I never saw the Housemaster in the common room and the garden remained a kind of empty dream, a dream for me because I had been brought up gardening with my gardener mother and gardens meant holidays, family, security, even if that was often boring.

The inside of the common room seems incredible now. I had found – or made – a relative privilege in my first school, as a winner of prizes, head boy, actor, choir boy even a bit sporty. Now we were the lowest of the low. The room was bare and quite small for 20 or so boys. We sat on low benches at long wooden tables to work or read. I remember thinking there was no room to spread out papers and write properly or do my homework. Other boys were too close, too close to breathe. Surely we were to be allowed to get on with our work? We had a locker each. But we soon learned there was a strong hierarchy in the room, corresponding to the order in which boys sat. Three boys – B, G and Y – who must have been a year or two ahead of us ran the room. G was large and fat with glasses, short hair, a rather cherubic face. He came up to us, too close, with a kind of wheedling intimacy, suggesting sexual secrets. When we lined up for meals the three of them policed our line, with slaps to the face and punches to the stomach and in G's case, with groping lower down.

Apart from the rituals, more of this later, I don't remember this casual violence happening to me, but I remember other sometimes smaller, sometimes more 'cheeky' boys writhing on the floor in pain. I also remember feeling sorry for them but also despising them. I wouldn't be like that, be a bully or be bullied. I would fight.

About a week into this nightmare, we all had to stand on a very narrow mantelpiece in the same room and sing a song, until someone said enough and everyone would throw books at you. Once this started you were allowed to jump down. Then, later, in the dormitory, in the house masters own territory, we were 'got', held down by a gang of our contemporaries, recruited by the loathsome Y, and had toothpaste smeared on our genitals which stung. Later we had to negotiate the outside window ledge of the dorm, above the forlorn garden. There was a lot of 'getting' in those years. As a birthday treat, boys were 'de-bagged' and their pants and shorts deposited on the roof to stay for weeks or be dangerously recovered.

I am sure my responses or defences to all this must have been important in forming my masculinity. I survived by being quiet, helped perhaps by my size and an inner certainty, that was perhaps conveyed, that I would and could fight if I had to. I did get two good punches into Y's face before he and the rest pinned me down in the dorm, But B was tough, a famed rugby winger at an early age and Y was very tall and wiry. So I guess some of this was/is bravado.

In truth I must have been very frightened because there are several remembered and vividly re-playable traumas from that time. And mainly I survived by being initially quiet and good. To much surprise but little appreciation I sang rather beautifully on the mantelpiece – a Shakespeare song 'Come Away Death!' Outside the house, I had support from a teacher or two but in The House, I escaped mentally, through elaborated fantasy worlds based on my reading - Eric Knight's *Lassie Come Home* and Maureen O'Hara's *Flicka* books especially. So while my littler peers were being brutalised I was somewhere off in the green grass of Wyoming or somewhere – coming HOME of course – between Scotland and Yorkshire. In both places there were real families, mothers, dogs or horses and proper gardens too. I remember my utter silence at mealtimes, especially when sitting next to matron. I wasn't really there you see. And didn't she see how unhappy we were?

The being good continued right through school days – and much longer. My defence was always to do better than expected or required. I suppose this was a way of not being a victim like hitting back or escaping.

First Time?

When I was 13 I was sent to a boarding school and I really missed my dog and my mum. My mum bought me grapes when I was ill and even peeled them for me, and my dog sat on my foot when I was watching TV. At this new school I didn't know anyone and people laughed at me cos I spoke with a Scottish accent and this was England, and they tried to mimic me which made me angry. (I lost my Scottish accent in my first term at school and have been speaking like I do now ever since.) Whenever I went back to school after the holidays I always felt really homesick, but never let on to anyone I was missing home, unless it was when I was pretending about my girlfriends at home. I had never had sex in my whole life and in fact I'd never had any girls as friends let alone girlfriends – all the schools I'd ever been to were all boys' schools and all my friends at home were boys and all the people I'd ever met were boys and all I'd ever had was a brother, even my dog was male, and I really craved girls. Then one time completely out of the blue when I was at school, I almost fell in passionate love with a young woman and had sex. I was on the school rugby team and we had just been playing a match at another school, one Saturday, and I went into the school kitchen to get a drink of milk and I was so happy cos I was away from school. And I saw this girl in the kitchen a few years older than me and I was wearing my rugby scarf and she came up to me and pulled my scarf, and I pulled her to me and kissed her and it was only for a second and I couldn't believe it. So I dashed out and told my friends about how this amazingly sexy woman had fallen for me, and then went back into the kitchen again and kissed her again just brushing my lips on hers and dashing away and going back again.

When we left to go back to my school, all I could think about was her and I told everyone I could about what had happened. I had a real girlfriend, I couldn't believe it. I then wrote a letter addressed to A, a maid, at this school hoping somehow it would get to her, and saying how much I was in love with her and incredibly it did get to her and I got a reply saying she fancied me. And then a few weeks later I arranged to see her. I was so pleased and told everyone. But I was also a bit scared, as I hadn't spoken to her really and did not know what we were going to say or do, and partly cos of this I went with a friend from school. My friend and I were given a lift from another friend's parents whose house was near the school where A worked. She was waiting in the place we had agreed to meet and I remember she wasn't as nice looking as I had thought. I can't remember what we talked about but it wasn't very much and she asked what was that in my top pocket and it was actually a packet of condoms, which I had bought for the first time ever, and she thought it was cigarettes and laughed at me being naughty and I didn't say it was condoms as it would have been too embarrassing. And then we went to a restaurant and had something to drink and then she said she had to get back to work, and I remember feeling relieved. I wasn't sure how to talk to her and was so glad my friend was there, and when she left we stayed in the restaurant until my other friends' parents turned up to give us a lift back to school and said we had a fantastic time, with lots of innuendos.

Playing Fair

I have this one memory of my school years that immediately comes to me. One of the reasons it recurs is probably because my dad has always brought it up when talking about my school years. He says: How was it that time when you were competing against K W?

Anyhow, I might have been about 11 years old and we had a competition in our English class. We all stood in line and our teacher gave us a word in Swedish and we were supposed to say it in English. I managed every word I got and in the end it was just me and K W left. K was a bit of a trouble maker, he was both a bully and bullied and I remember he used to fight in school. When we grew older he grew quite unpopular. He tried to please everyone, one day being a hip hopper, the next something else in order to get status. So it was just me and him left and I remember the kids screaming my name in support. We stood next to each other by the teacher's desk and I recall not knowing the word 'monk'. I think I won eventually cause he didn't know a word either but I'm not sure. I just remember how he seemed to triumph from the fact of competing against me and how I couldn't bear losing against him. I remember the line getting shorter and shorter and I was still in. It was as if everybody was expecting me to win and the fact that K was in was a bit of a surprise 'cause he wasn't supposed to be clever and excel. I think the classmates chanting my name is a very big part of this memory and that's the story my dad always wants to hear as well. I can't say whether it's a happy memory or a memory filled with suffocating expectations. A bit of both I guess.

Another memory that I sometimes talk of is that of the PE classes in school when we were playing basketball. I remember this since gender is very much at stake in this. Our PE teacher I was an older man and the only man at the school. He was very harsh and had somewhat more power than the other teachers. Sort of a mini-principle. When playing basketball it became evident to me and my girl friends in class that no matter how rough we played with the boys we would never get a foul. Whereas the boys, if they tackled us, would be taken out of the game immediately. I remember how infuriated the boys were that no matter what we did the teacher I always seemed to favour us. I remember us using this and playing really rough but at the same time we discussed when getting dressed how unfair it was that he thought so little of us, assuming we could never hurt somebody or intentionally play rough. I remember us talking of how he considered us so gentle and frail that we could never harm the boys. This memory is somehow linked to an episode where M was playing rough, being mad with the separate treatment for being a boy, and was consequently sent in to the locker room. He claimed the teacher had pushed him violently against the wall, something the teacher denied.

CHAPTER 6

Disruptive Bodily Changes

Vic Blake

INTRODUCTION

Whether our various bodily changes are regarded as disruptive or not is to a large extent a subjective matter and must surely depend upon who we are and where we are coming from. But the title – and this context – clearly implies something unwelcome, or at very least unexpected, something which knocks us off some chosen course and so has the potential to impact negatively upon our lives. More specifically - and like so much else - the changes to our bodies and the ways in which they disrupt our lives can really only be fully understood and dealt with within the context of gender relationships.

In our group of men we have listened to and supported one another through our attempts to cope with the effects of a wide range of such changes. These include serious heart surgery, the legacy of a major car crash, physical and mental breakdown, late onset asthma, deafness, prostate problems and much more besides. Again – as well as being hugely supportive – the impact and the relevance of each of these has been painstakingly understood by the group through the more analytical lens of gender.

One writer is quite specific about this. In his thirties and content in his masculine body he experiences a major car crash and is seriously injured. As a result he is forced to re-define himself and his sense of his own masculinity.

> The battered old warhorse image had a certain appeal but the pain was hard to deal with at times. Almost as an act of defiance I used six months of my recovery period training to become a carpenter and I enjoyed the ways in which I felt this enhanced my sense of manliness, strength and skill. Doing this in spite of my injuries added to this.

Eventually, however, he is defeated by the pain and forced to retire. Once again he needs to re-define himself but now the discussion probes beneath masculinity towards questions of 'self-worth'.

> By now, age 50, I was fully aware of how closely linked my masculine body image was to my sense of self and, more importantly, my sense of self-worth. If my body was going into decline how was I to cope with this?

He anticipates the group discussion that is to follow with a brief gender analysis of his own. Is this, perhaps, a lingering need on his part to hold on to control, to steal the thunder of the group maybe?

Other writers make no such attempt and focus upon their particular bodily changes while one member provides a very masculine backdrop to his story – age sixteen, a school rugby match in which he is picked in the centre. Again the story starts with a major head-on collision, this time with 'a really big brute' who succeeds in dislocating his shoulder for him. But the response this time is less defiant and turns instead to pathos:

> The pain was great, and the responsible teacher, Mr. ..., accompanied me to the hospital, with tears pouring from me, he held my hand. I was grateful; he hadn't been so soft before.

Once again he has to cope with a changed life course in which his injury and the associated pain are now a constant feature. He is shown how to put his shoulder back into place for himself but it is extremely painful and everyday activities such as feeding the ducks and even sleeping carry the risk of further dislocations and their debilitating after effects:

> I have to be kind to my left shoulder, to protect it and me from its potential for pain and above all draining of my energy.

Later he is let down again, this time by his back. One possible interpretation is that the injury mirrors in some way his let down in love. But then, on the other hand, it also has the benefit of distracting him from his preoccupation with his shoulder:

> It was a combination of high stress, from unrequited love, and from carrying very heavy suitcases when visiting my parents, with three children. Being laid down flat for six weeks, crawling to the toilet, showed me the body, my body, was bigger than the damaged shoulder. It was the whole of me.

Once again the story of his recovery begins with a scene of tenderness and the touching of hands:

> During the six weeks my unrequited love came to visit and we held each other's finger tips as we talked about the dire situation. I had to accept and do what I can, gently and if possibly firmly. After lots of years of exercise and changing my posture and relaxing, my back is now generally fine, is a friend, a respected friend.

In these two scenarios the writer moves from a scene of brutishness towards moments of loving tenderness, each of which precedes his developing ability to look after himself and to be kind to himself. Through learning how to deal with his injuries he learns how to be firm with himself but also to treat himself with kindness and respect.

In his final scenario, speaking now of his growing waistline, he speaks of himself with kindness, understanding and leniency. A note of gentle humour sets a different and perhaps more parental tone in which one can sense a palpable sense of resolution:

> It tells me every day I am older, and not so sleek as I should be. The stomach winks at my shoulder and back, cheekily, poking fun at the more obvious mechanical functions and malfunctions.

Another member marches proudly into his story:

> I'm proud of my legs and thighs, particularly in summer, when I can display them more. In the sun and heat, I like my brown, sun-tanned legs and thighs being revealed when I wear khaki shorts.

But treachery is afoot; he had thought he could at least trust his legs not to let him down, having been so badly let down by his upper body which had put him through such traumatic major heart surgery in 2006. And yet, somehow and in spite of all this, he keeps on going:

> my twangy, resilient thighs and legs seemed to keep on marching out into the world, re-affirming my temporarily lost vigour and energy.

It seems clear to me that this writer speaks of his legs as though they are his salvation, his means of his continuing connection to the outside world. Unlike his treacherous upper body his legs remain fully-functioning and he is conscious of their potency and their attractiveness. Once again, however, this story turns to extreme pain and for a while the writer feels unable to carry on. Overtaken by severe pain in his legs he now becomes unable (even) to walk.

But there is clear anger in this story too, as well as depression. Unbearable pain, broken trust and a temporary sense of defeat seem to me almost to reawaken in the writer the near-death feelings of his earlier collapse and major surgery. Is this IT - the end of my (useful) life?

> This numbness in my leg contributed to a general feeling of depression that I experienced round about April/May 2006. I felt that my world had shrunk to a severely constricted position. I could no longer expect my legs to carry me wherever I wanted to go.

Like those referred to above, this member finds a way of dealing with his debilitating pain. After talking to a vascular consultant he starts to walk through the pain and gradually he - and his blood supply - finds another way. He becomes able to walk again and with this comes a renewed sense of determination.

> I can't stride out now, like I used to, with cavalier abandon. I walk more slowly and cautiously now with occasional hesitation but I'm still walking.

These three stories could be said to be as much about maturity as masculinity as such. Each of the tellers finds his own way of facing down the pain: re-training as a carpenter; learning how to relocate a dislocated shoulder for himself, and walking through the pain of claudication of the arteries. For one the theme of a changing and adapting masculinity is clearly stated; for another it is perhaps implied in his particular brand of steely determination; for the third an extremely powerful early masculine image is something which slowly recedes into the past as his story unfolds.

The section is concluded with a reflection on well-being, and its recent and disturbing disruptions through new bodily changes and challenges:

The impulse to not-feel is profoundly de-powering.

I'm disturbed by this disconnectedness. I didn't realise it was such a strong part of my makeup. I would like to understand how this tendency to not-feel is tied to my masculine self. On the other hand, I'm very glad for the help of those close to me, especially my male friends to help find my way through these challenges. I think I know where I'm going now.

***

A NASTY ACCIDENT

At the time of my car crash I was physically very fit, though at 38 beyond my peak fitness level. I played squash regularly and would always run up and down stairs two or even three at a time. For the first time in my life I felt good in my body and had done so for about ten years. I was never big in any sense and I was always conscious of the wish to be bigger in accordance with common ideals of manliness, but this bothered me less and less now.

After the crash I concentrated everything on getting better again and, given the severity and nature of my injuries, I did very well. In a way I came almost to carry my injuries and my scars like trophies. The battered old warhorse image had a certain appeal but the pain was hard to deal with at times. Almost as an act of defiance I used six months of my recovery period training to become a carpenter and I enjoyed the ways in which I felt this enhanced my sense of manliness, strength and skill. Doing this in spite of my injuries added to this.

Within six years however the pain had become so bad, especially in my neck, that I couldn't carry this off anymore and I started to cope less and less well with work until eventually I was forced to retire. By now, age 50, I was fully aware of how closely linked my masculine body image was to my sense of self and, more importantly, my sense of self-worth. If my body was going into decline how was I to cope with this? This whole process really set off a long and often difficult process of self re-evaluation and I have really had to become a different person. In a sense I have to turn my frailty and my bodily disruption into a kind of strength and fitness so that I can feel intact again. And I can only do this by acknowledging it.

MY SHOULDER, MY BACK AND MY STOMACH

The first major change I recall (apart from puberty itself) was my shoulder not working. I had played in the junior rugby teams on the wing – I could run fast! On progression to the senior teams at 16, I was picked in the centre. The first game of the season – against HMS Worcester, I think – I found myself opposite this really big player. When the time came he ran at me and I did the right thing and tackled him head on. We collapsed down. I felt a searing crunch in my shoulder and I realised that something drastic had happened. Was my shoulder broken? It wasn't, but the arm didn't work. The shoulder, the left shoulder of course, was dislocated. The pain was great, and the responsible teacher, Mr. Winter, accompanied me to the hospital, with tears pouring from me, he held my hand. I was grateful; he hadn't been so soft before. After trying to replace [it], the medics eventually knocked me out and did it under anaesthetic.

The shoulder dislocated again and again, initially playing various sports. On the second or third occasion, I went to a different hospital and they showed me how to relocate it – it's an unpleasant procedure that involves putting the limp arm behind my back and then grabbing the hand with the other hand and pulling up – then it "clicks" back into place – it involves a lot of concentration, accepting the necessity of doing this pain and the associated pain, and afterwards leaves me in a little shock for the next few hours, and very tired for the next day or more. I used to use a sling in the aftermath, and have used flowered ties and so on in the past. For the next 10-15 years I tended to dislocate it about once a year; now with exercises it is much stronger and have only done it only done it only a couple of times in the last five years.

I've done it in many different ways, including throwing a stone into the sea and once feeding the ducks. The most dangerous time is when asleep, so I have to avoid sleeping on my front with my left arm above my head. It is an ever-present, knowing that this bit of me does not work as it should! I have to be kind to my left shoulder, to protect it and me from its potential for pain and above all draining of my energy.

In 1981 my back collapsed. It was a combination of high stress, from unrequited love, and from carrying very heavy suitcases when visiting my parents, with three children. Being laid down flat for six weeks, crawling to the toilet, showed me the body, my body, was bigger than the damaged shoulder. It was the whole of me. During the six weeks my unrequited love came to visit and we held each others' finger tips as we talked about the dire situation. *I had to accept* and do what I can, gently and if possibly firmly. After lots of years of exercise and changing my posture and relaxing, my back is now generally fine, is a friend, a respected friend.

For the last 15 years I have been *noticing* my waist. It grows slowly, defeats older trousers, and invites me to defy it and reduce it. It also comes and goes, I imagine I can exercise it to be under control and occasionally do so. It sits on me, a small bump, curved but not fully wanted or part of the younger me than I know so much better. It tells me every day I am older, and not so sleek as I should be. The stomach winks at my shoulder and back, cheekily, poking fun at the more obvious mechanical functions and malfunctions. I would like to run my stomach off; it sets a small identifiable body target to aim at.

PROUD LEGS AND THIGHS

I'm proud of my legs and thighs, particularly in summer, when I can display them more. In the sun and heat, I like my brown, sun-tanned legs and thighs being revealed when I wear khaki shorts.

I thought I could trust my legs not to let me down. My upper half of my body had become treacherous to me when in 1986 I had my sternum broken in order to have major heart surgery. But not too long after that my twangy, resilient thighs and legs seemed to keep on marching out into the world, re-affirming my temporarily lost vigour and energy.

In April/May 2006, my trust in my legs was exploded and a mounting fear that my whole body was collapsing threatened to take control of my life. A gripped, numbing ache had started in my left leg calf muscle and I couldn't ignore its limiting presence in my life. After about 300 yards of walking down the street to catch the bus, the gripped pain in my left leg was so intense that I had to stop walking and wait for the ache to disappear. I went to my G.P. and after cracking a joke about the Roman Emperor Claudius, he told me I had 'intermittent claudication' in my left leg. I was very puzzled by this but after consulting the 'Net Doc' on the internet I found out that I had a narrowing of my arteries in my leg that meant that not enough oxygenated blood was getting down to my extremities.

This numbness in my leg contributed to a general feeling of depression that I experienced round about April/May 2006. I felt that my world had shrunk to a severely constricted position. I could no longer expect my legs to carry me wherever I wanted to go. I could no longer stride out for long distances, without looking down at my left calf and pausing.

In June 2006 I went to the vascular consultant in the City Hospital, Nottingham. He confirmed that I had very little pulse in my left leg but he did refer to the fact that sometimes alternative, 'collateral' pathways could be opened up in my blocked arteries by regular walking. He suggested that if I walked into the pain and kept going through the persistent ache that other pathways might be stimulated to find other routes around my blocked arteries.

So all through late June, July and August I began to walk out in the evening along the towpath next to the River Trent. I was often accompanied by some of my friends and I would share a bit about my present state of achy numbness in my leg. I found that my concentration shifted from the state of my leg to the drifting conversations with my friends and, often, before I realised, I found myself down by the bench opposite the Yacht club, perhaps an hour and a quarter long walk.

Since then I've kept going, walking for about 35/50 minutes a day. My left calf has improved over that time. I no longer have that clenching seizure in my left leg. Instead I have a more gently painful ache, with a numbness in some of my toes at the end of the walk. I can't stride out now, like I used to, with cavalier abandon. I walk more slowly and cautiously now with occasional hesitation but I'm still walking.

WELL-BEING

I think what I've been reflecting on lately is the way I have responded to two major threats to my sense of personal well-being. These have been my diagnosis of prostate cancer and my ongoing difficulties meeting the expectations of my two bosses in my part-time job at the University.

In both these cases I've tended to go into an insulated state of denial, a kind of non-feeling. My internal dialogue has been "I'm okay, I can handle this, I'll be alright – it doesn't really matter." This last bit of self-talk is particularly telling because I think it might actually mean "I don't matter".

The truth is, of course, I do feel both these situations. One way this shows up is steadily worsening IBS – bowel problems, lots of wind, diarrhoea, general unbalance. The other has been a kind of mental sluggishness and incapacity. I find myself unable to analyse my situation and act accordingly. I haven't done much research into my cancer and my options for dealing with it for example. Even more tellingly with my job, I've not done much to confront my employers' expectations and create a dialogue for how these might be addressed. As a result, I am badgered and sniped at by these two women who feel frustrated I'm sure by my inability to meet their targets.

Now all of this is not especially remarkable – I'm certainly not the first person to respond this way to crises – but it intrigues me because it is so self-inflicted. The capacity to act is there but mostly unused and inaccessible. The impulse to not-feel is profoundly de-powering.

I'm disturbed by this disconnectedness. I didn't realise it was such a strong part of my makeup. I would like to understand how this tendency to not-feel is tied to my masculine self. On the other hand, I'm very glad for the help of those close to me, especially my male friends to help find my way through these challenges. I think I know where I'm going now.

CHAPTER 7

Sport

Zbyszek Luczynski

INTRODUCTION

> Sport like … work is central to men's sense of themselves …

The various experiences of sport reported were both positive and negative. Some enjoyed the competitive experience and team work, while other men were intimidated and turned off by sport. As one recalls: "Cricket was my passion. It was also how I gained acceptance from my peer group as a respected team member." He saw the link to the making of his masculinity through the sport he played and watched as a fan. But for another sport became "the main theatre of my boyhood feelings of alienation from the world of males." Yet later the same man writes:

> Later, as I grew up and became bigger and fitter, I tended to opt for individual and non-team activities. I enjoyed skiing, gliding, walking, swimming etc., and some individual sports such as squash – even karate, but my deeply ingrained reticence about competing physically against others meant that although I was quite skillful I was never very successful. This is quite ironic because I had become extremely fit, fast and agile by then.

His ambivalence was summed up in the comment:

> My thoughts about football are like those on organised religion; if only we spent that much time skill energy and dedication on helping one another instead, then the world might be a far better place.

There were plenty of references to the welling up of the heroic male sporting experience, for example, as in this description of a heroic incident from early rugby playing days: "I held onto the ball till my team's forwards eventually came round to support me." In something of a contrast, in later life he describes the pleasures playing bowls: "I enjoyed the perfect bowl using the bias of the ball."

In a further example of ambivalence, another man recounts a story when he was run out in the last over of a cricket match when his team were about to save the match: "We were clapped off the field by the whole team – almost heroes but almost tearful". And then, later in life he attempts non-competitive sport, playing squash with a friend without scoring: "It meant no one won or lost which was a great relief in and from the competitive world of work."

After a lifetime of not enjoying competitive sports, one writer says:

> Having to perform according to manly terms of recognition, to win and prevail be a hero was the bait; the hook humiliation at failure or defeat. More open terms of acceptance in a group of men is rare and was very special when it came. Or perhaps it is just that the rules of acceptance are different.

Sport has also been a feature of the banter of some of the members of our group. Two of us, visiting opposition football grounds, had to remain quiet when our team scored in case we were discovered as opposition supporters in the home team crowd. However as one of these says in his piece:

My sporting heroes are still in my life, but changing and contradictory men who challenge, give me support and have become like brothers, are my reality today.

Sport, even with its obvious masculinism, appears to be a world of contradiction and ambivalence.

***

Sport (Especially Football) Viewed by an Entirely Non-sporty Man

It is very hard to work out precisely how sport as such is significant in my life: like work, sport is one of those institutions which become so central to men's sense of themselves that it is hard to separate them out from each other. Unlike work, though, I suppose, a man can stop actually *doing* sport and yet still feel his involvement through watching and interacting with others.

For me, however, the process with sport never really got started. As a boy I was small, unhealthy and underweight – 'delicate' as they used to say. I was also extremely under-confident, having spent a lot of time in hospital. So mostly I was never really selected to partake in others' sports. 'Games' though, of a vaguely active nature, were another matter and felt much safer for me. I wanted to be bigger and stronger of course, to play football with the others because, through not being able, I never really felt that I was one of them. Sport, especially football, in other words, became almost the main theatre of my boyhood feelings of alienation from the world of males.

Later, as I grew up and became bigger and fitter, I tended to opt for individual and non-team activities. I enjoyed skiing, gliding, walking, swimming etc., and some individual sports such as squash – even karate, but my deeply ingrained reticence about competing physically against others meant that although I was quite skillful I was never very successful. This is quite ironic because I had become extremely fit, fast and agile by then.

Never having been initiated into the world of sport and football – and especially the *institution* of football – I find it strange and utterly incomprehensible, and entirely undeserving of the amount of energy and emotion, time and money invested in it. It is not just that I feel alienated from it, but that it is a strange and alien culture which has no appeal to me, and yet which still gets in the way of my relationships with male friends. It is something in which I have no interest whatsoever, but it is also something which my male friends still all seem to do together while I exist in an entirely different space. Therefore I have no actual football (or rugby, or tennis, or cricket) stories to tell. If I do then they are about being left standing shivering on the sidelines at school or being sent off to pick up litter, as if I were being punished for not being up to the mark.

My thoughts about football are like those on organised religion I suppose; if only we spent that much time and skill, energy and dedication on helping one another instead, then the world might be a far better place.

Two Times When Sport Had a Major Impact on My Life

My First Time … it was the first time I played for the Cricket 1st team, one of only two from the junior side to be promoted. The match was against one of those strong minor public school teams, Trinity, I think. In particular, they had one famous County level batsman who we were glad to dismiss for a modest 15 or 20. He had apparently scored hundreds. They amassed about 120 or 140 – in total, a reasonable but not an impossible score in those days. We started disastrously, and slumped to something like 32 or 35 for 5 or 6. Although I was a batsman, as it was my first game in the senior side I batted at 7 or 8. So I was thinking – is this what really happens in the top side? I went into bat determined to play defensively & not to be removed. We limped to about 48-9. Richard Evans, the main fast bowler of our team, came in at 11. He was acknowledged as the worst batsman. For the next 40 minutes or more he continued to play all sorts of flashy and lucky strokes, and we staggered up into the 70s. It was now <u>the last over</u>, but all the time I was conscious that there was a very good chance his luck would end and he would get out. I saw my responsibility to keep the strike. With two or three balls to go, he hit another cross-bat slog to the boundary; there was clearly three runs in it, so I would then have the strike to protect the draw for the final couple of balls. The fielder way out on the boundary happened to be the star batsman, he threw a very long range and perfect return to the stumps and I was run out by inches. We, Evans and I, were clapped off the field by the whole team – almost heroes but almost tearful.

His back was a worry ... after he had hurt his back, which had laid him up for six weeks and altogether three months recovering in the spring, he wanted to get back to some gentle exercise but was <u>worried</u> about risking over-exertion in competitive sport. With the summer gone and a new term starting, he discussed the dilemma with his colleague, Norman, a newish member of staff (with a special interest in China ancient and modern) and learnt that he wanted to learn how to play squash. Squash, that most maniacal and hyper-tense of sports, beloved by aspiring professionals, & where it is so easy to over-reach in the excitement of the moment, within the <u>four walls</u>. The conversation led to the idea of playing squash that was non-competitive. (He was friendly with John Bradfield at the time, an advocate and practitioner of non-competitive games and that may have triggered the notion.) This brought a strange pact between the novice & the ex-invalid on this basis. There was no scoring. He gave tips on how to play, tactics, difficult shots etc., and this worked well especially as squash is ideal for a more experienced player and being able to <u>make</u> the less experienced colleague run around the court back and forth with a few deft shots. The harmony was plausible, even tangible; it had a quiet and occasional vigorous rhythm. The non-scoring was novel and at times oddly emotionally moving, as each 'point' or 'non-point' had a little separate life of its own, its own narrative in the jargon. At the end of a longer or more stretching rally, he would check his back was OK. And then continue.

It also meant that no one won or lost which was a great relief in and from the competitive world of work. Norman had a special interest in China, both Confucian and communist.

Two Sporting Incidents

1. 1957: King Edward the 6th Grammar School

The first fifteen rugby team were without a scrum half. At that time I was playing football regularly for a local league side in Torbay. So when the school sports master put pressure on me to try and fill the scrum half gap, I wasn't interested. But after a long process of cajoling, coaxing and flattery, I gave in and turned out for the first fifteen.

I enjoyed kicking for touch and the occasional, theatrical, muddy dive pass to my fly half but there is one incident that I keep on coming back to through the years.

It was a sudden moment when the opposition pack broke through our pack with the ball at their feet. I suddenly felt very exposed as their beefy forwards charged towards me. The ball ran loose and I dropped on the ball, shaping my body as a defensive shield, curled around the ball, like a crescent.

The opposing forwards screwed their studs down into my back and buttocks trying to kick me off my bodily shield. Legs and feet flailed around me, wanting to prise me apart from the ball. Their forwards were the attacking enemy and I was trying to hold our beleaguered citadel against their ferocious onslaught.

My team's forwards eventually came round to support me. I let the ball go and the play moved away from the tangled bodies with myself at the bottom. At the interval, the sports master turned to me and said, 'Well done!'

2. 2001: Flat Green Bowls at the Forest Bowling Rink

Two or three of my friends used to play flat green bowls at one of the local rinks. It was always very casual and informal, with a great deal of talk about our lives while playing, arranging the mats on the green surfaces and rolling the white jack down to the other end. None of us were dressed in the regulation white trousers and shirts. Most of us wore jeans and sometimes khaki shorts on hot days.

What I remember about playing bowls was the precise way the plastic bowl would come out of your hand. A good bowl would flow out of your hand and stooping body. Sometimes I could sense the curving parabola of the bowl emerging from the line of my hand and body. Often, the more I slowed down the better I could control the gliding line of my curving bowl. It was as if the bowl's speed and direction came out of my breathing. If I was breathing jerkily the bowl would bump and zigzag out of my fumbling hand. If I breathed right down into the pit of my stomach, sometimes I could feel the bowl leave my hand like glistening silk.

I liked using the weight of the bias in the bowl to estimate the length and speed of the bowl. I particularly enjoyed playing backhand shots, arranging the bias in the right way so that when I let the bowl go it would begin to arc in at the point where the bowl began to lose speed.

Afterwards, we often shared tea and strawberries in a local hotel.

NOT THE SPORTING HERO

Reading our emails suggesting a topic I felt an immense resistance to writing on sport. Once there was a negative energy there to write critically about it; now there tends to be a nullity. So I don't usually read sporting pages, and only got a flicker of interest in the national-popular sport, when, my home town suddenly appeared in the Premier League after years of league-table depression. My partner is more likely than I to keep the TV on for 'Match of the Day' or the latest International. We both think that Rugby is a hilarious sport. So the sport question is a bit like the God question: not even important enough to get steamed up about.

Yes, it is partly because I never 'shone', after puberty anyway, in any game. The trouble was I did want to. I spent years of sporting battery in the rugby front row in a rugger-obsessed school, eventually becoming a wing three-quarter when someone realised I could run. But even then I usually dropped the ball or stumbled at crucial points or had to hurl myself at the opposing wing like falling at the feet of a galloping horse. And all in the search of approval of other boys and a very sporty housemaster. In retrospect it looks as though all sort of physical traps and opportunities for humiliation were offered here – and for the most part tackled or fallen into with what he called 'pluck'; but actually silently suffered. As for some intrinsic pleasure in the activities of the body in sport there was none.

As a little boy I could imagine that ill-coordinated effort was masterly performance. But even in my first school my boy friendships, which were quite passionate, were found in roaming, wrestling and running free, not in sport. Facing friends in a boxing ring was a troubling ordeal. Lose or win.

So I reckon now the aversion is partly about the intense male company and male collectivity of the sporting culture, not so much the sport itself, as its boyish setting and context. It did not feel safe to be naked in the showers, or really trust yourself to the roughness of their bodies or the crudity of their jokes. The sexuality of the changing room (my own) with younger boy's bodies in view was a guilty or spoiled pleasure.

The proof of this, perhaps, was my love of solo running in the 1980s and 1990s, a self-regarding, self-saving activity without sporting paraphernalia. And also walking and swimming with women friends, lovers, partners beyond the limits and rules of playing fields but with more real play nonetheless.

Having to perform according to manly terms of recognition, to win and prevail and be a hero was the bait, the hook humiliation at failure or defeat. More open terms of acceptance in a group of men is rare and was very special when it came. Or perhaps it is just that the rules of acceptance are different?

My Sporting Life

That ball was hard! My box took part of the hurt of the impact, but I felt the bruising blow around my goolies for some time. I doubled up felt sick, had a short rest to catch my breath then faced up for the next ball against Notts Cavaliers' fastest opener.

The next ball was even quicker. When my bat connected the shock waves up the handle trembled my hands and spread through up through my body and I just stood there quivering.

I do not think I lasted the over before I was out.

That was my last match for Notts Catholics back in 1966; the end of an illustrious career in schoolboy cricket as an opening batsman and first change bowler of medium pace.

Weekdays of practice in the nets after school, getting ready for matches against local schools from the age of 9 till I left for Uni at 18.

Cricket was my passion. It was also how I gained acceptance from my peer group as a respected team member. Playing together winning or losing brought us lasting friendships based on friendly ribbing and a degree of mutual respect and trust. It was lost once we all left to go to our separate ways yet strangely revived at old boys reunions thirty three years later.

I loved that feeling of a perfectly timed stroke for four through cover point, a six over midwicket, scoring fifty, bowling a hat-trick or getting five wickets in an innings. These were achievements remembered for life.

Adrenaline highs often followed by losing lows. These things mattered. They still do now, mediated through fandom and the externalised experiences of my home town football team Nottingham Forest, Notts cricket team, etc.

Sporting hero to watching heroes play sport forms a strong element in my masculinity. You were/are part of making history the team photos the privileges and admiration rewards; the skills successes and performances which built up confidence and self esteem; the training in responsibilities and loyalties.

The pressures daunting but exciting planning strategies also assisted in my career development, and in organising and leading community struggles as a Community Development Worker, which I have enjoyed over thirty eight years. All informed by my sport team work experience. They also enabled my becoming a leader/developer of a trade union branch in struggle, a conference delegate, speaker, and convenor.

The felt/imagined and internalised bond developed between the Forest team and me as a fan, echo the feelings from my cricket/football playing days.

The generations of players, as team members come and go became almost comrades my daily life. The successes/failures of the Forest team, Brian Clough, Peter Taylor, Tony Woodcock, John Robertson, Brian Roy, Stan Collymore and the rest of the heroes were all my imaginary brothers at times.

Their success was ours, but as they faded, so did our emotional attachments.

The main commitments in my life have been to political struggles, men's movement groups, love in partnership/marriage, fatherhood, and work. But these have always been balanced by playing and watching sport.

At times sport seemed to be life and death to me. I would talk to my sons about the match when Nottingham Forest won their second European Cup when they with stood wave after wave of attacks from FC Hamburg in similar tones to when my father described his battle against the Germans at Monte Cassino.

That love of sport is sustained by those great rushes of adrenaline and joy, when your team score or take a wicket.

Sport hooks you in with those near orgasmic highs which seem to make it a common language of emotions in a mass of mainly strange men. It's the only time men accept kissing each other breaking through their armour without resorting to well defended positions.

The brotherhood we have developed in men's movement groups over the last twenty years in middle age through to old age seems much more real and concrete.

So though I still follow Forest and play tennis regularly I am far less emotionally dependent on sport for my identity and self-esteem nowadays.

In the past when I did not have many real personal relationships with men I relied on my football team and their exploits for emotional nurturing.

This ceased to be so important once I developed personal relationships and friendships with men.

My sporting heroes are still in my life but changing and contradictory men who challenge give me support and have become like brothers are my reality today.

CHAPTER 8

Sisters

Zbyszek Luczynski

INTRODUCTION

Each member of the group was lucky enough to have sisters. We wrote of different levels of intimacy conflict and support, mostly from childhood days. In adulthood the dialogue continues. Many issues are still being resolved for us and them.

The bonds described between brothers and sisters were based on mutual support, jealousy and lifelong rites of passage. For one man, growing up in poverty and neglect from his parents meant "(a)s a result, my sisters and I formed a protective circle as best we could"; later he would learn to "wind up" his older sister. Another described how, though his family were poor, he was allowed to take up a grammar school place, but his sister was not. He also got twice the pocket money: "It was assumed I would not follow father into a factory, but other rules seemed to apply to daughters."

A number of men recalled sharing beds top and tailed with lots of warm intimacies, games and the start of first sexual feelings, for example, in playing "coal mining" under the blankets. As teenage years came, closeness sometimes developed into resentments, as when one man's sister thought she and her sister got "all the hard jobs", and sometimes into forms of admiration, even "reverence" for an older sister in one case. This author describes how as they grew up together relationships changed. From being organised by her at an early age, fighting her when she was a "tomboy", racing her and being at the end of her spitefulness, to later in their teenage years learning new social skills from her. He describes the conflict with their father and how he supported her struggle for independence. But once she married a "terrible" man and he was cut off, only for the closeness to return on her divorce some years later.

Somewhat similarly, for another there was mutual support wrought in childhood through life based on rebellion within a first generation diaspora: they were always a team looking after each other – his sister even supported him when he was talking to his mother on her death bed on choices for and against a having her having an amputation. Now that their parents are both dead he says "ours is the last blood tie that remains."

A third had an older more "worldly" sister who went on to read French at university, and became an existentialist and a fashion model with famous boyfriends. The matriarch of a spreading family, she was always one step ahead of him: "She had a way of dominating our quite large middle-class household" – "I loved and admired a version of my sister." "But I wish sometimes I could bring her home with me." Like others, the early bonds remained strong often despite being apart for long distances of time place and the separate family networks that formed.

Our stories illustrate the often lasting nature of brother and sister relationships and the formative influences our sisters have had on our development as men and the continuing influence sisters have on our lives.

***

GETTING BY

I have two sisters, one four years older than me and the other two years younger than me. A brother died at birth two years before me, hence the four year gap.

Our childhood was frugal and marked out by constant illness, cold and (I now realise) occasional neglect. Not only did we have very little, our parents drank fairly freely and often seemed to have very little idea of how to cope. As a result, my sisters and I formed a protective circle as best we could.

But there were still problems: my elder sister was picked on constantly by my father and we were too little to offer much protection or support. My younger sister, was deaf and very limited, and I, being a boy, wanted male friends and not to be 'tarnished' by too much association with them. I longed for a brother.

But there were cosy moments too. At times (I can't remember why) we were all bundled into bed together, which was a very cosy arrangement, and warm in the bargain.

We squabbled too, especially my elder sister and I who, because she was so much bigger, I felt justified in hitting if it came to it. But I usually came off worse. My response was to learn the subtle art of wind-up, which I did with such relish and style that she still (in a superficially nice way) resents me to this day. I remember, for example, getting her thrown out of Saturday morning pictures by playing the victim and pretending she had hit me and hurt me. I also learned later how to make tea so that one morning I delighted her by bringing her tea in bed. She hated sweet tea and I had put ten spoonfuls of sugar in it. I still laugh as I write this!!

We get on well now but sadly my younger sister is somewhat limited by her deafness and her experience and it is hard to have any kind of interesting conversation with her. Mostly we kind of look out for her but my older sister is far better than me at actually relating to her.

Heavy Action Down the Mine

It was just after the Second World War and I was about seven or eight. My two sisters were giggling and playing on the top of our parents' bed. It was Saturday morning and we used to burrow deep down under the blankets and usually play 'Coal Mining'. I had to hold my breath and dig out the coal at the face, where the bed clothes were tucked in at the bottom of the bed.

But one Saturday one sister turned towards me and shouted, 'Parachute Pants!' I'm not sure why she did it but it made me step away and look at myself again, wearing passed-down underpants that were too large for me. She was about ten and perhaps she'd had enough of me being the central coalminer who grabbed all the action, and she and my other sister were surface workers bringing the coal up in a bucket.

Sometime later our playing stopped and we began to take up separate roles in family life. I was still given all the heavy action roles, bringing in the coal, hopping splinters of wood to light fires, raking out ashes and carrying them down the bottom of the garden. My sisters helped Mum with the washing, washing up, setting the table, going shopping.

This division of labour stayed with us until Mum's death years later. Perhaps my sister was 16 and I was 13, up at my Aunt's and Uncle's house at the top of Maidenway Hill overlooking Paignton and Torbay. I can remember her unexpected rage at me one day. 'It's not fair,' she protested, we get all the hard jobs and he does nothing! All he has to do is bring the coke in and make sure the fire doesn't go out. It's just not fair!'

Sisters, A Moment of Trust

I was (and I suppose still am) big brother to my two sisters, some two years younger. I also have a brother, twelve years my junior.

I cannot immediately get back to memories from before secondary school age but I think all three of us were expected to help in some way with housework.

Perhaps too it was as early as that that differentiated pocket money scales operated: six pence for me, three pence for each of my sisters.

Differences became more marked as we moved towards our teens. Unlike them I went regularly with Dad to Celtic's football matches. I went to grammar school; they went to secondary modern. Later, however, as adults my elder sister and then I learned that she had been cheated of the grammar school place she had earned. Dad was also clear that he did not want any son of his to follow him into the factory: other rules seemed to apply to daughters. At any rate he did not foresee them either as factory workers or as professionals.

Suddenly an earlier memory. Our tenement house had only two rooms and so until I was about ten my sisters and I shared a double bed, me being at one end and they at the other. When my cousin came to stay over with us, which he did quite often, he joined me at my end of the bed. I think there were moments of pleasure as my legs touched those of my sisters in the middle of the bed. There were also kicking moments, never I think in anger.

I am resisting adding this, but dammit I trust you. As a youngish teenager I found a woman's swimsuit that my mother never wore. I put it on occasionally when I was at home alone. Once I did it when my sister was there and went to show her. As I remember it there was no hint of condemnation from her. I look back on it as an important moment of trust between us.

SENTIMENTAL STORIES

> 'Sisters, sisters, there were never such devoted sisters.'

I remember seeing the Beverly Sisters live when I was a child, and thinking they were gorgeous. We went with the whole family, that is, including Deidre ..., my sister ... four years my elder.

Apparently when I was very young – two or three – she would dress me up as a girl – so the family story went. I really don't remember it well, except the feeling of *being organised* by her.

She was always known as a 'tomboy', with a bad temper on her; that was blamed by my parents on having to live through the bombing and then the evacuation from London in the War. She was given a bad press and I usually came off worse in any fighting.

When I was five or six, we were having a semi-organised race in the garden, in which I was given a 'start' and to my surprise I was still ahead as we approached the finish at the back of the house – when she pushed me from behind, so I smashed into the brick wall at the back of the house, drawing blood.

For much of my young boyhood I lived in part fear/part reverence for her. She was not to be messed with, especially with her renowned 'spitefulness'.

Then there was a change – I became a big boy and she became a teenager. There was an odd transition. One day the whole family went to the seaside and got somewhat red and sunburnt, before the days of compulsory suntan lotions. That evening at home my mother and sister were suddenly giggling and then Deidre appeared naked on top with an obvious <u>un-suntanned</u> strip across her breasts singing 'Bridge that gap, bridge that gap, bridge that gap with Cadbury's Snack.' It was all a bit confusing. Then at my mother's instigation I was encouraged to 'do the same back', so I took off my pants again with the obvious un-tanned strip across my loins and sang with my mother's encouragement 'Bridge that gap, bridge that gap, bridge that gap with Cadbury's Snack.'

During Deidre's teenage years I came to admire her, her piano playing, social skills and strength, ability to get boyfriends and ability to annoy and confront my father. He would sometimes chase her upstairs. One day after a particularly uncontrolled confrontation between him and Deidre, my mother told him very firmly not to behave that way again and he became much more passive thereafter.

By 18 or 19, he had calmed down, she had won a holiday camp beauty contest (of which I was very proud at the time) and she was calmed down too, as she was with her future husband – to become apparently passive and thus 'lost' to me for 30 years, as she married a terrible man, apart from when we were alone together at my father's death. During that time there was no point in visiting her. When she divorced 11-12 years ago we became close again and she was there for me when I divorced. And she still is, even though I only see her, say, once a year.

A Strong Bond and the Last Blood Tie

We have been a team for a lot of years together. Even though we have lived at least a thousand miles apart for the last thirty five years, our bond is as strong now, as when I defended her from verbal attacks from father when he tried to stop her seeing unsuitable boyfriends or when he found out she was taking the pill.

She has developed a protective older sister persona even though she is two years younger, defending me as I left the Catholic faith behind.

This mutual protection and support has grown further following our mother's death.

Mother was in hospital in agony, gangrene galloping up her right leg, the surgeon was offering to amputate to stave off her death. I was torn apart by feelings of losing her, wanting her to live a few days longer no matter what and supporting her in refusing surgery, letting go, accepting that her time had come to go.

It was my sister talking to me at my mother's bedside by mobile phone from Switzerland who gave me the strength to counsel my mother to say no and accept death. In fact she heard me talking it through with our mother as inadvertently I had left the phone on whilst she talked through that final decision. I only realised this when I heard her voice say 'Well done', as she heard my mother say she did not want a drawn out painful death and accept that it was too late for surgery.

There has always been an element of parenting each other, from a young age I would often follow her lead. I had girlfriends after, married after, settled down and had children after her.

Now that pattern has been broken, the bonds have been loosened and caring for our mother no longer unites us.

I am looking forward to building a new accommodation with a more distant sister, as we move to our post children post work phase of our relationship, with more space for connection. Ours is the last blood tie that remains.

BIG SISTER

She was always a step ahead of me – well two or three usually – five years older, and always, it seemed, much more worldly and sophisticated. Her projects – which were many - had a way of dominating our quite large middle-class household, whether it was keeping Persian cats, painting and drawing, reading the latest novel or theory, re-designing her bedroom in black lino, white paint and striped rugs, going to university and becoming an existentialist (she read French). Me and my brother, ten years her younger, took many leads from her, especially intellectual and artistic ones. In these respects, she was much more our familial model and inspiration than either my mother or father. We only had one cousin, one aunt and one uncle so our sibling relations were relatively undiluted and intense. She read aloud to us, gave us books (e.g. *The Uses of Literacy*) and was an early traveller, initially accompanying my father on his buying trips in Holland, France, Italy and Spain, later as a translator, fluent in French and Italian. At 19 after leaving a posh Hampshire boarding school she was a fashion model for a year or two, was 'presented' at Court, and went to Hull University where her boyfriends included Roy Hattersley.

I loved and admired a version of my sister, my own version of course: clever, independent, socially very competent and confident, elegant, tall and beautiful. But the five year gap was more than years, important in our different self-formation too, for, to my eyes, she missed out on 1960s liberations, popular music and dance and on rebelliousness, feminism especially. Instead she met, fell in love with and married a wealthy Italian, a leading surgeon from a conservative Veronese gentry family, having winkled him out of a preferred bachelorhood. She was also a passionate and sincere convert to Catholicism faithful as a wife, a protective mother but always my sister too.

I visit her in their villa and vineyard on the edge of Lessinian hills. She teaches English and French at home, writes stories and novels (not yet published) and is the centre of an ever-spreading family. But I wish sometimes I could bring her home with me.

CHAPTER 9

Food

Randy Barber

INTRODUCTION

The theme of food revealed itself to be a very rich one in the writings of our group of men. Like other themes we explored, memories associated with food were both positive and negative but for most of us cooking and eating was a pleasurable experience.

Not surprisingly, memories of food dated from childhood. Also unsurprisingly, given these older men's ethnic and class backgrounds (British, mostly lower middle or working class), early food experiences tended to be of rather bland dishes, simply prepared. Sometimes, these were fondly remembered but many of our men recalled despised items like fatty, gristly meat, milky puddings and lumpy mashed potatoes. For many, these kinds of early experiences laid the ground for later pleasurable "discoveries" of more exotic foods and more elaborate and sophisticated cooking methods.

Mealtimes were frequently the scene of childhood conflicts. Food could be withheld as a punishment or else our young boys could be forced to eat foods they didn't like. This coercive use of food occurred both in the family home and at school.

For all of our men, early experience taught them that food preparation was a distinctly gendered activity. The kitchen and all things in it were in the female realm. When their fathers made a meal it was an exceptional and memorable event but, for those who wrote about it, memories of dads cooking were constructed as indicating their fathers' dedication to the family and family life. One man recalled that his father missed a significant football match rather than forego the midday meal he unfailingly prepared on New Year's Day.

Later, food experiences grew more complicated. There was food as part of the dating ritual and later still food as an important component of child rearing. These were men whose partners worked when their children were growing up, and domestic duties like cooking tended to be shared. This, of course, was quite a shift from their own family experiences and was often seen by our men as demonstrating a commitment to feminist principles.

Lacking in kitchen skills, most of our men struggled with preparing food for their children. Perhaps anxious to avoid the strict discipline around eating of their own childhood, several of our men tried to cater for their kids' different tastes and preferences which made the whole business of cooking even more fraught.

Another problem was performance anxiety around preparing food for the family. Some of our men felt unsupported by their wives in their efforts to share the cooking load. Criticisms from this quarter were keenly felt and confidence in cooking easily shattered. But to their credit most of the men in our group persisted in their attempts to share kitchen duties. Almost all of them are now quite capable cooks who enjoy preparing food for family and friends.

***

THE MOST DANGEROUS ROOM IN THE HOUSE

The kitchen is the most dangerous room in the house, said my psychotherapist; of course, the bedroom is dangerous too. I thought about it first. Then I felt my way into his comment, and am still doing so.

Yes, I think he is right. The kitchen is the place of primitive, mythic distinctions. The uncooked is edible, honey; the overcooked is inedible, ashes. Clean and dirty have to be kept separate, as far apart as civilisation and savagery. Why does my partner have to put the top of the swing bin on the work surface? We prepare food there, you know. I did ask her once. She finds it easier to pick the swing-top from table height than from the floor. It feels as if it is her kitchen and she will do what she likes.

The kitchen and the preparation of food is the difference between men and women, and it stretches back into childhood. Dad, the shift-working tyre builder, had a custom for New Year's Day, ever a bank holiday in Scotland. On Christmas Day, however, he had to squeeze going to Mass into his journey to work or his journey home wearing his rubber-stained jeans.

On New Year's Day he always cooked the meal: chicken, a real treat. My sisters and I would plead with Mum to serve the meal onto the five plates (no serving dishes on our table) for Dad did it so slowly. Meticulously. She said, "Shush!" and Dad did look totally absorbed. He seemed proud of what he was doing. Perhaps it made him a good Catholic man to give his wife a holiday on one of his rare days off: he had less than two weeks for his summer holiday. Perhaps it separated him off from so many of the other men: down at the pub as soon as it opened; leave the missus to get the meal and look after the weans.

It wasn't easy for him, I now realise, being a man in that world. He even missed the Celtic-Rangers match on New Year's Day, though a season-ticket holder. How dare I expect that going into the kitchen in 2006 might be less dangerous!

"Do you want a hand, Love?"

"Stop fussing, will you!"

SCRAPS FROM THE TABLE

1946: I was comforted by Puffed Wheat ('Shot from guns') breakfasts eaten from a large bowl filled with creamy milk and piled with sugar. I used to enjoy digging down with my spoon and scooping up sugar from the sludgy bottom of the bowl. This was food in a house where my mother loved me. I could taste her love for me in the Puffed Wheat sludge.

1955: Marrowfat peas out of large, catering tins sitting on fried bread was slammed down in front of me in the boarding school. I was hungry for food after football and I didn't think the combination of peas and fried bread was strange. I just wolfed it down, even though some part of me sensed that this was institutional food, devoid of human warmth.

1969: I cooked fish fingers and chips for my kids in Todmorden. The fish fingers I did under the grill and we had a special chip pan full of congealed fat. It was always a race against the clock. I had to get food down them before we could all move on to the next part of what we were doing.

1979: France. Near the Lot Valley. I was a bit puzzled by encountering this French delicacy, ceps, for the first time. They were prized by French people as a rare fungus. But I didn't feel comfortable with their exoticism so I asked for Ceps on toast as a familiar, English way of converting ceps into mushrooms on toast.

1988: I spent a lot of time in preparing 'Hearty Hotpot'. I used to soak the black eyed beans overnight and then boil them up with onions, carrots, parsnips, swede, tomatoes out of a tin, potatoes, finished off by red wine with thyme and tamari. It was one of my precarious ventures into the world of making food in the kitchen besides spaghetti Bolognese. I wanted to pull my weight in the domestic labour of the kitchen.

But my partner's response to my 'Hearty Hotpot' surprised and eventually undermined me. She said she was bored by the hotpot and she found it dull and worthy and not to her liking. I felt rattled by this and could sense my confidence and belief in myself as a cook ebbing away from me.

2003: I decided that I wanted to be more assertive around the ageing men's group. Usually we had brought food and drink to share but this had developed into a small feast of enticing foods. I wanted to combine having a midday rest with eating and I decided I wanted to eat a more simple and plain meal, that became oat cakes, an apple and some fruit juice.

Without wanting to deny myself, sometimes I like the unfussy simplicity of cutting down on food and moving away from making eating into a special, fancy event.

2005: R, a friend of mine, helped me to broaden out the range of my cooking. It felt good to be around somebody who wouldn't judge me harshly for practical incompetence and lack of confidence in the kitchen area. We made risotto Milanese together. I did it falteringly and with some frustration but it was good to learn slowly in a context of support. I really enjoyed the first mouthful of risotto eaten out on R's verandah. It was melting and glowing in my mouth.

FOOD: MY LIFE STORY

Fuck. Is a four letter word. As is shit.

The memories are too many. The earliest might be the rationed banana from under the counter, because the greengrocer liked my mother – that is apart from the breast, I suppose. More substantially, I remember toad in the hole as a favourite standby, or steak and kidney pie as a more luxurious alternative or even tinned salmon on high days and my father doing the Sunday lunch roast with roast potatoes as his special sweaty contribution. Then there were the party foods of jelly, milk jelly, blancmange and trifle, with all the layers together, wonderful. But occasionally, the horror foods of crystallised ginger sweets and the terrible pease pudding of my grandmother on the occasional stays at her home round the corner after school. Disgusting! Later, with sport, especially with adult men, came the hearty pub food – with pies and chips and lashings of baked beans, accompanied by jugs of beer, to be consumed and then sometimes sicked up – though not so often by me.

Courting and dating with food, that was an ordeal – I recall once having a particular tense Chinese meal with a new girlfriend, V, before going back to the ritual snog. There was always the risk of going out on a *food type date*, of being next to some other couple who sat too close and were definitely listening in on all your "moves". Another Chinese meal, this time with R, this time unusually at lunchtime and so rather special, only to find we were sat next to another student and her boyfriend, who I knew slightly but not well enough to feel comfortable to be next to AND she was called Daffodil!

Marriage and babies and children and <u>more</u>, much more food. Lots of it. Two things stand out. One was the fact that for much of the family time there were five different food regimes – one full vegetarian (not even biscuits with animal fat + reading the labels), another more or less vegetarian (me), another wanted to be vegetarian but succumbed to meat, a fourth normal meat eater, and a fifth advanced meat eater – liked raw meat. The other was that there was at one point an intricate system of child sharing after school and this meant the voluminous twins also came on Friday evenings and it was my responsibility to feed them vigorous teas – with lots of potatoes. I got fed up with cooking for children so much and repeatedly, especially if I was criticised.

Then a new life began – at the turning point we ate macadarme nut ice cream just because it was so nice and I learnt that it was possible to buy special foods that I really liked even if they cost a lot more than baked beans. And in another country a whole new menu appeared – lots of mushrooms (both bought and picked fresh), rye bread, lots of berries, smoked reindeer, great fish, smoked nieria (for special occasions), mustard herring, even skagen röra.

I would still rather have a tin of sardines in tomato sauce on delicious bread than some exotica.

FOOD OF LOVE MY MOTHER GAVE ME

These are the messages my mother and culture gave me. Eat my food if you love me. I love eating you through the food you lovingly prepare for me. I will go without to feed you. It is the most important thing I do for you, it shows I love you. Have some more, shows I love you lots. If you refuse I will get upset.

These messages gave me a healthy/unhealthy comfort zone around food. It gave me a healthy curiosity and interest in all the different cuisines. It's a big part of why I go abroad to try new restaurants. I am driven to broaden my taste. It gave me the motivation to try a new dish, create my own experiment. It motivated my scientific approach to cooking, mixing ingredients, looking at people's reactions and for their praise.

Yet fatty salty food in this nurturing diet my mother fed us and which forms our Polish cuisine is largely responsible for my father's early death at 76. It caused the arteriosclerosis from which my mother died, my own high blood pressure, and other heart and circulation problems.

Yet that awareness of food power together with my strong scientific training gave me the willpower and belief in eating my way back to good health (with a lot of help from my dietician). That and the extra exercise, meditation, relaxation, de-stressing work life balance attempt based on the bedrock of food power (vitamins, minerals etc.) turned my life expectations around.

I have found that this largely female domain of food preparation, behaviour control, worked positively for me. It was liberating to own my own diet. Controlling what I eat helps me care for myself. I often amaze mainly women colleagues when they see what I bring to eat at lunch. They are full of praise for the care I am showing for myself. I'm sure it has helped me deal with the many stresses at work and at home.

Our family have a caring attitude to food. Our sons look after themselves as I had to learn by myself. They had a good role model in their father. In contrast to my own traditional father who left all the cooking to his wife. I have found responsibility for the planning of meals, purchase, preparation and cooking a creative arena for my relationship with my partner, my children, friends we dine out with or have round.

This cooking responsibility has always been one of the ways I have consciously demonstrated my pro-feminist attitude. It stands alongside the changing of nappies, feeding baby, cooking meals for each member of the family. Mealtimes are when we communicate. We are inspired by Polish, Scottish, French, Indian meals. We seek out restaurants that are interesting. Last week my son insisted we go to a Polish restaurant in Manchester for his 22nd birthday. It was a difficult journey from Fallowfield to Altrincham. Going round the outer ring road the wrong way twice we arrived at Lech Cafe exhausted, but expectant. Our juices and expectations were ignited by the sight of the menu and the nuances of the conversation on difference and familiarity of tastes brought us closer in warming love enjoyment of our family celebration of the love of food.

On Food and Fads, A Very Emotive Subject

My relationship with food is interwoven with some very important aspects of my childhood. My family were quite poor and though we never actually went seriously hungry, food was never especially imaginative and seldom appetising. Some of my fondest memories therefore are of simple things; toast and butter, bread and dripping, corned beef and tomato sandwiches. I thought at one stage that we were highly privileged because I could take a round of toast and butter with me to school – not realising that other people ate this wonderful substance too! The upshot of this (one upshot) is that once I realised there were other things out there I developed a fascination with what for me was the 'exotic' (mushrooms, for example, and blue cheese).

But food was also wrapped up in scary expectations and threats of retribution. Food for me came very close to becoming a conduit for discipline and control: "You can't go out and play until you have eaten it all up"; "I spent ages preparing that, now eat it or you will get a smack"; being forced to eat mouthfuls of rubbery, un-chewable fat until I gagged – to drink sterilised milk by my jack-booted Nan. This process was worst at school though where sadistic dinner ladies wreaked havoc upon me by keeping me behind after everyone else had gone out to play and then force feeding me the offending and offensive items: fatty, chewy meat, lumpy spud, watery greens, and worst of all, custard and other milk puddings. These things still have the capacity to make me feel ill for just thinking about them. To make things worse they would even insist that I was given custard on my pudding even though they knew it made me physically sick. You had to have it – that was all there was to it (so they said).

So when I started work as a butcher's boy and later in what was actually a very ordinary delicatessen by today's standards., at last I found that I could explore what was good and exciting about food; different cuts of meat and bacon, dry or wet cured, continental meats, sausages, pates cheeses and other 'delicacies'. Now that I think about it this is why I took to cooking so enthusiastically. Something in me was saying, "No-one will ever force me to eat what I don't want ever again; I'll feed myself." In practice, over time, I came to feel less anxious and even learned to enjoy some of the things that earlier I had learned to hate. Just experiencing these things properly prepared and cooked was all it took. But I still hate milk puddings, never have cream on my fruit, I still hate fatty meat and I'm still none too keen on the plain mashed or simple boiled spud.

My boyhood fantasies about warmer and sunnier climes, desert islands etc., where people caught and cooked fresh fish over a fire and finished off with delicious fruits, sparked off in me a particular love of fish, especially whole fish - that actually looked like a fish not the featureless stuff of my boyhood, served up with lumpy mash and lashings of hot milky parsley sauce Properly cooked, of course, it is now a dish I enjoy hugely.

A Very Fast Cook

I don't know whether to write about cooking or eating, but then I realise they are related. It's an exchange. You cook FOR someone even if it is yourself. Your food – even industrial stuff – has been produced by someone, sold and eaten.

To be a cook is important genderwise too. She cooks, he eats, it's the perfect arrangement. Though, with my partner I often cooked before the children 'arrived', in workaholic middle life, with her at home then part-timing, she cooked and we ate, lovely food actually, with an experimental edge for its time, especially in the line of puddings.

When she went back to teaching – about 3/4 time and in Special Needs - and the children were 10 -11- 12, I started seriously cooking again. But these were days of cooking horrors, pressure, shrieks and tears.

Around 4.30 or later, two days a week, I would rush back from the campus, calling in at the supermarket, usually with no plan. It was always hard to wrench my mind away from the latest departmental excitement or disaster. Oh God, what on earth to cook? For some reason, we seemed to have to eat at 6.30. Was it just a shared rigidity? Or some real need? I might have 45 minutes to get a meal. This time between school and supper became famous for noises from the kitchen and the need to stay well away. Even today they tell jokes about it. Bangs and clatters of saucepans and plates, curses and shouts, smells of burning and things going wrong. Usually, it did work out OK in the end. I used to cook pasta, chicken, fish a lot and I learned to cook very very fast. But emotionally it was too complicated. Did I resent cooking for them at all? Was it only out of 'pro-feminist duty' after all? Was my partner resentful at my messy kitchen incursions? Her advice (common as she had decided views) seemed like deadly criticisms to me. Meals that were not prepared in love could be eaten in silence. I do remember after particularly hectic days weeping over cooking and somehow, at the time, we didn't manage to make enough of a joke about it and I was too obstinate to give up, or eat out.

As I went part-time from 1990, things grew more relaxed and I encountered a friendly household with a strongly foody culture. My best memories of food at home date from later, from our 12 year old current household, especially when my Mum was there. Having given up cooking (perhaps she was my first cooking teacher) she treated us like a rather splendid restaurant, revelling in good food from three cooks, though grumbling if it was late 'What **are** they doing' she would say to me if one of the others were cooking. When my big younger brother came to stay he said after the first meal "Do you always eat like this?" "Yes, they do" said my Mum "you wouldn't believe it".

We have definite spheres of influence now. I cook Indian vegetarian food, Chinese, occasional pasta and risotto. R has some good staples (cookies, chowder, good salads). C is the brilliant all-rounder, inventing from whatever is in the pantry and fridge.

The anxiety sometimes comes back on special occasions – dinner parties and the like. But if things get tight, I am still a very fast cook!

No Picnic

Without any planning for food or for the day – we both brought picnic sandwiches (just in case) and both brought fruit and I brought some nibbles – *cantuccini* in fact (which were her favourite! fantastic) – but after all we ended up going for a delicious sushi, eaten outside, by a delightful stream, with two light beers, and yes sharing all day the higher class of water bottle with the plastic nipple.

CHAPTER 10

Intimacy with Men

Randy Barber

INTRODUCTION

Several things struck me as I read the stories on the theme of intimacy with men. One, strangely, was how very short they were compared to other stories we had written together in the group. It seems to me this may be an indication of the difficulty we men have in writing about our personal experiences of intimacy.

In writing these, we focused on intimacy with men, so a notable aspect of the five intimacy stories was that they all focused largely on male to male friendship and love. This might go some way to explaining why my impressions of the intimacy stories were most strongly of the sense of danger, the feeling of risk and impermanence. A related but still slightly different theme was that of rejection, of intimacy scorned.

Some of the men recorded experiences of intimacy where their affection and trust had been betrayed. One recalled an incident of opportunistic sexual abuse from a stranger he had befriended briefly before the beginning of a concert. Less dramatically, another of our writers recounts his feelings of bewilderment and pain when a man he thought of as a close friend suddenly began attacking him for perceived faults and scornfully rejecting other people's compliments on his attempts to speak Spanish.

Sometimes overtures of friendship would meet with unexpected coolness and withdrawal. One of the memory group writers recalls his sense of hurt and disappointment when his attempts to form a more intimate friendship with a black man with whom he shared political activism were politely but firmly rebuffed.

In this latter instance, the story's author wonders if perhaps it was his eagerness to deepen the acquaintance which had led to his friend drawing back from him. This was sentiment expressed by another of the writers – a sense of awkwardness in pursuing closeness and intimacy. I think that our men reveal a willingness to go beyond the usual rituals of male bonding in their stories which might account for some of their frustrations and disappointments. This is clearly illustrated in the episode where one of our writers tells of accompanying his friend to the dentist and holding his hand during the treatment to calm him.

Despite the negative experiences with intimacy in this group of stories, none of the men said that they were prevented from continuing to seek closeness with others and, in particular, with other men. I find this deeply impressive.

***

My History of Challenging Relationships with Men

Best mates at school. At secondary school I always had one best mate. These were intense often short-lived pairings. Sometimes they were based on an unhealthy, dependence which led to jealousy once I was abandoned for another boy. I needed a close and intimate buddy, someone I could share exhilarating moments listening to music playing cricket watching football matches and then joining the safety of an extended gang.

The middle years at university and before long term relationships with women. Intimacy grew up a bit. Political activism, reading Marxism, crystallised around left group membership relationships with leading hero comrades.

This sense of belonging was strangely hollow as we mouthed the mantra of the personal was political whilst trying to get female comrades into bed.

After my first big love rejected me, I politicised out my personal feelings in activism. Personal needs for intimacy were seen as a diversion from the struggle.

Trade unionism took over and more affairs provided a balance of sexual needs.

Men were more formal comrades than friends.

An activism challenged by feminist partner, becoming a father and then meeting profeminist men the Men for change and other men's groups.

My respect and love for my two sons and for men in men's groups have grown over the last twenty years.

It has made me feel more safe and rounded.

At last I have a warm supportive platform of brothers from which I can support and challenge other men with confidence I never had before.

In the past I would try to force male friends to like me.

This did not work as I scared them off. I felt hurt then, but as I reflect on this I realise that intimacy needs space and patience to develop. It cannot be forced out of other men.

I have learnt to listen more. Wait to hit the right chords and respond to opportunities in a relaxed manner.

One man was very self-sufficient and did not want to be intimate. I felt hurt, but as I reflect back, the need to give space for intimacy to develop, seems a lesson I have learnt.

Hearing is with the ears but listening is with the mind, and this seems appropriate. To which I would add, intimacy is listening with the heart and mind.

These opportunities often pass me by as I drift through days of pressure at work with no space for me.

That's why I appreciate the men's groups and one to ones so I am setting myself the task to slow down appreciate friendships and get some balance into my life.

Intimacy is nourishing and sustaining in the context of giving space and attention to it.

I feel more self-sustained and no longer crave a claustrophobic reliance of being a teenager or young adult. What I have is more mature equal and self-realising relationships with my fellow brothers. Enjoying the challenges of sharing feelings and thoughts that may not always be welcomed, but will be listened to by you.

SOME VERY CLOSE RELATIONSHIPS

Some of my closest relationships with men have come via men's groups. However, the first man whom I really kissed was Alan. He taught me it was OK to do this, and in fact he was pretty promiscuous in his kissing and so that included me.

The next, there was Brian – he was a Francophile; kissing him was easier, more relaxed. I remember the first time he taught me that for us to meet did not need an excuse to come around for afternoon tea. Then Colin, who was avowedly very heterosexual, but on some new year's eve decided to snog me. Later Dennis whom I would kiss goodnight after the group pronounced that he loved me.

The most intimate group I was in was a closed group of six of us. I only knew one of the others at the beginning, but we all became very close. I met Eric when he was a student, and taught him on various courses, but it was only after that I got to know him well in that group. There was a real mixing of the personal political and public political there. Gay and bisexual sexualities were high on the agenda, and all of us recognised the gay part of ourselves. It was different to other men's groups I had been in before. A high point was when we all went to the very large anti-Section 28 demonstration in Manchester.[2] It was the kind of group that couldn't contract or expand. So it was hardly surprising that the group ended when two of the group moved away.

Eric was gay or perhaps bisexual and later trained to be a priest. When he moved away I naturally visited him. We had a very confiding relationship. I stayed with him a few times, partly as I didn't want to spend long weekends at my mother's. Visiting her for the day was so much easier. At first he lived in a small flat that was part of a bigger house, there was no spare room and no spare bed. When I stayed the first time he offered me to sleep with him in his double bed, so I did. So I always slept with him in his bed, which was very cosy and slightly exciting. The same arrangement continued when he later moved to his own place. It was good to talk before sleep, with or without an arm around one of us, then kiss goodnight and sleep soundly. I did wonder if he might try and seduce me, but he talked about his sexual exploits in a very different way to this, so this was very unlikely.

There was only one night when I remember stirring in the middle of the night as I became conscious he was stroking very gently my thigh or was it my lower back, I don't remember but I think I may have shuffled around a bit and he stopped. We were in a trusted situation. And it was very precious and intimate. I don't think we talked about the stroking but I could be wrong.

So, when he visited me for the weekend and my partner was away he naturally slept with me in my double bed. That night one of the children had a friend staying over as well, and the friend seemed a little surprised when they wandered into the bedroom the next sunny morning. They had clearly never seen two men in a bed together before.

Then Eric got together with Flynn and they moved together to a larger flat in London, so when I visited Eric there was a spare room, and Flynn (who was very nice and a very good cook but not my friend particularly) was there, and so I slept on my own. Something was lost in the visiting and it was harder to find time to talk to Eric in private, confidentially, intimately. But we kept in contact. One day when I visited Eric I mentioned a new intimate man friend I had become very fond of, and Eric asked "Do you want to fuck him?" I was bit shocked by his direction.

---

[2] For a succinct account of events around the anti-homosexual Section 28 that was made law in May 1988, see Janine Booth 'The story of Section 28', available at: http://www.workersliberty.org/node/1531

THE CHALLENGE OF INTIMACY OF MEN AND MEN

Over the last few years I've become aware of whiteness as a key issue in my life. My friendships and contacts with men are multiple and a major part of my new sense of personal and social connectedness but I'm also aware of the narrow, even claustrophobic range of men I'm making contact with. Most of us are white, middle class professionals. There is an absence of black men that I'm close to.

About a year ago, another man and myself set up a local community, men's health group. The neighbourhood men's health group started in the local Scout hut, one February evening. In that first group of seven men exploring the theme of 'Loss, bereavement and men's health', one of the men was a black man who called himself Bunny. We got on well in that first meeting and Bunny came across as warm, questioning and extremely thoughtful. The following day Bunny rang me (we only lived two minutes away from each other) and invited me for a cup of tea.

It turned out that Bunny was a magician in the entertainment business, and came from Jamaica from a middle class family. He told me he had done a sociology degree and talked to me about magic. He then showed me a few tricks that involved ripping up newspaper and then putting the fragments back together again. I made it clear that I'd like to have regular cups of tea at both our homes, and I felt really glad that a friendship seemed to be developing between us.

However it didn't turn out like that. After I'd rung him a few times and invited him around and encountered a few excuses, it started to dawn on me that my expectations were very different from his. One day meeting Bunny out walking his dog Marley, he admitted that he wasn't in to meeting for cups of tea. I felt a bit deflated but realised my expectations of openness, honesty and shared intimacy were a bit Eurocentric. I began to realise the differences of his survival strategies in a racist context. Perhaps openness and honesty were dangerous in that kind of context? Perhaps he had learnt that he could only trust his immediate family and long-standing, black friends? Perhaps he sensed that my interest in him was a bit idealised and politically correct? Perhaps he could only meet strange, white men through controlling the terms of the encounter? Perhaps he couldn't give up being a magician and performer in front of me?

Anyway, we now bump into each other all over the place: on buses, on the towpath, outside his house while he's washing his car. We both say a lot to each other but it's mainly about the outside world and never about anything personal. That disappoints me but I don't know what to do about that or how to change things.

We now meet each other regularly in the anti-war movement. At the candle-lit, peace vigil outside the Primary school, he lights my spluttering candle after it has blown out in a sudden gust. He smiles at me and says goodbye. I meet him again in the organising meeting for Stop the War in our local, community hall. Politically, we seem to have a great deal in common but I can't get rid of the sense that he's wary of me, wanting to keep me at a distance. Our contact is never about trusting me with his personal life. It's always about social action and strategy. Perhaps I'll have to wait much longer for him to want to come to my house for a cup of tea?

INTIMACY—INTIMATELY TOLD

For a large part of my life I found the issue of intimacy to be extremely difficult and risky. As a child my mother was never especially close and usual examples of physical intimacy – such as cuddling and holding – I have no recollections of. My father on the other hand was bullying and intimidating and did everything he could to put me down. Phrases such as 'You make me sick!', for example, still ring painfully in my ears. To add to this I was a small and sickly child with serious respiratory problems and was picked on mercilessly throughout my school years. Not surprisingly I found it hard to get close to people – but I was also frightened of doing so (this writing in itself feels like a piece of real intimacy for me).

In short, achieving intimacy for me was always very difficult and extremely risky and my enduring expectation has always been that at some point in any relationship I will be dumped and/or hurt. Of course, as an adult and as one who has spent a lot of time on both sides of the therapeutic fence, I have learned to address this fear and mostly now I manage intimacy very well and certainly better than many I know. However, when I *am* hurt I become really *deeply* affected. I seem to completely fall apart inside and find it very difficult to get my confidence back.

Ten or eleven years ago, at about the time I was retiring from teaching, I met a new friend and his new Spanish partner. We were both very much into men's issues and he had also very recently retired from teaching. With so much in common we became close friends and exchanged many close intimacies in the way that two modern-thinking, 'right-on' men might have expected to. I remember once that he had to have some very invasive dentistry done and he asked if I could go with him to the dentist and be supportive (he was genuinely very frightened). I held his hand during the procedure even though the dentist and his female assistant clearly found this very unusual. I didn't mind; we were close friends and it seemed a perfectly natural thing to do.

Over time we shared more and more of our inner lives with each other and were both very supportive towards each other, always taking time to listen, always being honest and sensitive, always proud of the fact that we could be intimate and gentle as men. But then things began to change. I began to notice that his observations and comments about me were, for some reason, taking a critical, even spiteful edge. By this time he was living in Spain and I had been spending a lot of time there. 'You always have to be right', was one such observation that came right out of the blue and really hurt me. He clearly began to resent it as well if people complimented me on my Spanish and he would often shun me afterwards. On one occasion he rounded savagely on a woman who complimented me which embarrassed me terribly – and her. The next day a crowd of us spent the day on her husband's boat, he (my friend) spoke the local dialect all day, leaving me completely out of the conversation.

It left me very angry for a long time that he changed in this way towards me but, interestingly, it has not made me shy of intimacy as such. I suppose, in short, yes – it hurts when it goes wrong but I wouldn't be without my intimate relationships.

CHALLENGES, INTIMACY, MEN

There seem to be rules about this kind of stuff, rules that have dark origins that are dangerous to explore.

That evening at the Kings Theatre in Glasgow has something to do with it. I suppose I was fifteen or sixteen and being at the theatre alone was already part of some solitary exploration of my own, a breaking out from the practices of my family and my tribe. Acceptable music at home was Bing Crosby or Frank Sinatra. Acceptable going out, apart from going with my dad to the men's world of supporting Celtic, was visiting one of Paisley's seven cinemas. But here too there were rules that came from other places and older people. One of my dad's aunts in the USA had sent him a warning about a film that was coming, "The Seven Year Itch". He was to make sure that neither he nor any of his children went to see it in all innocence.

I was beginning to do what nobody in my world had ever done: going to concerts of the Scottish National Orchestra to hear whole pieces that I had briefly met on Family Favourites (Rachmaninov's Second Piano Concerto, Ravel's *Bolero*); operas (*Carmen, Samson and Delilah*); the Citizens Theatre (*The Cherry*

Orchard, J.M. Barrie's *Baiche Chiarivari*). Some of my school friends or my mother had once gone with me, but never for a second time.

So it happened that I was in the standing-room-only at the Kings to try out *The Merry Widow*. The man standing beside me had been friendly and chatty before the operetta began. He wondered what the minister sitting a little way in front of us would make of the can-can scene.

Then, the lights down and some way into the spectacle, he took my hand and drew it down his penis. I drew back. Somebody standing behind us moved into the space between this man and me. There were limits I did not want to cross in my explorations.

CHAPTER 11

Love

Jeff Hearn

INTRODUCTION

Here there are five powerful memories of different versions of love. While diverse in character and style, they are often written in a less detailed and less concrete way than some other topics.

The Topic

For some, this topic of love is a valid and unfortunately neglected topic in its own right: "a subject that we don't really talk about", and especially so in that "men talk about love even less than women". For others, the topic is questioned: is this a topic to talk and write about at all? As one writer puts it, it "is not a topic I'm inclined to write about", as "(t)o put "it" on the page is not quite right. It reduces it". To be direct, love is "the wrong subject". Loving and being in love are undeniable, but "it is the person, not the love, that is important in the memory".

Types of Love

Many types of love are addressed: romantic, sexual and sex love is most obvious, but there is also love for family, the intimate bonds of friendship, non-sexual love, love of the self and self-worth, and being loved – and the relationship between some of these different loves: "(n)ow I know people can love me because I love myself". Love can be extended to the person and beyond the person, to "the natural world":

> What I loved about Peter, at about the ages of 7-11, was his passionate energy and involvement in the world of animals, birds, nature and all living creatures. He was totally unsentimental about animals. ... I loved his full-blooded engagement with living things and the natural world.

Dependence and Complexities

Love is represented as often about admitting dependence: "honesty openness, vulnerability and the confidence to say what I really feel", risk, and a lot of giving and receiving. The complexities of love are also recognised: "over time [I] have had to learn how to be separate from and with someone at one and the same time". Somewhat similarly, there is the admission of "how much I love her, not constantly and certainly not to overload her with it ... But during quite ordinary and mundane moments". Accordingly, the effort may be reported "to let my partner know".

Time and Times

Not surprisingly, time figures strongly. Indeed learning and learning about over time, sometimes too late, are key themes of these memories. Almost inevitably, this also invokes loss, regret, sadness and devastation at times, as with the death of a loved one. Love is also connected to very particular times and moments). Time also recurs in terms of giving time and careful attention. To return to Peter, he:

> ... was the person who took time and gave me tenderness by taking me out into the woods or down on the beach, to point out details of the natural world that I hadn't paid any attention to.

Romance or Not?

There are there also other tensions, between romanticised accounts and what might be called their questioning, even their debunking, whether speaking of sexual love or other forms of love, as with the so-called golden-memory stories that may be used to push unsettling things away or lay ghosts. More conventionally, "(h)e admired [her] from slightly afar. The beautiful gorgeous Stella. She was blonde, bright eyed, smooth skinned, and well developed and curvaceous for a 16 year old – encircled in a sheen."; "(a)nd on a park bench the first wonderful, honey-tasting kiss. She was a beautiful kisser, very soft and succulent."

In contrast, the non-romanticised memories stick out with incongruence: "They kissed and then he moved his hand up her leg, and then, "oh shit" he came in his trousers. He rushed upstairs to mop up. Came down a few minutes later, and talked, with some embarrassment, "You know what happened?"". Or ... "(h)e looked at her bottom ahead of him. "Is this love?" he thought."

And finally, love often goes along with loss. Very sadly,

> He died a stupid, wasteful death. He was snorkelling in the sea off Gasworks' beach and he vomited up a recently eaten lunch into his mask. He couldn't breathe and died through asphyxiation. It was a wild, rushed death and I grieved for his loss, his sparkiness and the distance between our lives when he

***

LOVE: THE WRONG SUBJECT

… is not a topic I'm inclined to write about. To put "it" on the page is not quite right. It reduces it. Love is the *wrong subject*. Of course, I memorise being in love, but it is the person, not the love, that is important in the memory.

***

So, he was on holiday with his family, just 16, so it must have been the summer of 1963. They stayed in a caravan on a caravan park near Rye in Sussex. By that time, Bobbie [his sister] was holidaying away from the family, so it was just him and his younger brother. In a neighbouring caravan were another family – with two 16 year olds, a girl and a boy, and a younger boy of 12 or less – the Bains, with a Scottish mother, M., a fine handsome woman, and an English father, perhaps G., a jovial good humoured Londoner. The families mixed and mingled. He admired the daughter from slightly afar. The beautiful gorgeous Stella. She was blonde, bright eyed, smooth skinned, and well developed and curvaceous for a 16 year old – encircled in a sheen.

On the last night, the two families went to the nearby beach through a scrubby sealand area to make a bonfire on the shingle. This was the other father's idea; his own would not do that, too much like wild life. They made the bonfire from driftwood and sundry wood and vegetation & a few cartons. It burned with flames in the dark, the sea quiet nearby. Some food was shared, probably some sausages on and potatoes in the fire. He and S. were near by the fire, some pleasure and similar in being alongside. It was time to return to the caravans & walk up the <u>narrow</u> path through the scrub. The party strung out, with them at the back. They bumped and then held hands. He was <u>in love</u>. He knew she too. It was late and on reaching the caravans, the families said Goodnight. Next morning was more Goodbyes.

On getting home, they wrote. She used pinkish paper. They arranged to meet – it was not so far away where she lived. And on a park bench the first wonderful, honey-tasting kiss. She was a beautiful kisser, very soft and succulent.

They continued writing and meeting and kissing over several months, being in love.

But he noticed a slight boredom arriving, a difficulty in thinking what to talk about, an understanding that she was not so knowledgeable on certain things. But she still smelt and tasted sweet and sweetly, and he still desired her. He realised his love was reduced to almost gone, but wished still to touch her more. The last "date" was staying at her home on Saturday night; her parents were out for the evening; they stayed on the couch "to watch television". She was as desirable as ever. They kissed and then he moved his hand up her leg, and then, "oh shit" he came in his trousers. He rushed upstairs to mop up. Came down a few minutes later, and talked, with some embarrassment, "You know what happened?" "Yes, I think we should stop before we do anything more", she replied. They sat with not so many words; the parents returned; it was obvious something was up. They wrote afterwards they should stop seeing each other. That was the last date. They met again once or twice after that when the families had joint gatherings. It was a little embarrassing, but on one occasion they both stayed to talk in the front room whilst everybody was in the back room. She was a nice decent full-faced girl, not his type at all any longer. No love.

LOVE: A TEN-THOUSAND-LETTER WORD

I think this is a subject that we don't really talk about. By that I don't just mean *men* but everybody. But I do think that men talk about love even less than women. Somehow or other we seem to think that it is more important to talk about the practicalities of life, whereas our deeper feelings become glossed over and tend not to get aired. I think that one of the ways we deal with this is by getting overly sentimental at certain times, when watching films for example, and especially when it comes to poetry and song. Then we really lay it on thick.

There was an item on the news last night about a guy who had killed his partner. She had decided to leave him and he just couldn't deal with the hurt. He stalked her, then he started to threaten her, and eventually he drove her car off the road, smashed the windscreen to get at her and then killed her. Was it because deep down he loved her, or was it just that he needed her too much and couldn't bear to be without her? Or was it the pain of rejection? Love can be very damaging if we are not careful with it.

It has also been hard for me to separate these three things out in my own life, especially where the line is drawn between loving someone and needing them. I know that I have a deep need to be intimately involved in a relationship, that it hurts me to the core when things go wrong, and that I have always very quickly become involved with someone else when things break down. Unlike the guy above, though, I have never reacted badly to the person concerned in any way. But I do know that for much of my younger life this deep neediness of mine could push others away and that it took me a very long time to become sufficiently self-assured not to jump into things too quickly or with the wrong person.

But acknowledging this deep need doesn't mean that I didn't genuinely love the people that I was involved with. If anything it meant that I loved them too much, unrealistically, so that I swamped them and invested far too much of myself in them. Of course this was more about me than them. So over time have had to learn how to be *separate from* and *with* someone at one and the same time. Blimey, this is complicated - because I have also had to learn *when* to be entirely *with* a person as well! Sometimes that's really important too. I guess I'm saying that there has to be space within a relationship for the individuals concerned to grow, or else they become pot-bound.

Something else that I learned, far too late in life, is how much others have loved me. This realisation was a real shock and it just hit me one day. I think of all the times that I have let women down or hurt them badly in some way, sometimes rejecting them before they could reject me - rather than working the issues through. Something in me felt that it was OK to do this because surely no-one could be hurt that much by me leaving them – because surely no-one could possibly *love me that much;* I was un-lovable so therefore I must have been *un-loved.* I know now that this was a big mistake and that it went on for far too long.

This realisation has meant that I now make the effort to let my partner know how much I love her, not constantly and certainly not to overload her with it. But during quite ordinary and mundane moments I will just remind her and let her know. I know that she loves me too, even though I can be a pain in the arse sometimes. That's a good feeling.

"Is This Love?"

After they had been to the second bar some of the group were starting to fade. The other two of them made their excuses to leave. She asked him if he wanted to go to the nightclub in the same building. "Yes, of course." That evening he was wearing his favourite coat, pale blue floppy collared shirt, and dark green fleece. They went in together and to his astonishment and great pleasure she took his hand leading him to the music and onto the dance floor immediately, with coat and all. The disco staff followed them and insisted that they leave their coats and bags at the cloakroom and pay for the privilege. They went back, deposited the coats and bags, then went back towards the dance floor.

Having no coat herself, she asked if he could take care of her bulging wallet. "Of course". She gave him her bulging wallet, to put somewhere, so he pushed it tight into his jeans pocket, but then decided he shouldn't take off his fleece, as that *covered* the bulging pocket. It was no kind of place to leave clothes around safely anyway. And he actually didn't feel excessively hot, but actually cool and relaxed. They moved towards the music. She took his hand a second time, leading him to the music. He looked at her bottom ahead of him. "Is this love?" he thought.

Whenever he sees the coat, that fleece or shirt, he thinks of her and the disco.

Love in My Life: Homily

> I love loving someone, loving relationships. To me it is about caring for them as if not more than myself.

> Love is an unconditional promise to be there for someone no matter what they do to you or others but within limits.

> Love can be because sometimes the loved one does not love back. The two way interaction completes the loving process.

> To be loved is nurturing, feeling unconditional support and caring from someone makes my life worth living.

> I have felt this love from my parents throughout my life, from my sister my partner my sons and some male friends.

For me sex love is different to that love. Again I've been lucky to have felt that in a number of relationships, with lust mixed with possessiveness and fear of losing that passion.

When I was younger I felt a religious intensity based on chanting and ritualistic singing which evoked feelings of joy and elation, a spiritual love. This intensity of feelings still return when listen to some music. My own intellectual criticisms have removed the religious links.

Whenever I lost the love of a partner I was devastated because that intense trust that comes with love was shattered. Feelings of betrayal, being abandoned bereft were much more hurtful than any physical beating.

This taught me to be careful in the love stakes. I went/ego in for building a strong caring relationship lustful but also based on respect caring and nurturing.

Love is a risky business which requires a lot of giving and receiving. I learnt you have to be confident about your own self-worth, love yourself first before you can be loved for being yourself.

For me honesty openness, vulnerability and the confidence to say what I really feel lie at the centre of my loving relationships. When I was in relationships without that; the love and relationships died very quickly.

Now I know people can love me because I love myself. Care for, trust myself to give the same to others. That is why I can feel happy to live life with confidence that I can love. Love keeps me going.

LOVING PETER

Just after the Second World War, I found myself living in a rented house in Paignton, South Devon, as a part of a semi-evacuation arrangement within our family and friends. My father had been away for most of the war working as a firefighter in London.

From about six or seven I became closely connected to my two cousins, Michael and Peter, who were both living under the same roof as me. First, Michael, who was about ten years older than me, showed me the intricate world of making and flying model aeroplanes. I went along with his interests for a few months but it was with his brother, Peter, that I developed a much more intimate bond.

Peter opened my eyes to a wild, natural world on our doorstep in Devon, in the fields, wood and beaches. Unlike Michael who went to Torquay boys' grammar school and then later worked at Farnborough, having a hand in researching and designing planes, Peter failed his 11+ and he looked on academic work with contempt.

What I loved about Peter, at about the ages of 7-11, was his passionate energy and involvement in the world of animals, birds, nature and all living creatures. He was totally unsentimental about animals. He loved dogs, ferrets, birds with a rough embrace but he would also kill animals and paunch them, ripping the steaming entrails out of rabbits, without apparent care or compassion.

Peter was about seven/eight years older than me and as an adolescent boy growing up he was very much a poacher and rebellious outlaw. He got into trouble regularly with the Police, nicking cars, stealing things and was sent to Borstal for a short while. But to me, Peter was the person who took time and gave me tenderness by taking me out into the woods or down on the beach, to point out details of the natural world that I hadn't paid any attention to.

I can remember the day when he took me down to Gasworks' beach. We were walking along the sands and Peter told me to imagine that I held a camera in my hands. He told me that to get close to wild life you need to sneak up on them and make no noise. As an example he pointed out to me four or five dunlins edging their way, nervously, along the shore.

We slowly approached a large, seaweedy rock further out to sea. Peter told me to hold my breath and carefully creep up on the birds to 'photograph' them on the far side of the rock. I can remember the hushed approach, the bulky, black-backed gulls on the rock and then the clanging alarm calls of black and white, oyster catchers as they wheeled away. I think I framed them between my fingers and thumb.

Later, Peter took me on walks where weapons appeared. I remember something of the soft, dusky wait in the pine trees for the pigeons to come back in to roost. I couldn't see much because of my short-sightedness but Peter would point upwards, slowly raise his twelve-bore gun onto his shoulder and then the evening was shattered by the loud roar of the gun going off. A bleeding pigeon fell through pine branches, flapping and scuffling. Peter used to kill them quickly and effectively.

One day Peter invited me to use the twelve-bore but I refused fearing the kick-back and the startling explosion. But he also had an air gun and pressured me into carrying it. I gave in to Peter's request and one afternoon out in the woods with him, I shot a sparrow with the air gun. I was confused afterwards, feeling both pride for the accuracy of my shot and also a flinching away from the dead bird. When I wrapped my fingers around it I felt the tiny heat of the dead body with its fluffed up feathers.

Much later I began to wonder about Peter. I realised that he liked to show things to younger, more innocent people. And that he wasn't very good at adult/adult relationships.

My love for him was very intense for a short time before I went on to Grammar school and University. I loved his full-blooded engagement with living things and the natural world. But later I became aware that perhaps I looked up to him, at that particular time, because I lacked a proper, intimate relationship with my father who was absent for too much of my early life, through no fault of his own, to ever be allowed to get back in.

When I was in my late twenties, Peter came up to see me when I lived with my first wife in Settle in North Yorkshire. I tried to re-kindle our previous contact by taking him for a long walk with his dog. But Peter found the Yorkshire Dales too bleak and treeless after Devon.

I never saw him again. I was away on the island of St. Kilda when he died in his early forties. And I was only told about his funeral, which I missed, after I had got back to Oban.

He died a stupid, wasteful death. He was snorkelling in the sea off Gasworks' beach and he vomited up a recently eaten lunch into his mask. He couldn't breathe and died through asphyxiation. It was a wild, rushed death and I grieved for his loss, his sparkiness and the distance between our lives when he finally died.

CHAPTER 12

Saying Goodbye to Mothers

Dan McEwan

INTRODUCTION

As I re-read these stories in order to write this introduction, I have a strong emotional response. The realisation that I am not far from tears is rooted in re-visiting the experiences of men I have known for at least ten years and have grown fond of individually and collectively.

They/we have written these stories about our mothers often with concrete details which both recall a particular private experience and paradoxically reach towards a general, shared, perhaps even a universal experience.

I am reminded of the first of two workshops when a woman shared with us a session of memory work. On the topic of "hair", she recalled being one night alone at a London bus stop with a skinhead youth. She felt nervous. She found herself wondering what childhood experiences had so damaged the young man that she felt afraid of him. Suddenly he smiled to her and her anxiety disappeared. Later she asked herself whether, in imagining him as a child, she had perhaps first smiled to him. Our memory-men work was richly evocative beyond its single-sex home.

As I re-read our stories about our mothers, I recognise myself. Obviously I recognise myself in my own autobiographic story; but, more surprisingly, I recognise something of myself in them all. Perhaps when an author is true and honest to the particularity in his own story, he (and presumably she, when a woman writes) gets closer to something universal. Also, interestingly many of the stories in this section initially had almost the same title of "saying goodbye" or "separating from mother", or something similar. There seemed to be a real convergence of themes and issues here.

A tension or contradiction is present in at least some of the stories. One man calls it "anger and love" as he explores thirty years of tearful separations from his mother at airports. Another calls it "vengeful" when his busy life compels him to leave his mother protesting on the floor that she cannot get up; and he looks back to leaving for boarding school "harbouring unspoken feelings" and further back to the tough parenting of a "strict" nurse. The same tension seems to lie behind a third's "feeling stifled" by what he now recognises as his mother's own needs, recognises and understands better. Perhaps too it lies behind another's childhood expectation that his mother would always be in his life, "but I was very wrong". Would it be too fanciful to call this contradiction "love and hate", somehow coexisting but not cancelling each other out?

The separation that death brings is connected with earlier separations. One account hints that the final separation is prefigured in the extended separation from family culture that developed during his grammar school years. Another looks back to the closeness of being breast fed, while wondering if what he is in fact recalling is the memory of his brother, six years his junior, being fed. That experience returned later for him in a different form: after visiting his widowed mother with his own son, they found themselves on a train opposite a young mother breastfeeding: he looked the other way while his young son, "my surrogate," talked with the young woman.

One memory specifically talks about the role reversal of mothering his own mother as he prepared food for her during her final years. He had to keep her alive so that she would trust him to let her go when she had to decide about the invasive surgery that would keep her alive or half-alive for longer.

In some cases deceptions were used to "protect" the closest participants in these dramas of separation. The mother of one man simply disappeared from the family home when he was eleven-years old. Nobody told him that the GP had recommended that she be separated from the burdens of child care because of her heart problem. Then when she returned to the family home with an aunt looking after the children, the aunt sent him during the night to fetch his uncle. When he returned, his mother's body had disappeared, the Lucozade bottle still beside her bed. Similarly, another memory tells of the man's extended family gathered around his mother's hospital bed, but they had agreed not to tell her that she was dying. This left him and his father wondering if she had known but they had denied her the chance of speaking about it.

While many of these stories look behind the separations to older histories, one memory is more focused on more recent times, specifically recalling the closeness amongst the adult children gathered around the bed of their dying mother. Then, as they later go to telephone their partners, one sister stands lonely against the wall. She has no partner. "Who is going to hold me when I die?" she asks.

***

Separating from My Mother

One of the biggest pleasures I recall is sitting on the floor as a child beside my mother in her armchair. In those memories she is always running her fingers through my hair.

There seem to be two movements of separation from that childhood experience. The first seems to last the whole six years of my secondary school education. The school was so close to our house that I always went home for lunch and that frequently was time alone with my mother. My sisters, two years younger than I, either went to our more distant primary school or later to their even more remote secondary school. My shift-working dad either seemed to be at work or asleep after nightshift. I don't remember how my brother, twelve years younger than I, fits into this picture.

During these lunchtimes I was growing too old for head rubbing, even if now that seems a poor reason for its stopping. Those lunchtimes were precious. Mum seemed to be there for me. Looking back, I hope that I was there for her, listening and not just speaking. "Desert Island Discs" was on the radio once a week at lunchtime. It played an important part in my moving from the family culture of Bing Crosby and Frank Sinatra into what seemed the richer world of "classical" music. When I ran the risk of going to orchestral concerts in Glasgow usually on my own, Mum once went with me. I enjoyed that concert hugely, precisely because she was there sharing it.

All that came to an end when, aged eighteen, I left home. But Mum was still there to visit in the summer or, less frequently than Dad, to write me a letter. Both my parents had left school at the age of fourteen. Dad's letters seemed more fluent and more correct but hers were better at keeping details of my past alive: "I'll just stop there. I don't know what to get for tea. I'll just go to the shops."

The second time of separation came when I was in my late twenties. They told me my mother was in hospital. She'll be OK but it would be good if I could come home.

Once home, I learned that she was dying. Everybody, however, was clear about one thing: we should not tell her what we all knew. It certainly felt false telling her that her eldest sister, my Aunt Helen, had come back from the USA just by chance.

Looking back I am almost certain that Mum knew about her imminent death. For a dozen years, since she had been seriously ill (something to do with her blood), our old family GP kept popping in to visit her on his rounds although she was living a normal life well able to visit his surgery. Did he and she share a secret which they kept from us? Certainly after her death my Dad wondered about that. I still do.

ALWAYS SAYING GOODBYE

Why have I always been saying goodbye to mother? I immediately think of repeatedly saying goodbye to be sent away to two different boarding schools. But maybe I didn't say goodbye; I mean maybe I just left, harbouring unspoken feelings. Then I think of my mother dying. My brother and I and our partners by her bedside, in my home, holding her hand, her breathing becoming discontinuous, great gasps of air and a final long sigh, and a definitive leaving. She lived with us for ten or so years when my Dad had died, and I was always leaving her, though we also went places together. 'Where's B?' she'd ask the others. And 'Where are you going now?'

Often my leaving was an ordinary independence in a busy life, but it could be vengeful too. Once, when she was out of breath, I asked her to lie down and she couldn't get up. I could not raise her and there was no one else in the house. She wasn't comfortable. "I'll have to call an ambulance" I said and she was adamant I mustn't. So I left her on the floor, walking out of her room angrily. When I came back she was in her seat again, but shocked, white. I remind myself that her final decline, aged 93, followed my refusal to take her to Canada for a great nephew's wedding, leaving her at home. She took it as a sign she had become a liability, a burden. Did she, a woman of many insights, sense the anger in this refusal?

Then last week I saw a TV programme on three ways to bring up babies- an old-fashioned routine-based, they-must-fit-in, leave-them-in-the-pram-to-cry version, a Dr Spock more flexible version, and a version based on the inseparability of parent and baby. Perhaps because she was of that generation and we each had – me, my brother and sister in a socially aspirant family – a famously 'strict' *nurse* to look over us when tiny, I was 'left' as a baby too, long before the boarding schools. I also remember a story told by my older sister: she, the first, had bad colic as a baby so she was 'sent back to hospital' until she got better, something hard to grasp in parental culture today and painful to think about in terms an infant's psychic needs.

So maybe I had an enduring impulse to leave my mother as my mother left me, without saying goodbye, or not forgivingly. If so, how weird that I behaved – sometimes, so baby-ishly to my clever and loving mother as an apparently grown up man. Maybe also this pattern founded feelings of worthlessness – why was I left or sent away? What had I done? This may have had other consequences, of striving so anxiously to be 'good'. Worth considering anyway ...

SAYING THAT LONG SLOW GOODBYE TO MY MOTHER

My Relationship with my mother has almost always been two-sided. For as long as I can remember – given that I spent a large part of my early childhood in and out of hospital – I suppose I always had to be able to get along without her for long periods. Therefore I could easily alternate between being obsessively clingy and becoming self-contained. None of this was in any sense her fault of course – it was just the bad luck of the draw.

It wasn't until I was well into adulthood that I realised that there was another aspect to this. It began to dawn on me that we were in fact quite poor, even by post-war standards, but also that we were impoverished in another way – by my parents' immaturity and naivety. Thus we took it as normal, for example, that we would be put to bed early so that they could leave us alone and go down to the pub for the evening.

She had married when she was twenty, at the outset of the war, and had been looking after her grandmother for many years prior to that. Her own mother had died when she was relatively young. The upshot is that she was actually very needy herself and I think I sensed this from quite an early age. I suppose this could be part of the reason why I never felt especially close to her, since when I was close to her it could feel like I was being there for her reasons and needs, rather than for mine.

One incident in particular springs to mind: we were in a shop and there was something that I wanted which she also clearly wanted, but presumably we didn't have the money for. I don't remember what it was now but I vividly remember her whispering to me, urging me to steal it – which I was reluctant to do. She persisted but I don't think I did.

I can't really ever remember being close to her. I have no memory of being kissed or cuddled, though I am sure I must have been. My one most enduring memory is a general one – of feeling stifled and, above all, kept as a child. I must have been the last boy in our street, and the school, to go into long trousers. This happened when I went to secondary school at the age of 12. The toys we were given were almost always 'below our years' and this pained me terribly the older I became.

Even now, eighty seven years old and in a care home, she speaks in clichés and catchphrases from game-shows and television programmes going right back to the 1950's. Still this makes it difficult to actually talk to her as a person, to get close to her – the real person behind the superficial defence.

TRUSTING ME

She had felt tired of life for over a year now. I had visited her at home every other day for two to three years as she slowly stopped eating much, shrinking slowly into death.

I tried to encourage her fighting, to hang onto life with tasty meals brought round or cooked for her at home. But she did not want to eat them, reassuring me, "Later son, I'll eat it later, when you're gone".

She who really loved her family through food, always inviting C., me and the boys for Sunday dinner, now could not bring herself to cook or eat. With the roles reversed, mothering my mother, I became obsessed by my food care for her. I had to keep my mother alive. So when that final decision came to be made I knew she would trust me to let her go.

In the final days of her life she suffered blockages in the arteries of her feet which quickly turned blue with gangrene galloping up to her hips. The surgeons offered to start hacking her limbs off, but I had seen my uncle have both legs cut off and live bed-bound like a vegetable. So I did not think she could live being like that. So we discussed options and she agreed reluctantly not to be mutilated like that. She knew she could only last a few days without the operation but submitted herself through a haze of morphine to my loving advice. She refused the op reluctantly trusting her life to me her son.

A DEEP SEA DIVER

The gaps between her breaths were getting longer and longer. She was grey, and had been unconscious for 24 hours. I cried when I realised 36 hours earlier that she had started to stare into space. Her body was there, her eyes were seemingly looking at me but she was no longer seeing me. M. comforted me by rubbing my stomach, making gentle circles on it. It was a gesture I was not familiar with, but it was oddly soothing, getting to the eye of my pain. My three sisters and I had been nursing her day and night for a week and we were *willing* her to die. Mi. was at the bottom of the bed gently sobbing; her face was screaming: 'Don't let her suffer anymore'. I did not think Mi. could stand much more. C. and M. were each holding one of my mother's hands (as my mother had requested when she was still conscious and knew she was dying). I was behind C. and had been holding my mother's right hand for the previous two hours, which she had been squeezing for days beforehand – not wanting to let go of me – but now her hand was lifeless and grossly swollen, looking like a sea creature. My back was hurting from that still position, slightly twisted towards the bed. Her whole body was putting in a last effort to catch her breath. She reminded me of a deep sea diver who has to come up for air. Every time, her body raised itself slightly to breathe. We were silent – rocked by Mi.'s muffled crying; when the lungs appeared not to be filling up, we would look at each other, all thinking: 'Is this it?' I have never seen a human being pause for so long between each intake of air, but somehow, her organs were not giving up. Her mouth was open, and I could see deep inside her throat; she looked quite inhuman. Then, a longer gap, we conferred with each other by means of glances. Our own bodies were filling up with a sense of relief, but then she breathed again. There was almost laughter amongst us, except for Mi. Sleep deprived and emotionally exhausted, we were near to hysteria. After that surprising last intake, nothing. We said (I can't remember whom: 'It's the end'). It was weird, having watched over her body for so long, in the middle of the night, for signs of life, to see a motionless corpse. Time was suspended. And then another long breath from deep inside her body. C. almost jumped up, startled. We did not know it then, but it was to be her last manifestation of life.

Because we had been preparing for her death, we had been told by several quarters that at the moment of death, the brain is still active for up to a few minutes and therefore, she may hear us. We had pre-arranged to do this. M. was the first one to speak, accompanying her one last time with gentle words, telling her we loved her and thanking her for the life and the love she had given us. I can't recall if the remaining three of us uttered anything. I had discussed in advance with my sisters that moment, and requested that, before we let the world in and started phoning our other three siblings, the nurse, the doctor etc. we would take time to be together. The last eight days had brought intense intimacy (one we had not known since living under the same roof as children) with fits of laughter, occasional irritation with each other, but always respect between us. Our codes as a non-tactile family had been reinvented. Mi. and I, giving each other physical support, allowed C. and M. to do the same with each other, and eventually with all of us. So we stood, forming a circle around my mother's death bed, holding hands. C. and M. took turns trying to close my mother's mouth, but every time they let go, her mouth gaped open again, as if it had a life of its own. Mi. kept telling them they would not succeed in closing her mouth, but it is as if they were not listening, and did not want to be defeated in affording their mother that last dignity. I had prepared some words in my head and talked about the intense experience we had lived through, how it had brought us together, and also addressed my mother – but have forgotten what I said to her. We then had individual hugs. I was touched because M. who is tiny, let herself be wrapped up completely in my arms. By contrast, C. was so, so rigid, it took me back; it was like hugging a dry wooden stick. And then we let the world in. I contacted the nurse to officialise the death. We all made phone calls and rang family, partners, and children. Mi., who is partnerless, stood lonely against the wall. She did not have anyone to contact to let them know that her mother had died. I went up to her and she whispered in agony: 'Who is going to hold my hand when I die?'

BEING WITH MUM, NOT BEING WITH MUM

To find a memory, one memory, seems difficult. It is the overwhelming ordinariness of my mother *and* me, my relationship to my mother. It is *snippets* that come back. So break the rules.

I wonder if I do remember the smell of her breasts and her breast milk – but I think it was from my brother being fed as a baby, when he was born at home when I was six. The sweet sickly smell offended me, though still slightly intriguing. In photos then she was a thinnish pretty woman. She was always there, but not warm, almost functional. When I was young before going to school, we would visit my grandmothers and aunts. I preferred Gran-round-the-corner; the walks to Gran-at-Greenwich were more demanding and tiring, I protested a little, and arriving there I knew the smell of the old people and the old people's flats – not 100% clean, a bit musty, food, perhaps cabbage, also slightly sickly. It was generally boring being there with my mother-companion, though the walls of Gran's flat were hung with large brown photos of relatives, including my dead Grandad – some slight mystery. A different time and history. I liked the bulky green vases, ugly and reassuring. Mum and Gran just talked, I waited to go home. Mum held my hand then, especially the time I fell over and had to have stitches in my chin which bled so profusely.

She did not hold my hand or kiss me that I remember when I was a "big boy". I had to learn to say goodbye to all that. I was becoming normal.

Now as adult, my father suddenly fell ill – I rushed to the hospital, by his bedside, he was dying. My Mum and brother stayed in the next ante-room talking, not throughout, but for the last moments, minutes, too long. My sister and I stayed by his bedside until he died. I kissed him on the lips when he was dead.

We drove back home, all the Christmas cards, were written and in a bundle, Mum said to post them anyway. We stopped the car at a postbox, I jumped out and sent them off, through the aperture.

Next day or so, she and I went to the Registrar's Office to record the death. We approached the town hall type building with many entrance steps. Another couple, clearly in mourning, approached slowly. "Quick", my mum said, "we can overtake them if we're quick", as she rushed up the stairs. I followed slowly in disgust and amusement. I knew she was in shock, but at least she could pretend not to be ...

The next few years she did not wish to travel and visit us on her own. So I took it in turns to take one of the 3 children on my own to visit her. It was a long train journey and a good way to be with each child in turn *on their own*. One journey with S., my son, involved us sitting opposite a youngish mother breastfeeding. I tried to look the other way, to not pressure; S., who was by this time about eight, engaged the mother in conversation, including about breastfeeding. He was my surrogate.

After this, I then interviewed my mother several times on tape. I realised it was time to re-educate my mother to actually hug me and to kiss me hallo and goodbye. Doing this is not especially pleasant for me. It seems, still seems, after 20 years now, unfamiliar territory for my mother, as she tenses her upper body on anticipation of the hugging contact. The mundane kiss is also ambiguous, perhaps on the lips or to one side, a thin lipped kiss, not wholehearted, like most hetero men who kiss men. It is a bit of a shambles but worth the uncoordinated effort.

This summer I arranged to stay overnight with S. and then planned to go to see my mother from there, perhaps as a surprise – oddly, without telling, he had <u>separately</u>, arranged to visit her the same day. So we went together for the first times as adults. We couldn't surprise her as that would have panicked her food plans. She was very pleased to see us together, for *the long afternoon*. Then we said goodbye, a little relief it was done.

I Never Said Goodbye Properly

I never said goodbye to my mother. That's a part of the problem. The story went like this: when I was 11 my mother vanished from my family home. Later, I learnt that she had been diagnosed with a very serious heart problem and that her G.P. had recommended total rest apart from all the chores of being a loving mother; that meant spending 6 months away from our demands. But after that 6 months, she came back to our home, where she spent the time on a day-bed in the front room of our house.

My Aunt came down to look after the house and us kids. One evening I was nearly asleep with my aunt working in the kitchen below. Suddenly, there was a loud, panicky shout from down there, David! David! Get your clothes on and come down here. Quick!'

A bit groggy I tiptoed downstairs. I hovered at the door of my mother's room. I glimpsed into the darkened interior but only saw a motionless lump in the bedclothes. There was only silence and darkness. I managed to whisper a worried, 'Are you O.K. Mum?' But there was no answer or movement inside the room.

The next minute my aunt had swept past me and closed the door of my mother's room. 'I want you to run up the hill and fetch your Uncle Bill,' she hissed. 'Do you hear? Go as quickly as you can and bring your Uncle down here. O.K.?'

I didn't know what to say. I just remember that panting, aching run up the lower slope and then the hill up to where my Uncle Bill was.

When I got to the house I banged and shouted at the front door for a few minutes with no answer. I was nearly sobbing. But then a light came on at the back of the house.

Bill's usually reassuring face was dark with a puzzled anxiety. It took him a long time to get ready and get the motor bike out at the front of the house. He told me to hang on tight as I rode on the pillion seat down to my family home. When we got there the darkness in the house had disappeared. Lights were full on in every corner of the house. It was as if we had decided to throw an impromptu party in the middle of the night.

My father was back from his night shift at Torquay Fire Station. All the members of my family were gathered around my mother's room, the landing and the kitchen. But my mother's body had vanished. There was no sign of her. The Lucozade bottle was still beside her bedside but there were no traces left of her.

I was never able to hold her in my arms and kiss her goodbye. I never had the chance of saying a proper goodbye to her. I didn't know why she left me to struggle on, alone. I assumed that she would be there for ever in my life, soothing me, praising me, protecting me. But I was very wrong.

The funeral was held the following week. In the photograph that I have showing the chief, family mourners, all the people are showing a glassy, fake smile. My Aunt has her mouth open in a hysterical yell. Nobody there told me where my mother had gone. I just felt an impossibly wide crater open up in front of me and swallow me down, legs waving.

ANGER AND LOVE

Me and my mum, yes, what can I say about our relationship? Mostly, I'm angry with her though I seldom if ever display it.

She has this way of telling stories about people she knows but I don't. She will relate in endless, excruciating detail the minutiae of their lives – the things these people, these strangers like to watch on TV or what they did on their recent trip to Seattle. Stuff like that, always completely insensitive to me, to what I might want to know or might find interesting. She does this a lot.

And I feel trapped, unable to tell her to stop because I am her favourite, her first born. There is never a harsh word between us.

Over the past thirty or so years while I have been living in various places, my mother and I have shared a series of perhaps twenty tearful greeting and farewells, usually at airports. When we part I always say "I love you" and I do but I also look forward to not seeing her again for another two or three years.

This is my solution to dealing with anger and love.

CHAPTER 13

Political Moments

Richard Johnson

INTRODUCTION

The theme chosen for this sequence of stories was 'formative political moments'. Although we all wrote about episodes in our lives that had formed our political outlooks and practices in some way, as usual we wrote about this in very different ways.

Two of the stories focus on youthful political formation and the subsequent continuity or rethought recurrence of some feature derived from that time: "laying down a pattern that has continued all my life". These two stories are, however, very different in tone. The first tells of the student movement at the University of Louvain in 1968 and is careful and measured, the writing matching the theme of investment in a kind of academic or educational politics, which is work-place based and 'cerebral' and in a university (or a school). It was only later, that the author himself, responding to discussion in the group, wrote about the intensely emotional character of that time – with personal rebellion and unease against a chosen life of clerical chastity connecting with the other excitements of 1968.

Another story is also about the origins – here from the age of ten! – of a political outlook, already named as 'socialism'. By contrast, however, this story flares with emotion and up-front feelings: fury with a Conservative father round the dinner table, disappointment with a lover whose gender transgressions were not matched by a left-wing politics. The oedipal nature of these feelings – the identification with mother and anger towards the father – don't require much analysis to uncover. The continuity here is an interesting and psychologically convincing one: the story is about unease in the discrepancy (and by implication comfort?) between loving someone and disagreeing (or agreeing) politically with them. By implication there is a craving for the comfort of loving someone you

119

can agree with, being fully 'at home' in a way impossible in your family of origin?

Both stories, then, the first in its absences, later revealed, the second more explicitly, tell us about the close connections between loving and hating, identifying and dis-identifying, and the more formal or articulated political positions we take up in the world. It is interesting that both these writers became educators in their later lives.

Two of the other stories deal with issues of becoming politically active in later life, with politics and ageing. Again, however, the theme is treated in different ways, according to the particularities of two lives. In the first of these, 'Challenged to be politically active', there are painful oppositions that run right through the account between activity, running, speaking and doing something on one side, and silence, immobility, waiting and inaction on the other. The narrative (and the life?) finds a way of reconciling these oppositions and of breaking through the inaction, tellingly through a form of action that actually involves silence and immobility: the silent vigil. This is a locally-based solution that is possible within the limits of relative physical frailty and brings its own sense of courage, pride and achievement. This complex story seems to tell of desires that strongly oppose, but must accept, the physical limits of ageing, a 'retirement' that is forced, sometimes accepted and sometimes rebelled against.

A second, ''Doing something about it' – getting 'political' again post-11 September 2001', belongs to roughly to the same historical turning point – the War on Terror including the wars in Afghanistan and Iraq. It is another old-man-becoming-politically-active story. Retirement here, however, is presented as a moment of release and even exhilaration and while the first story is alive to the necessary limits of ageing activism, there is more than a hint of conventional male heroism in second carried in a kind of adventure narrative. Much of this is, interestingly, projected onto a younger man, a student who leads the way from academic politics to lively urban scenes of anti-war and anti-globalisation politics. This story too is about retirement – and the death of a cared-for mother – but retirement as the releasing of constraints, the activist possibilities that is, of ageing. One possible interpretation of this story is that this writer has for a long time – since 1968 perhaps – lived his political life through his students, and the excitement is about becoming more of a political actor himself.

The remaining three stories all concern men's politics or Men's Movements in different ways. Two are similar to the two youthful stories in that they concern formative moments of feminist or men's movement consciousness. The memory, 'A political awakening', while questioning that there can be a single moment of formation, identifies a key contradiction in an earlier Marxist-feminist formation, where an angry woman uses very sexist language to attack a gentle male teacher. Men, the story seems to say, can also be victims in the gender order, have their own vulnerabilities, so that there is 'a distinctive men's agenda' which a feminism, based in women's experiences, has not, perhaps cannot address. It's important to stress that the temporary partial reversal of power relations which is remembered here, qualifies or extends, rather than inverts the commitment to a critical gender politics.

'Thanks J for that slap!' is similar in that it constructs some part of political commitment to a particular gender-laden episode, though this time the angry act is presented as a justified correction, not as an insult. The slap administered by a woman for a sexist remark is still remembered with gratitude! The author is very clear about his feminist convictions, taking the side of women, but this story is much more complex than this, and is perhaps best read as a story about the contradictions of anti-sexist men's politics (or white anti-racism). It acknowledges and explores both guilt and resentment: the slap is welcomed but is also 'a bit over the top'; guilt about privilege and sexist or racist attitudes is acknowledged but the guilt itself is also questioned. It seems to me that here and perhaps also in the previous story, there is often a subtext of Romance, even of Courtly Love, in the narratives of men who are also feminists, the need perhaps to get beyond love as worship or the idealisation of women as altogether superior beings, who are justifiably our guides or muses. Greater wisdom seems to come with ageing which allows some relaxation in the fierce self-accusatory inner dialogues of a more youthful self.

'Being active in Finland' is not about the origins of commitment to feminist men's politics, but about a later adaptation to a new national and cultural context. How is it possible to continue and develop a men's politics in Finland from an experience of Anglo-American traditions? One solution the story explores is a straight transposition of the White Ribbon Movement's ways of opposing violence towards women, sparked off by the visit of the Canadian activist Michael Kaufman. The limits of this transposition are carefully analysed. By comparison there is excitement in the story as a form of 'profeminism' (including the word in Finnish) is invented and seems to work, gathering political momentum. This is not quite matched by a move into opposing the sex trade which is 'disappointing in some ways but definitely OK'. The narrative ends with a celebration of political friendship, working together and laughter, a warm coincidence in short between commitment and loving.

All three stories about men's politics open up the question of the complexities of feminism for men, a complexity always shaped in a particular historical and social space. It is important to recognise the retrospective nature of all these narratives. They are all making sense of past events, picking them up as significant indeed, in the light of current concerns and commitments. They are records in short of an *ageing* male pro-feminism, a learning, that is, from experience and experiment. This learning is of course uncompleted: writing the stories themselves, reflecting on them, having others reflect on them, reflecting on others' stories, are also now parts of the learning.

***

AN IMPORTANT PART OF MY POLITICISATION

It was 1967-68. It was a Continental university, Louvain in Belgium. I, a young priest and friar at the time, was doing a postgraduate degree in theology.

As students we had come to feel that our lecturers, for all that they were introducing us to international critical scholarship, were failing to confront the big radical questions of the day. So in our faculty the students formed themselves into a representative body linked to the general student union. I became the representative of my year in the four-person steering group.

We dealt with two main issues. The first arose from the specific circumstances of "la contestation universitaire". The authorities had decided that despite the linguistic tension in Belgium Louvain would continue as a single university offering every course in both Dutch and French. The Dutch-speaking students demanded that there should be two separate universities and that the French one should be built a few miles from Leuven in the French-speaking part of the country. By the end of the year the latter option won the day. It felt like a victory for student protest, though clearly it was more complicated than that.

Before the decision was made, however, the lived experience was of rowdy demonstrations in the streets confronted by armed police and water cannons. With the agreement of the other two members of the steering group I was able to contact I set about organising a debate introduced by a speaker from the two linguistic communities. The Dutch speaker had agreed to use French, as it was the common language of the international student community. The event was to take place in a beautiful eighteenth-century college. The chair of our committee returned from his doctoral research to explode about the foolhardy, ill-informed scheme I had set up: the riots from the streets would pour into our meeting and we could be responsible for thousands of pounds worth of damage. In fact it all went ahead, an oasis of calm discussion secluded from the violence on the streets. Probably the presence of a large number of foreign students helped to create this atmosphere. A French-speaking student sitting beside me told me that he had never realised that the Dutch speakers had a reasonable case but that once he was out on the streets again he would lose all awareness of that. I was not surprised by his ignorance of half of the debate for by going to the student union of French speaking students I had realised that nobody outside the small Faculty of (postgraduate) Theology and the big Faculty of Political, Social and Economic Sciences had any grasp of both sides of the debate.

The other main issue we dealt with was the idea of theology as a separate academic subject. We organised a small number of lectures by professors from outside our own faculty and invited all of our lecturers to attend. I remember in particular two outstanding presentations, one by a psychoanalyst on the mythic dimension of theological concepts and one by a philosopher on the questions that twentieth-century philosophical movements were putting to theology. We had the impression that some of our older lecturers did not grasp what was going on but that the younger ones were very excited and certainly several of our teachers went up in our estimation when we saw them perform in that challenging context.

Looking back I can see that those experiences were laying down a pattern that has continued throughout my life. My insertion into politics has always been around the place where I was working and generally of a debating, cerebral sort. Yet I can also see strong emotional elements. Identifying with Flemish aspirations seemed to connect with feelings of being Scottish and of working-class origins in a United Kingdom where the dominant power seemed to lie elsewhere. More concretely all those activities helped to form a warm friendship with a female student from Antwerp who (oh, innocent pleasures!) introduced me to the thought of Ernst Bloch.

A footnote is that amidst all those distractions from studies I had better results that year than any other.

The Author's Later Own Reflections on This Story

Re-reading my story in the light of your [another group member's] comments I can see that most of it is indeed a factual, detached account of events I was involved in: it is only towards the end, when I look back on those events that more personal aspects appear. I am also surprised by the sexual connotations of my language pointed out in that final part. You also suggest that there might be a lot of anger bottled up in me without, however, referring to the text for this.

Perhaps you were just guessing at something to see what would come out if I responded. In any case, here goes.

I was aware at the time of the events that there were sexual undertones to my politicisation. For one thing the four-person steering group I belonged to included one of the two female students in the faculty and so gave me opportunities for friendship with a woman. Such opportunities were not legion in the unnatural world I was inhabiting. Also political sympathies and activities did lead to two other warm friendships with young women at the time.

As young priests who had been introduced to the more optimistic theology of Eastern Christianity as distinct from the more guilt-ridden Western tradition that developed after Augustine (arguably the inventor of original sin) we had a different attitude to our celibacy than our more "traditional" colleagues. They saw their virginity as something to preserve at all costs to the extent of shunning the company of women. We viewed our virginity as something to be preserved, yes, but as having its value especially as a single-minded devotion to taking part in the collective struggle for liberation and world justice which we saw as part of the coming Kingdom of God on earth. All this meant that I was living through in my mid-twenties the adolescence that "normal" young men dealt with in their teens.

Do I think there's a head of anger behind all this? I am aware of anger about growing up in a deeply Catholic and constricting family and about what I imagined I was missing as a result. This is unfair on several counts. I also gained massively from my family and Catholic upbringing. My parents sincerely knew no other way to bring me up. They encouraged me, in fact, when I started to go to the dancing for they did not want me to be some naïve seminarian. But then feelings don't have to be fair even if our actions should be.

Perhaps there is anger about the restrictions my celibacy involved, but I don't think so. I chose that way of life and all it involved as consciously as I was able.

I think there is anger though not surprise at my father's lack of comprehension when I left the priesthood and married. My mother was dead by then. I think I left only partly because I realised that what my partner and I felt for each other was incompatible with continuing to be a priest and friar. I was also finding that clerical structures could not contain the person I was becoming. I could explore that further with the sociologists amongst you if that is of interest.

I suppose there is something about changing masculinities in all this. Come to think of it, the Christian tradition of virginity and celibacy has for centuries offered alternative images of masculinity and femininity even if in practice it sometimes produced grumpy bachelors and spinsters, neurotic individuals and even (sadly) sadists and perverts.

I'll stop there. I feel that your friendship and our work as MemoryMen have enabled me to delve a little more deeply.

BECOMING A SOCIALIST ABOUT TEN

I think I was quite precocious politically. I was born into a Tory family and became a socialist when I was about ten. I don't know why but it was then that I started criticising the royal family, inherited wealth and public schools, one of which I was about to be sent to.

From around then, and certainly through my teenage years and beyond, I had many ferocious arguments, especially with my dad and usually when we were eating in the evening. He was like a red rag to a bull, his face reddened as he launched into a critique of communism and that made me more convinced than ever that I was a communist, and more angry with him. I couldn't stop myself nor could my dad, in spite of my mum's attempts to calm the waters. And what made these arguments so horribly compelling for me (they were horrible, I remember shaking with anger and disbelief that my dad could be so heartless and pig-headed and unmoveable and when they ended we didn't speak to each other for ages) was that it was my dad, who was always telling me not to do things, who was so obviously wrong. Also, although I was closer to my mum than my dad, I wanted to be close with my dad and with these arguments I felt I was driving a nail into the coffin. Although my mum agreed with my dad she sympathised with me, and I always thought she wasn't really right wing, not underneath, and as she got older she got more radical and hated Thatcher and the Falklands War and I was so proud of her.

I expect people with whom I'm close to not to be right wing, and am shocked when they are. This was the case with a British woman I met in Botswana with whom I had a relationship. I liked her partly because she was really earthy and laid back and enjoyed taking the piss as well as being sensitive, and she had two daughters who were really funny. The first argument we had was provoked by me and was about politics. I'm not sure how it came up but she said she wasn't sure whether to vote Tory or Labour when she returned to Britain, and I couldn't believe she said this. I assumed we must be on the same political wavelength. She was surprised at my reaction, and thought I was making a mountain out of a molehill, as if our politics weren't really that important. But one of the reasons we got on, I Assumed, was because of our politics – at least our gender politics; neither of us were wedded to conventional ways of being male and female, and, I imagined she had to be like me and hate any kind of conservative politics. I feel a bit intolerant and judgmental writing this, as if I expected her to be my clone. But partly I liked her because we were very different in lots of ways, though how could she vote Tory!

CHALLENGED TO BE POLITICALLY ACTIVE

The combined U.S. and U.K. invasion of Iraq in March 2003 had just begun. Rumsfeld had promised the 'Shock and Awe' bombing campaign on Baghdad. I was waiting with mounting frustration, anger and increasing despair, watching and listening to news bulletins. I found waiting difficult for a retired man. An itchy restlessness moved over my skin as I waited for another night's raid over Baghdad. But it didn't come that night. Nor the next night.

And then there it was on the television screen the following evening. A flame-red, choking smoke was rising in billowing plumes. Through the screen of green, night vision cameras the trajectories of tracer bullets were lighting up the dark sky. There were cracking detonations, thunder, silence. There were people, children down there in that silence. But in what condition?

That silence unnerved me. I couldn't just wait around feeling useless and not do something with that murderous silence filling my ears. But I have to admit that silence is sometimes difficult for me as a retired, ageing man. Sometimes 'doing something' can be a way of trying to escape my despair and my fear of silence.

I wanted to protest but, in talking it over with a close friend, I decided I didn't want my protest against the war to be a conventional one. I wanted to protest but also work within my emotional and physical limitations. I knew that I couldn't go up to London to voice my dissent through a march. I didn't have that kind of stamina and emotional energy any more. But I still wanted to do something.

So I chose peace vigils in Nottingham market square. Before and during the Iraqi war I joined these silent vigils in the heart of the city's noise. To keep a silent, anti-war vigil in the buzzing heart of the shopping and skate-boarding territory was new and slightly scary for me. I couldn't use my voice or my arms and my legs to protect myself. I just had to stand there for half an hour and reflect on what was going on in Iraq. I had to use my heart and my head but in an unmoving position.

The peace vigil formed a large circle while shoppers and curious kids eyed us warily. Some of the people joined our circle, some abused us, others laughed at us. Two boys joined the group and then started giggling and then shouted 'Let's bomb them!' Then they burst out laughing.

Next week an Asian man in the circle brought his two kids and enormous, plastic, black and white Dalmatian that floated up and down before our vigil. More boys shouted at us.

Sometimes I would get to the Market square and find that I was the only one there. I felt nervous and exposed. But soon other people drifted in with banners or candles, and then we had enough to ignite our courage and we would form a small circle and face the boys again.

I missed the vigil where the boys threw apple cores at the silent protesters. But I was there when one or two of us decided to break ranks and try and talk to the boys. But the boys wouldn't keep still. They jeered at us, shouted and swore at us and then ran furiously away.

It was only later that I realised that it might be some of these very same boys who might be turned into soldiers in the next military skirmish or war.

'Doing Something about It' – Getting 'Political' Again Post-11 September 2001

When we closed our course in International Cultural Studies for a year, before starting a new programme, there was one applicant who refused to accept that this had happened - and just came. He came from a first degree in Chicago, where he had been involved in anti-globalisation and other kinds of politics. He was, in my eyes, incredibly young-looking, with pink cheeks, spiky hair, gentle and restless and keen, as it turned out, to be involved in left politics in Britain. As I got to know more about his political style, I found it hugely attractive, especially in contrast to the flat, masculine landscape of the local left. He was open, fascinated to learn, winning rather than hectoring, scooting off everywhere on his bicycle, careful, even reserved in meetings, but leading by example and by encouraging others. Not at all a know-it-all, he was vulnerable and uncertain and also thirsty about knowledge in an American working-class sort of way.

And he demanded to be taught. So bearing in mind the old programme, we each had to design something special. So he and I met regularly to talk about theory and politics. He wanted to know what Gramsci had said about revolution and activism. He brought stories about organising with students and trade unionists in Chicago and later about the Nottingham scene. At first at least, he seemed to think I knew everything, not only theoretically, but from some vast political experience, which I don't have at all. One time he asked me whether he should fast for peace in the Town Hall Square – which he did eventually. It was post September 11th, during the Afghan War, just when Bush had declared they would drop food parcels as well as bombs. He wanted to experience what it was like to be hungry and to make this point to eager consumers in the city centre. Later he started his own website – which he called 'Counterheg' – the first item being an essay on Gramsci he wrote for the course.

I think his effect on me was to make me want to live up to his imaginary image of me, or something more like. *He* was also an example to *me* especially in his own border crossing between academic work and political activity off the campus, only with the stress on the other side to me, more politically engaged outside the university than I had ever been. I think he also restored my faith - in a way my son does too - in *young men*, not the macho hero at all (though I hero-worshipped him a bit). It was probably important, given my past politics and relation to older men, that he was **a** *student*.

11 Sept and the Afghan war had already triggered my more usual responses – writing on Bush's and Blair's (anti-)terrorist rhetoric for a (very) academic journal and organising a teach-in on Afghanistan. But he pulled me into Stop the War and meetings for the Florence Social Forum. I met other members of his 'Student Activist Network' and on his initiative was invited to speak and do a workshop for Nottingham Stop the War - it was now the run-up to invasion of Iraq. Eventually I did the sensible thing, stopped trying to straddle two cities, and got involved in Leicester rather than Nottingham, mainly as the liaison person between Leicester CND and Leicester STW.

Retrospectively I can see that his extraordinary accidental appearance coincided with a political and also personal turning point. The millennial turn in US foreign policy and the new forms of Empire were becoming clear. Working on Bush's and Blair's late 2001 speeches, I got an inkling that something critical was happening before reading about the neo-cons Project. I shared that widespread anguished disbelief that 'this could be happening at all' – 'this' being the 'War on Terror' as much as the attack on the Twin Towers itself. And, very importantly, my mother died in June 2001, quite quickly at the age of 93 but struggling hard and terribly painfully to keep her dignity and not to leave us. Her death had an extraordinary impact on me: along with the sadness and some guilt, there was a kind of release, a certain wildness. I didn't have to hurry home on Tuesday and Wednesday evenings to see if she was all right after a day on her own. Instead I could go into a city, largely unknown to me so rather exciting, and go to meetings, to lots of meetings! Besides, this was my last chance wasn't it, to be 'involved' outside the academy? I had 'planned' this, quite firmly but still only in theoretical anticipation, for when I retired, but sometimes you can't choose can you? Anyway my feeling in those first mad months was exhilaration – 'At last!'

A Political Awakening

My political watershed isn't really defined by a single discrete moment as such. But I do remember a particular incident which suddenly flipped my perception of the world – gestalt fashion – and which then completely changed how I perceived my previous life and many of its more memorable events, as well as all my future relationships.

Until this point I had regarded myself as a Marxist and a feminist and as such I actively supported and encouraged all allied and associated causes. I even chose to do my masters influenced by the fact that it was a Marxist-feminist M.A.

Throughout this course I went right along with feminist thought and diktat, and read the right things, did the right things, thought the right things, even though at home and elsewhere, including in the M.A. itself I was being bombarded and sometimes troubled by contradiction.

One day, after an evening seminar, I was in the bar with one of the (male) teachers and he noticed a woman of about our age with her female friend. In passing, and very politely and inoffensively, he commented that he hadn't seen her earlier in one of his seminars. She instantly rounded on him with the words, "fuck off you little cunt", at which the lecturer, clearly deeply embarrassed, smiled back benignly and bemused, not knowing what to do or say. Suddenly all of my assumptions about gender issues re-shuffled themselves and I found myself holding a very different hand.

I thought her behaviour was way beyond the pale by any standards and I spoke to my lecturer about this later. It was clear from his response that he felt unable and/or unwilling to respond appropriately a) because she was a woman and b) because he was an avowed feminist and c) a man.

From this point on I saw gender politics in a very different light and could no longer take everything quite so easily on face value. I also realised that there was a distinctive men's agenda which had barely been touched on and needed addressing. The idea put forward by some at that time, that all women were OK and all men were of dubious, if not bad intent, no longer held true.

I still get angry when I think of this incident. My lecturer was a lovely and gentle bloke who deserved better respect.

Thanks J for That Slap!

One evening in the early seventies when I was twenty-four I was watching "Top of the Pops" with some friends, when I said "That Tony Blackburn – he's just like an old woman."

Then CRASH! I received a slap on the head from a female friend.

"Don't say things like that you sexist."

I realised I wasn't as right on with women as I thought.

That incident stays with me to this day as a turning point for me.

That slap knocked some awareness into me that made me develop a self-awareness policeman inside me I still use today.

I am a lover of women and support their struggles in daily contacts, in my work with community groups, and in most situations.

However I still think it was a bit over the top and a bit of resentment lingers alongside a feeling of guilt of being exposed as a sexist deep down somewhere.

I've had moments of feeling a racist as well when I felt a black person was given preferential treatment. Things have been overlooked. I haven't challenged things for fear of being called a racist.

These fears of being labelled as a racist, sexist, homophobic and generally full of oppressive behaviours are always there in the background for me, despite all the work I have done on challenging myself and being challenged by women, black people, gays, lesbians etc.

Policing my fear of others different from me does not seem very healthy to me. So by speaking about these in a safe group as this I am asking the other men, "Am I different or do you have similar internalised messages that you want to get rid of?"

My feeling is you all have worries but like me your fears prevent discussion except when you do challenge it feels good for a while.

As I grow old this internal dialogue and struggle becomes easier as I admit inadequacies and become less senatorially critical of myself.

I can thank J though for focussing my self-awareness with that slap those thirty odd years ago.

BEING ACTIVE ABROAD

On moving abroad I somehow assumed that there would be some kind of activism there for me to fit into. This was of course naïve. The experiences I had had of men's politics didn't translate very easily, and the kinds of men's politics that I came across there seemed to be about other things, fathers or something else. After a year or so I got an email from Michael Kaufman that he was visiting the region partly to try and encourage the formation of White Ribbon groups that commit men to oppose men's violence to women. He came and stayed at my place and naturally I went along to the open meeting. About 12 men and one woman came, and a group was formed. I went to the meetings over the next year or so but got increasingly disillusioned, as the main discussion seemed to be about how to make the message of opposing men's violence to women more palatable to the man in the street. This included trying to make it easier by including opposition to men's violence to children alongside violence to women, by using psychological explanations of men's violence, and by saying that men were welcome to join regardless of their views on feminism. The argument was always that we should appeal more widely.

After about a year of this, four of us decided to organise a demonstration against men's structural power and violence. We called ourselves 'profeministimiehet' ['profeminist men']. And we were genuinely unsure if this was going to work.

The week before we produced banners, circulated information on the demonstration, produced fliers, and decided that the demonstration should ironically be *silent*. On the day we 4 gathered about an hour before, had coffee in the nearest café, and distributed fliers. To our surprise 30 men came to the demonstration, and this was in mid-winter with snow and sub-zero temperatures. The main national newspaper came along to report and we agreed to do a 'collective interview' with first names only.

Since then we've organised six or seven more demonstrations, they're always silent, set up a website, completed a poster campaign (rather unsuccessfully), written articles, made postcards, done media interviews, virtually always collectively and no photos of faces, and so on.

Most recently, we decided to try and do something on what is currently a very topical issue in Finland, namely demonstrating against the sex trade. We went through what is by now a fairly well known process – clarifying the focus of the demonstration, giving advance warning on email lists, designing the fliers, doing a press release, re-emailing various lists, doing the posters, and so on. During the week or two before the demonstration, for the first time a very extensive & antagonistic debate developed partly on our email list but mainly on another 'more general' men's list. One of our members formally resigned; other non-members set up an attack around the problems of defining sex trade, pornography etc., the rights of some women to prostitute themselves etc., etc. 40-50 emails zoomed around.

We felt more nervous on the demonstration day. It was a lovely warm summer day. This could mean a good turnout or it could mean men might find better things to do, as it was the last summer weekend before the autumn. In the event it was the latter. Our usual 20-30 members and supporters shrunk to 13. Being against men's violence or even structural inequality is easier than being against the sex trade. This was all disappointing in some ways, but still definitely OK. As usual, passers-by were generally interested, though some men, especially young men, were abusive.

At the end of the demonstration, which happened to be held on the same day as a collection for war veterans, some of us mingled with some of the young soldiers, collecting money, alongside their armoured car, which happened to be immediately adjacent to our usual demonstration plot. I took photos of the mingling, for our website.

We don't know what we achieve. Whatever the "success" or not, we often joke that at least we have coined a new word 'profeminism' in Finnish.

I love these men and our laughter.

CHAPTER 14

Power

Richard Johnson

INTRODUCTION

Sorting out the men in the boys! The most obvious features of this sequence of stories is that they are more about being on the receiving end of power than about its exercise and are more about relations of men to men, or men to boys than men to women.

One account is about being under the sway of a bullying and insecure father. Another focuses upon the complex power play of schools, male teachers to students, boys to boys. A third, an exception in this regard, examines the relation between a driver wife and a navigator husband, in which the narrator, as navigator (in version 1) loses his 'crown.' In a further memory a father maps a life course for a son, who rebels and yet conforms in different ways. And the final recollection starts with power as somehow an alien concept, more difficult to write about than 'agency' and ends with an account of victimisation in the army and his own discomfort as a boss.

One feminist reading of these stories might conclude that they show how unconscious many men are of the power which they themselves exercise, especially in relationships with women, unconscious too of the systemic nature of male privilege. Instead, so it seems, we focus on male-to-male struggles, and especially, but not exclusively, on our own subordination as sons or pupils, or in masculine practices like sport, or all male institutions like the military. The one cross-gender story, 'Navigator extraordinaire', seems to be preoccupied with a loss of potency in the context of marriage.

All the stories are, however, a good deal more complex and self-reflexive than such a critique would imply, and there is, perhaps, more to learn from them for a pro-feminist perspective which takes men's experience seriously. As one man in 'Power – not always what it seems' puts it,

> I know that down the years this [memories of early subordination] has made it difficult for me to see my own power so that I have imagined myself to be power-*less* when in fact I may have been in a very powerful situation.

If men behave oppressively to women or to other men it seems to be because of feelings of weakness or vulnerability. At the subjective level, male power and patriarchal control are fueled by fears that are then converted into the urge for power or control. This is made most explicit in the story of the bullying father. Here the author begins to realise that 'in spite of my father's brutish exercise of power he was actually very weak, frightened and insecure', protecting himself from the prospective the power of his children 'should we ever grow up independent and self-assured'.

A different kind of power and vulnerability of a father in relation to a son is seen in 'Not the ARTIST? Father and son story (1959?)'. Here the father lays out a course for his son, and enforces it against artistic deviations, because of his own feelings of loss for an education he never had. In this context, the son's response - to say he will join the family firm and not go to university – delivers a nastily accurate wound to the father and also a self-harm, which can't in fact be sustained.

Other stories explore the complex play of power between men and/or boys in particular institutions. "Don't funk it, boy!" focuses on the play of power in two different schools. Here power is seen as pervasive, boy on boy and teacher on pupil. Teacher power, seen from boyhood memories of traditional forms of schooling, seems rather straightforward here: based on the fear of corporal punishment, exposure to ridicule, commands not to 'funk it' and 'gold dust' rewards from a competitive ordering of academic success and failure. Ultimately of course teacher power is premised on anxiety about the unruliness of boys and girls. What boys (or one boy) made of these environments of power is complex, many sided: finding spaces for skills and recognition in (different) sports, succeeding academically, but also having a tough friend to negotiate bullying, winning a playground fight, but later having a group of friends who were successful in school-based tasks. In a more working-class milieu it is probable that the 'toughness' noted in one context and a collective resistance to the school routines would have played a larger part in the acquisition of power and status. with school and peer group criteria pointing in different directions. And how do these dynamics work out in a co-educational school?

'Some kinds of power' is a rather gentle story that contains an episode of some brutality. Here again the main context, like the grammar school, is an all-male institution- military training. As we know from many stories and statistics in Britain today, this is a context in which personal problems and individuality are systematically over-ridden by rules, strict obedience and formal hierarchy. It also gives opportunities for bullying and all kinds of sadistic abuse. Here the author clearly feels his life was threatened and this helped to form his later attitudes to exercising power himself. The story raises the interesting general question of how our early experiences of being oppressed shape or disturb our later exercise of power, as privileged men in unequal relationships or hierarchical institutions. Under what circumstances do our memories and self-narrations predispose us to conform? Under what circumstance can they steer us on more rebellious or reforming courses. At what point does identification with the bullied school child or subordinated sibling become identification with the systematically oppressed?

The story, 'Navigator extraordinaire', is the exception in this sequence in that it directly tackles an aspect of cross-gender relations, albeit obliquely in an apparently 'safe' area, that is, the driver/navigator relation. There is an interesting complexity here around identity, power and, especially, skill. First there is a reversal of a traditional (but now much broached) gender division of labour: he drives; she navigates. Second there is the building up of skill, pride and pleasure in the role of navigator and planned-for trips and journeys: 'I get great pleasure out of looking at maps'. There is power involved too: as we all know, the driver can rule, but here there is a power in conscientiously planning outings and best routes and advising someone who isn't always geographically well-informed. Finally, however, there is the difficulty of the wife/drivers' more instrumental and less pleasure-seeking attitude to travel and the inevitable mistakes in navigation. These risk demotion – Sat-Nav or 'loss of the crown'.

Overall then, while tempered by a certain knowing innocence and by its humour, this is a story of opportunity, loss and shifting relations of gendered power in the process of men's ageing.

***

POWER—NOT ALWAYS WHAT IT SEEMS

Looking back on it now, issues to do with power have had a profound bearing on all of my life. Mostly this has had to do with my feelings of being the subject of other people's exercise of power – or with the memories of that experience. I know that down the years this has made it difficult for me to see my own power so that I have imagined myself to be power–*less* when in fact I may have been in a very powerful situation.

My father played a very large part in this; his frequent outbursts such as, *'You make me sick!'* or *'That will teach you not to be so clever'* were, I now understand, designed to prevent me from ever, in his eyes, becoming more powerful than *him*.

I took this constant humiliation into myself and became a natural victim, bullied, easily intimidated, excluded, and then, later in life, even as my confidence grew, I found that I was all too easily reduced to self-doubt and feelings of hopelessness when challenged.

Over time I have become more able to deal with this, as I worked hard to understand others – but also myself – better. I began to realise that in spite of my father's brutish exercise of power he was actually very weak, frightened and insecure. His apparent 'power' had a purpose, and that purpose was to protect him – and especially to protect him from the imaginary power that he felt we might potentially hold over him should we ever grow up independent and self-assured. His 'power', therefore, was born out of his own terrible weakness.

Once, when I was in my early twenties and at college, I contradicted him on his use of the word *'chromometer'*, telling him that it should be *'chronometer'*. He became, once again, angry and abusive and when I showed him the dictionary he declared that the dictionary was wrong and (not for the first – or the last time) threatened to leave home when I wouldn't back down to him. He got his way; the 'challenge' to his sense of authority was dropped in order to keep the peace - but was he *powerful,* and if so was his power as such restored?

This was hardly an isolated incident and I now understand that each time he forced his emotional power over us in this way he actually weakened himself all the more. Conversely I came to learn that the opposite course could be empowering; that by being able to face up to my own feelings and fears, no matter how irrational or inappropriate, this would help to strengthen me in ways that he never was able to do for himself or for me.

One of the more complicated contradictions that I have had to deal with and work through concerns the ways in which working as a counsellor placed me in a potentially very powerful situation vis-à-vis other males (my clients) who may have been feeling disempowered by the encounter and/or vulnerable. Ironically, the more I tried to work with this by acknowledging my own actual frailties and vulnerabilities, the more empowering I found it was. I felt therefore that I had constantly to live with and work through this contradiction at the heart of power as I had come to understand it. Perhaps the difference is between my sense of self confidence, on the one hand, and the exercise of power on the other; the one, in other words, does not *necessarily* become the other.

'DON'T FUNK IT, BOY!'

So spake Mr. Dacombe, the feared French teacher, who seemed to love to humiliate us boys. I remember he often threatened corporal punishment, but in practice rarely delivered. Once he called me out of the front of the class, and 'beat' me with a piece of string. I felt soiled and ashamed and humiliated, even though it was funny.

My School, my grammar school, was suffused with power. Mr Boardward, the headmaster, was especially feared. He seemed to relish corporal punishment. He was very tall, probably 6 foot 6, his voice was loud, very loud.

Power was everywhere and every day, with the two mainsprings: sport and academic success, or application. That was, either way, how you got status – both from the teachers and between most of the boys. There were so many aspects and events, it is hard to know where to start.

One was the practice of bullying new pupils, first years, 'weeds' – the older boys, especially the second years, hitting them, with knotted handkerchiefs, often on the heads. I don't think I joined in, but I certainly didn't intervene against this, just kept clear. I later made it my business to befriend Manning (very appropriately named). He was a large thuggish boy and an outstanding rugby player, but also surprisingly good at Science, sometimes even a gentle giant. Hanging around him on the edge of his court was recommended, even though occasionally he would threaten or worse. I remember him thumping me on the upper arm for fun, and bruising, as a friendly warning. This was on the steps during the morning break, and for no other reason. It was marking his territory and his wider gang. I never experienced any problem with bullying from others after that.

However, most of my time was from then onwards was spent in a small group of four of us – Gardiner, Royce, Davis and me. We always referred to each other by our surnames. Royce was from Liverpool and was something of a cheeky northern novelty, who joined in the second year; knowing him brought status. Davis lived near to him and was the reasonable middle class fall guy. Gardiner was my closest friend. Chris was a good ally to have, as a high performer, academically outstanding, getting exceptional exam results, and captain of the rugby XV. He was unusually fast for a second row forward and totally committed in play, including frothing at the mouth when in the thick of the action.

Manning and Gardiner were leading members of the school rugby team. I was a member of the 1st team up until the senior level. Up to that point I was a regular but marginal member of the team, on the wing, as one of the smallest in the team but also a fast runner. Posing for the team photo when I was 15 I managed to deliberately expand my neck so that I fitted in on the page. Every time I look at that photo I see my neck.

The most obvious display of power was inter-house rugby. The School modelled itself on a minor public school, even though it was a state grammar school. The most brutal matches were the senior inter-class matches. In my final year, and to our amazement, we won, beating the feared Lucas House, with its collection of tough leading players. Power.

I don't remember power at my primary school though presumably there it was lurking between teachers, boys and girls. My friends were mainly the girls.

At the boys' junior school power gradually emerged. Two memories stand out. One was in the 2nd or 3rd year when I was about 9. I didn't see myself as at all tough, I wasn't, though I liked playing games, especially football. I was rather meek. On the other hand, there were a few boys in my class, the top class, who were noticeably tough. They were a little feared. One day, and I don't recall why at all, one of them, Baker, a boy who was slightly more thick-set than usual and had close cropped fair hair, got into a tussle, a small fight, with me. It might have been over who won a game of cigarette cards but I cannot be sure. We wrestled on the ground of the playground. Baker seemed to have the obvious advantage. To my surprise, and I think by luck, I managed to get on top of him, subjugate him, and so I had 'won'. A crowd had gathered around and acclaimed it, before it was broken up by one of the teachers, Mr Ding I think. My reputation suddenly grew, even if it was luck, and another boy, who understood these things, I think rightly, said to me that if the fight had gone on longer Baker would have won.

The second memory is of the final year in the top class of six classes; I was in the 'baby boomer' years with about 210 boys in all, and what happened around Mr Charman, who was always the teacher of this class. He was an army man, a Lieutenant Colonel, who had served in India, or so we understood from his stories. He was terribly strict and terribly feared, using corporal punishment occasionally, and threatening more often, if only in his demeanour. But if he liked you, you were gold dust to him. I was expected to come near the top in the final year exams. There was David, a friend of mine, but usually slightly better than me in his work. He was the rightful top student. In the event, I managed to come top overall, again by chance, beating the star pupil, and only because I did very well in Art with 8 or 9 out of 10, and he was rubbish at it, getting 4 or 5. It was a painting of a boat, a lifeboat, in a very stormy sea, and the art teacher liked the expressive movement of the waves. David was strongly resentful; I remember now his annoyance that he had been beaten by way of the 'not real' subject of Art. Competition and his irritation and my guilt. I was very glad I had won, but I felt I had cheated a little. Power and success.

NAVIGATOR EXTRAORDINAIRE

It was about the time that I had to give up driving. I think. It was 1989 or 1990 but I'm not certain of when it was exactly. But I can remember my glaucoma getting worse and my sight getting blurry, particularly in my right eye. Also I recall my anxiety increasing as I struggled to see properly especially on night journeys. So later on I sold my VW and took to public transport. I think I felt some loss but it was mingled with relief from an increasingly screwed up tension that I experienced when driving.

But my wife was still driving and, occasionally, we took long trips on holidays. That's when I seemed to intensify my sense of needing to be a good navigator. She had always been a bit hazy about the geography of the U.K. and I became the person who generally told her which way to go. Although in the underground car park in Nottingham's Victoria Centre (where she had lived in a flat for a year), she was totally in charge of the directions.

So picture this scene; we're going on a short trip to Morecambe in Lancashire to stay at the newly renovated Art Deco, Midland Hotel. I'm the passenger in the front seat being driven by my wife, with a large map book open on my lap and other guides littered around my feet. I've already researched which is the best way to get to Morecambe. I've already looked at the different, possible routes, either keeping to the East and going up the A1 and then crossing the Pennines and getting over to the West by taking the M62. Or should we take the A50 route towards Stoke and then up the M6 to Morecambe?

I like knowing where I am and being in charge of the routes we're taking and the direction of where we're heading. I get great pleasure out of looking at maps. And I like discovering new places, new routes, new viewpoints. But my wife often gets fed up and tired of driving so far and she doesn't like to clock up extra distance when we're trying to discover unfamiliar churches, tea-shops, bookshops and Neolithic, burial sites. She prefers to get to where we're going in the quickest, possible way. Fair enough. For example, as a part of planning the route I've bought the Ordnance Survey's map of Kendal and Morecambe. I've discovered, from another guide, that there's the Lancashire dining pub of the year at Whitwell in the Trough of Bowland. I'm intrigued by the possibility of driving back to the M62 via the moorland road from Lancaster to Whitwell. Vaguely, I suggest this to my wife but she doesn't sound very interested and on the day when we're going back, it's raining all over Lancashire. So I give up, shelve the scheme and together we decide to stick to the motorways going back.

As I approach 70, I can't drive anymore but I can take control of the navigation. I can be a useful route-finder but it's when I have to express uncertainty that I often get into difficulties. My wife wants fast, clear directions particularly in confusing situations at unfamiliar roundabouts where I haven't had time to marshal all the available evidence about routes and directions. So sometimes I get it wrong and we have to re-trace our steps or turn around after a few miles when I realise we're going in the wrong direction. That's when she accuses me of being a hopeless navigator and threatens to swap me for a Sat-Nav.*

Author's note: When I shared this writing with my partner she suggested the present ending ('... threatens to swap me for a Sat-Nav'). But what I had written, originally, was, 'or having lost my crown of being a good route-finder.'

So you have a choice of two possible endings.

NOT THE ARTIST? FATHER AND SON STORY (1959?)

'No, you are not going to art college. What do you think I paid for, for you to become some kind of bohemian art student in London? Besides you can't go to art college as well as Cambridge. I am not supporting that. You might as well join the firm.'

My father was at his most adamant, provoked into his own challenges. We locked gazes, this 19 year 'artist' and his businessman father. It was a real showdown, but not as usual around the dining room table and about politics and religion, but in my father's 'study' and about a choice I'd made, perhaps the first significant choice I'd made 'for myself': to go to Goldsmiths to do an art degree. In the two years waiting to go to Cambridge (delayed because of the ending of National Service) I'd taught at a private school (art, drama and English), got lots of recognition from the previous art teacher, built up a portfolio, and had been accepted. I remember walking out of the room, slamming the door, not speaking for several days and my mother's distress. But I didn't leave home, did not do what I really wanted, or continue the direction (towards art and social conscience) begun in an A-level-free year at school. Instead a few weeks later I told my father that I wanted to join him in his business, in the family firm importing fruit and vegetables.

I think my father was as confused as I was by this 'decision', half gratified, half appalled, since he wanted for me the education he'd never had. Perhaps, he saw it as a temporary thing he had to live with. At the time I saw it as a life choice. Perhaps he thought I would get to Cambridge eventually, something I had dramatically foresworn.

So it was that I spent the summer of 1959 selling cases of fruit and veg to the retailers on Humber Dockside, learning all the tricks of the trade from my Dad's right-hand man on the street. I never got to the office or discovered more about his actual work. I just used to see him steaming past, on the way to the trade club for lunch, a busy little man with a rapid walk, who whistled as he thought, and jangled keys or money in his pocket. So my stories, partly imaginary no doubt, about his battles with dockers, in which I took their side, remained more or less intact.

I don't remember how and when my 'decision' was reversed, though my father's support, of course, meant money as well as ambition. But I know I went to Cambridge the following October.

SOME KINDS OF POWER

Power is a theme or topic I have a bit of trouble relating to. Maybe this is to do with my conception of power which is, I think, of a coercive force, something which you find you have to do whether you want to or not because of the threat of unpleasant consequences. This quite distinct from notions of agency, the capacity to act to express yourself through doing. I would write quite a bit about agency in my life but power as I've conceived it, only very little.

I'm not sure why this is. Maybe culturally, coercive power is somewhat alien to me. Canadians aren't much give to the exercise of power in this sense – it's not something that's valued. With the important exception of native peoples Canadians have never been people to be feared especially.

Anyway, I don't know and don't want to muse on this abstractly. I do know that I have ambivalent feelings about power. I'm uneasy with it either exercising it myself or having it exercised over me. Here's a personal story about power.

There was no compulsory military service in Canada when I was growing up but one summer, as a way of earning a bit of money, I signed up for a term of duty with the local militia (I think this might be the equivalent of the Territorial Army here). There was lots of coercive power exercised over us new recruits in this but mostly I able to put up with it quite well by just keeping my head down and doing what we were told. But I had a nasty brush with the reality of power one weekend when we went away for exercises at a nearby army camp.

We were all billeted in a barracks, a kind of large dormitory hall with a screen door on the exit which we were warned not to let bang shut if we decided to leave the building after lights out. Anyway, I had an asthma attack on the second night we were there and decided I had to go outside to catch my breath. In my hurry to leave I let the screen door swing shut behind me and it closed with a loud bang which attracted the attention of a NCO who happened to be standing nearby. This fellow came over and after telling me off decided I needed to be taught a lesson. So he ordered me to jog double time around the camp perimeter.

I tried to explain why I couldn't do this but he just yelled at me to shut the fuck up and doubled my punishment to two circuits of the camp. What followed was pretty awful as you can imagine and I was probably lucky not to be hospitalised but the whole episode made a very powerful and lasting impression on me about being on the receiving end of power.

I think I have deliberately avoided ever being put in such a position again in my life. I have also been very reluctant to exercise coercive power over others which I've mainly had to do as an employer or manager. I've had to discipline and occasionally sack people under my authority in different work situations and I've struggled with it at times. It's an aspect of being the boss I don't feel comfortable with.

It seems to me this kind of power is a kind of weakness when you have to use force to get your way.

THE STING (2007)

Full of fear and panic, cornered in the open.
I wanted to surrender but had nowhere to go.
I just had to face down that barrage of bullets,
That invisible ambush,
That relentless venom as they blasted me down to the floor.
Once on the ground they continued to shoot at me,
Launching my mind into a desperate abandonment
Of all living things.
That paintball shot into the middle of my forehead
Left me with a stinging, rounded lump, which
I wore like a medal for many weeks.
It captured my hatred of war games
But yet gave me a hero status
Among those young warriors I had taken
With me to that painful encounter in the woods.

Chapter 15

Violence

Zbyszek Luczynski

Introduction

The question of violence is a vital one in any focus on men and masculinities, and is addressed here in a variety of ways. Two memories address violence done by the writers. One describes difficult two incidents in a marriage of over twenty years when he struck his partner in the middle of an argument. He feels shame, and though they separated many years ago they are still on good terms. Another talks about the violence to a child borne of an exhausted father of which we are all capable in moments of great stress. They speak of how they have tried to avoid it but still feel capable of it.

A third account has a more oblique relation to violence in telling about the violence he hates with the scars of bullying still raging inside him.

A complex violent episode is found in another's recounting of an incident in which his vulnerability through poor health exposed him to becoming the victim of a physical attack by an irate father. He had shouted out when a child bumped into him in a park. His reaction of self-protection led to greater violence.

Then there is the ritualised violence of boxing. Specifically, one man learnt to box and used a counter punch technique to survive. He recognised his anger and temper came out in arguments with his father, his first wife and academic debates. Gradually he regained control using a pause to think technique in these situations. Learning from becoming a profeminist and in new relationships and campaigns he urges us to reject the counter punch; pause and negotiate.

A further account tells us of another man's violence rooted in seeking peer approval and power. He makes reference to the violence built into the predatory capitalism we are living in and the need to transform society to rid it of the oppression it begets.

Violence

Each of the examples they cite leads these men to conclude that change for a better society involves a struggle to avoid violence. But as the last author states from his experience this will not happen without a fight

Finally, there is a story from a man who could not remember any violence impinging on his life. He says: "I fear it, I avoid it, I'm repelled when it happens to others. I would see it as primarily a defeat or failure in myself and others."

Taken together our stories illustrate the all-pervading intrusion of violence in our lives, our relationships between men, towards women, in our families, and in the structures of how society is organised. The stories illustrate our struggles to eradicate violence and its threat in our relationships as we change and become more profeminist in our attitude and behaviour.

***

Hits

I don't want to write about this. Sometime during the first year of being married, I remember being in the antic room of our flat with my wife. It was a good sized room set into the roof, if a little dull and sparsely furnished. She was often a very emotional and excitable person, and that was certainly partly what attracted me to her. One evening she became what at the time I could only describe as "hysterical". I don't know exactly what it was about, except it wasn't directed towards me. It may have been about her mother who lived fairly nearby, and who would sometimes drop in without warning and with difficult consequences. Anyway I had not encountered this before, and it scared me! What do I do in this situation? What am I meant to do? Those old Hollywood black and white films flashed to my mind, and I slapped her face, hard enough to surprise her, and break the spell. She broke off from the hysterical rage, and continued talking, complaining about the initial problem prompt. She seemed to take it in her stride: the source of the rage seemed to override the slap. For me, I didn't think this was a good way. It had the desired result in one sense, but I felt bad. We were not in a film.

Maybe seven years later, I have a memory of us arguing in the back room near to the door to the kitchen. It was mid-evening. It was a house we like very much, and the room was one we were especially fond of, with particularly nice rose-coloured lamps on the wall. Again, what the talk was about I do not recall. It may have been that I had come home later than promised. In the course of the argument I hit her once on the back of the head. It was a glancing blow with my open hand that seemed to have little impact. It was thus obviously very *controlled.* Whether the argument escalated or subsided after that I've no recollection. It probably continued verbally.

Twenty years later, when we were separating, prior to divorce, I asked her how many times had I hit her in our long marriage. "Once" was her answer, said firmly. I presumed it was the back of the head occasion, but, with some relief, I didn't enquire further. I think we get on well now.

Not Totally Out-of-Control

My first thought is: violence, that is other men. But then I remembered.

Our first-born cried every night, several times. My wife, who was already pregnant with our second child, would put the baby to the breast. Then it would be my turn, walking up and down with a baby that just kept crying.

As if this is not challenging enough for learner parents, we had overheard the landlady next door telling our new landlady that our baby was disturbing her tenants: whenever one of her tenants became pregnant she would tell her to leave.

My wife checked our rights at the Citizens Advice Bureau. In those days, if told to leave we could appeal and have three months more of secure tenancy: a further appeal might have given us three months beyond that; but that was all. And I was unemployed.

And still the baby cried. I changed her nappy as best I could while half asleep, and still she cried. Suddenly I lost control and slapped her on the thigh leaving a red mark. I could have punched her stomach, which would probably have killed that few-months old baby. Child killers are not necessarily some kind of monster; just perhaps sane men driven beyond reason by lack of sleep and an unreasonable infant.

It might be that I was not totally out-of-control and so slapped rather than punched. I hope so. Other fathers I have shared this story with have sometimes told similar stories of throwing their child but onto the bed rather than onto the floor. The distinction between child abuser and respectable, loving father is less clear than I used to think, and still do in a holier-than-thou default position.

Men and violence has recently come into my life in another form. My same daughter, now a professional in her forties, told me about being trapped in unemployment. Outside the meeting of about thirty job-seekers, who were being instructed in c.v. writing and how to spend forty hours a week walking round shops to look for work, she saw a shell-shocked member of the group. She asked if he was alright and learned that until two weeks previously he had thought the unemployed were all benefit- scroungers. Then suddenly he, a specialist engineer who had worked for the same company for thirty-five years, had been made redundant. He was being humiliated by the instructions in how he had to spend his weeks walking from place to place pleading with employers who had no need of his skills. He was the victim of the systematic violence which government is imposing on people who want nothing more than a job.

I suspect the two examples are connected in several ways.

Violence, A Nasty Business

Not an easy subject for me to write about. I hate violence and deep down I am terrified of it. I so want it to be something that exists only 'out there' so that I can turn my whole being against it. But it is not and so I can't.

I know that I have a lot of buried anger in me and that a lot of this is to do with my experiences of violence against me - by my father and other children at school and on the street. This is sometimes really hard stuff to live with. But this 'interpersonal' violence is different from the larger scale, more calculated violence that we see so much of in the media. So are there different violences - or are they just different manifestations of one and the same problem? I am not sure I know.

My hatred of violent people, of bullies and despots makes it difficult for me to have to sit by and witness the kinds of crimes against other people that we see all the time in the media. I feel the need to fight back against them, even forcefully if need be. And then, at these times, I experience the capacity for violence within me and if not careful I end up hating myself almost as much as them.

I think this is why I spend so much time thinking about and railing against the likely *roots* of violence - the ways in which the worst elements of our psyches are nurtured and cultivated by systems such as capitalism, politics, consumerism, the media, religion and so on.

Incident: I am about eight years old and walking through the park on my way home from school. It is a warm afternoon, probably late spring. I come across a group of boys from school and thy start calling me names, prodding and shoving me. When I resist they seem to get angry with me and more serious, as though this is becoming my fault and not theirs. One of them stuffs his wet chewing gum into my hair. I take a swipe at him, red now with rage at this completely unprovoked assault. Then they push me over. There are three or four of them. They pick me up struggling by my hands and feet and start to swing me, backwards and forwards. When they let go I fly through the air briefly and land in the middle of the thorn bushes while they run off laughing and calling me names as they go.

It hurts so much. And the more I try to struggle free from the bush, the more the sharp thorns stick into me, my hands, legs arms, neck and face. I am crying hopelessly. I feel utterly humiliated. But I also feel uncontrollably angry - violent.

That evening my mum has to cut my hair to get the sticky chewing gum out and she spends ages picking at and pulling out all the sharp thorns that have embedded themselves deeply, all over my throbbing body. I am crying and protesting and the anger is rising up in me again. I feel as though, given half the chance, I could take a sharp knife to all four of them - anything to get rid of these awful feelings. But of course it never would. The thorns have long gone now but those feelings are still there, sticking in me just like the thorns. Now though they are buried that much deeper beneath the veneer of responsible adulthood.

So for me violence isn't just something that exists out there – unfortunately. It lives on within me and I hate it.

'SHE'S ONLY SIX'

I was coming across the park having been shopping in a local supermarket. I was day-dreaming and slightly dozy, thinking about war, militarism and the peace-loving writings of Cynthia Cockburn.[3] I should be meeting her this evening in Leicester and I was looking forward to talking to her.

All round me in the park there were families and kids, playing, running around. I was enjoying the Summer sunshine as I made my way slowly across the park towards an exit. When suddenly something walloped into me from the side. I was surprised and shaken by the force of a scooter suddenly hitting me when I was unguarded and thinking about something else. It took some time to make out what had happened but it turned out that a young girl, about six or seven, had lost control of her scooter and had slammed hard into my day-dreaming body.

I was so startled, like being woken up from a lazy contemplation of the world, that I quickly lashed out at the young girl, speaking loudly and sternly about what she had done and yelling at her:

'Why didn't you look where you're going !'
The girl, crest-fallen already from the crash, dissolved into tears and quickly began a loud sobbing.

---

[3] Cynthia Cockburn is a leading British feminist activist, researcher and professor who has written extensively on such as issues as equality, work, war, militarism and peace-keeping, especially in relation to the Balkans and the Middle East.

I heard an enraged shout come from behind me. A burly, young man, probably the girl's father, was running towards me, shouting abuse. But he was closely followed by another young man who was trying to calm him down. The father finally reached me, bellowing : 'What do you think you're doing? She's only six!'

And he started to finger-prod me right into my unsuspecting chest. I knew I was about to be hit by the father's ferocious onslaught. But before he could really set about me with his fists, the other man had squeezed himself between the father and myself and was holding on to his upraised arm.

I felt a great wave of anxiety and fear sweep over me as my heart began to go faster. I doubled up in pain at the sharp, digging-in, finger-prods and felt nervously breathless as I collapsed onto my knees. I was struggling to regain my breath when a young woman, perhaps a nurse, joined the huddled group. She held my hand and reassured me while the other young man gradually led the angry father away. But it was obvious the father didn't want to move away so quietly. He wanted to pummel me into submission for what he saw as attacking his innocent daughter and making her cry. A few moments later the father had gone with his daughter and friend, leaving me still on my knees but still with the young woman's support, thinking about what I had done.

After some time I re-gained my breath and picked up my shopping. I realised that with my vulnerable heart I might be dead now, if it hadn't been for the sharp interventions of the father's friend and this young woman who was still coaxing me back into a calmer state.

Later that day when I got back to my home, I rang Leicester and explained that I wouldn't be coming this evening. Perhaps I needed more time to re-consider the tone of voice I had used with the scared, young girl that had frightened her into tears?

Learning Not to Counter Punch

I learned a kind of physical violence as a boy, aged eight or nine. Boxing was compulsory at my Prep School and there were public boxing bouts before the whole school in the Winter Term. This, I have to remember, was the late 1940s – post-war, austerity, private schooling under a military shadow. Our boxing teacher was a jovial, working-class ex-NCO called 'Mr Maggs.' I don't think we called him 'Sir'.

In my first fight I was 'matched' with a much older boy who happened to be about my weight and also the headmaster's son. There was evident consternation about this: my parents even came down to Berkshire from our home. The fight was stopped very soon fortunately, but the thing about fighting in a ring is that you can't run away.

I kept on fighting though in and out of the ring. I learned a fairly classic style, straight lefts and counter-punches. I won later fights this way, both against boys I was friendly with and definite 'enemies'. My boxing career ended as it began however in my secondary school (also private) with a particularly humiliating defeat this time by a younger boy, very aggressive, who didn't wait for counter-punches.

I am sure something of the character of the counter-punch was lodged in my body and my feelings for much of my adult masculine life. Responding with anger and aggression usually verbal to a threat, real or imagined, was a feature of my not so grown-up behaviour. It was expressed in arguments with the passionate beliefs of my father and later in academic contexts, in critique or counter-critique. It was expressed most unhappily at time of conflicts with my first wife. On two particular occasions I pushed her to the ground and hurt her physically; more often I shouted or threw things at walls. Always these were responses to being 'attacked'. Because of the milieu in which I lived, including my domestic space, the physical violence, though symptomatic, was rare not systematic. I am not sure my gender violence was about control in an intentional way, though in a patriarchal context it may have had controlling effects. It felt more like desperation, being trapped. If I had been in a context where violence was more acceptable, life more desperate or physical challenges acute, I would probably have been more violent.

As I grew conscious that my own violence and the violence of men was a larger problem, I began to reflect on it and, very gradually, to change. It was already a theme in the radical feminist critiques I read in the 1970s. But the main 'solutions' came later: particularly involvement in peace movements and living with a new partner who had many psychoanalytic and other insights about emotional life. Today, the issue of men and violence is central in the feminist revival and is rightly insisted on, in many different respects by feminist friends and allies.

The link between forms of masculinity, violence and war is something I now to try to understand, write about and act against. We need to understand the willingness of leading men to go to war, the evident fascination with glorifying World War I, the incidence of violent misogyny on streets, homes and internet and the predominance of men in crimes of violence including those against other men. I don't want to divorce this from my own experience.

Obviously men have violent feelings and may act violently when they feel attacked. They also end up visiting their own violent feelings on Others, whether they are really 'enemies' or not. Sometimes this production of enemies is fantastical and can arise from mere difference which is perceived as an attack. It also interests me that these counter-punching feelings and strategies can also be given an ethical character, as moral sentiments, justified feelings, as legitimate self-defence.

I still have feeling of anger and 'fighting back' and I can think of this as standing up for myself. But something interposes in the desire to strike back, some equally learned pause, a certain calm. The hope is to contain the other's aggression, if it is real, or still my own fast heart beat. The pause – which might also apply as a truce or a negotiation instead of an imminent war – allows time to learn of the other's sense of being attacked, his/her vulnerability. Perhaps this is a means both of reconstructing aspects of masculine identity, and also a protocol for settling larger conflicts: pause, think, don't counter-punch.

MY EXPERIENCE OF VIOLENCE

When I was at secondary school in the sixties the only time violence seemed to be necessary was fighting whoever was my best friend at the time. Early teenage years were often spent that way.

Usually a best mate and I would wind each other up to the point of having a good "fisty cuffs" in class or in the playground. Feelings of jealousy mixed with defending your position in the pecking order lead to these display fights in front of the rest of the class.

In my twenties there was the violence of political protests and demonstrations at which by that time I tried to avoid any physical confrontation. I remember the picket of the National Front meeting Red Lion Square Conway Hall in 1971 surrounded by cordons of Mounted police. As some comrades tried to buck the horses to unseat the police I decided to move away to the back to avoid the violence. The same thing happened when I was at an NF counter demo at Leicester University in 1973when the International Socialists linked arms and charged police lines, I just let them run past me. That is how I have dealt with violence doing everything to avoid it, never wanting to be at the receiving end.

This stance contributed to my involvement in feminist issues when I was involved in setting up of a refuge for battered women about this same time campaigning against domestic violence. It also led to my meeting my life time partner and later involvement in the pro-feminist men's movement.

The taste of violence in our lives. Under neoliberal's speed up at work welfare cuts permanent wars abroad we taste the violence of "savage capitalism", see it in our newspapers and on TV. It feels like we are tearing ourselves apart across the world. Cushioned in a baby boomer's privileged retirement largely protected from these forces I am a lucky man who is again avoiding such violence.

Yet the knowledge remains that such an oppressive system will not be changed without resorting to violence as those in power are not going to give it up or share it without a fight.

All that remains to be done is to continue as before in that fight as best I can.

VIOLENCE AT SOME REMOVE

I find myself amazed that in my long life I can think of practically no incidents of personal experience of violence. Oh, of course, I can remember a few times in my childhood when I was physically punished or disciplined by my father or a (male) school teacher. But these seem completely ordinary events, probably not even especially traumatic at the time, and almost trivial when I think of all the violent things that do happen to people even in our relatively safe society.

Now, don't get me wrong. I have no wish to have first-hand encounters with violence and I'm sensibly careful to avoid situations where that might happen.

I accept, in a theoretical way, that I am capable of violence myself, but again I think I must, consciously and unconsciously, avoid situations where I might confront this. This does not seem at all difficult to do but I probably have led a very privileged life that way.

It's strange because violence seems to be everywhere. The way the vulnerable and weak are treated is often violent, if not physically, then in other ways which involve intimidation, humiliation, and distress. I know this but usually at some remove. I hear about it, read about it, watch a TV program, sometimes but not often speak to someone who has been put in this situation.

I know violence is highly gendered. Men are more likely to commit violent acts than women. I've certainly met men who seemed likely to be violent and I always avoid them if I can. I don't understand this impulse to violence even if it's apparently normal as in violent sports like rugby or boxing.

I've tried to think how I might be persuaded to violence. Maybe military service in times of national emergency, maybe self-defence if I or someone I loved was attacked. I don't know. I think I would be frightened, maybe even overwhelmed by such situations.

That's it. I can't think of anything else to say about violence. I fear it, I avoid it, I'm repelled when it happens to others. I would see it as primarily a defeat or failure in myself and others.

CHAPTER 16

Fathers and Fathering

Randy Barber

INTRODUCTION

Fathering was another difficult theme for our group of men. In one way or another, all of the writers express feelings of disconnection or distance from their fathers. For most, this is recalled with melancholy but one man, deeply scarred by his father's psychological abuse of him as a child, experiences actual hatred.

Many of the men suggest that they wanted to be better fathers to their own children but none of these writers feels that he entirely succeeded in this wish. The individual, referred to above, who had been severely abused by his father as a boy found to his dismay that he was behaving in some of the same hateful ways with his children and says that this was partly behind his later decision to leave his family. Others write of inadequate efforts to nurture and emotionally connect with their children, often as a result of giving priority to their work.

Sometimes these narratives of guilt and regret are challenged, however. One man recalls a recent revealing conversation with his daughter who tells him these attitudes are keeping him from forging closer bonds with his grown up children. Another of our writers delights in his close relationship with one of his daughters which has continued and even deepened as the years have passed despite the breakup of his first marriage.

The elusive, largely unspoken nature of father/son relationships is poignantly expressed in two stories. In one the author recalls some rough horseplay behind the couch (which he remembers as being slightly unpleasant) and another time when his father expresses his surprise at his teenage son's intellectual prowess. In the other story the writer tells of a memorable freewheeling overnight bicycle trip with his stepson and later of his startling realisation of his own father's role in recording a cherished moment in his childhood.

Another, and altogether more positive, portrayal of fathering is presented in the story of the meeting between the writer as a young man and his dad. Here, we

Fathers and Fathering

have an almost apocryphal tale of the son sitting down with his ageing father and declaring his independence, in this case from his parents' Catholicism. The separation is achieved with love and respect on both sides and the writer is able to recognise and cherish his father's legacy in his own life.

***

OEDIPUS VEXED—A FATHERING STORY

My story of fathering can only ever really be about one thing: how desperately awful my own father was at the job. Then there were my own – often clumsy and inept attempts to outgrow his influence. In therapy it took me a long time and a lot of angry discussion for me to drive home the point that he was in truth a thoroughly nasty, spiteful and selfish man (nasty, brutish and short is the phrase that always comes to mind) and that I wasn't just afflicted by deep-seated Oedipal hatred of him.

This was the man who psychologically abused, cheated and exploited his wife as well as his own children. We each dealt with this in our different ways. While our mother worked hard to keep the peace and not to upset him, my elder sister escaped and got married as soon as she was nineteen and I left to join the army when I was eighteen. But my younger sister - left alone now and deaf and highly vulnerable, disengaged from herself and the world around her and learned always to please and play safe, divesting herself of all personal desires, ambitions, needs, opinions and ideas which might in any way conflict with his. To this day it is difficult to know what she really wants or likes or thinks about anything.

He stole from us and from my mother, rent money, pocket money and meagre savings, Christmas club money, and then, when he died, left my mother in debt which we had to sort out for her. But he also stole or destroyed our independence, our confidence and our self-respect - or at least he tried his very best to do so. We had it constantly drummed into us that we were, stupid and worthless, pathetic and selfish, and - in order that we should never grow up and so one day present a challenge to him, he did everything he possibly could to keep us as children. Most of all, though, he robbed us of a decent father, something I so badly needed.

One instance always springs first to mind. As a young teenager I wanted a guitar. The first Christmas he bought me a toy ukulele which lived out its short life, string-less and neglected at the back of a cupboard somewhere. But I persisted and so the following Christmas a cheap guitar appeared from a local department store. On Boxing Day, to my utter dismay, the back started to come away. *'I'll have to take it back and change it,'* was what he said; what he actually did, while I stood and watched, was to take it back to the store and pocket the money. End of Christmas present; end of guitar.

I hated him then, I still hate him now, and I need have no conscience or guilt or 'better-informed' doubts about doing so (I have also been a psychodynamic counsellor in my time).

How could I shake such a person off when it came to being a father myself? Truth is I couldn't. Naïve and unworldly, I didn't know where to begin and so made a real hash of it while desperately wanting to learn from his mistakes and be a kind and loving – truly fulfilling father to my own children. Instead, and in spite of myself, I became angry, selfish, domineering and even heavy-handed, just like him. *'The bee stings and then dies itself,'* I wrote many years later in a poem. I knew it was happening, I hated myself for it and desperately wanted to change, and then I went on and repeated the whole damaging exercise all over again. My leaving when my two boys were age ten and six was in a significant part intended to protect their interests and their well-being from me. I wish my father had had the decency to leave, though he frequently threatened to when he couldn't get his way.

I have little idea how this affected them in reality; my sons and I get to speak only on rare occasions. I have learned so much since then and I have changed out of all recognition – though of course my father and my volcanic inner demons still remain buried beneath, held in place (I like to think) by the better, holding and loving father that I have since learned to become to myself.

I want my sons to know this – to know that it wasn't them who were at fault but me – all the way down the line. But if we can't have that meaningful conversation I guess they will never know. This hurts me a lot.

Of course my father had his own inner demons to deal with. The most significant difference between him and me, though, is that he never did *deal* with them but gave in entirely to their sadistic and greedy appetites. At least I *have* made an attempt, if rather belatedly, so if only in that respect I am sure I have made a better job of it than he did.

FATHERING: THE SECOND CHANCE

My first fathering experience was a flop. From about the age of 23 to 33 I didn't pay enough attention to the different needs of my three kids, Peter, Melany and Kate. I was too engaged in school work as a Secondary school teacher to be usefully available. I didn't change enough dirty nappies. I didn't cook very well –

chips, fish fingers and beans were about my bravest adventure into cooking for the family. No nourishing stews. No exotic salads but things I could do without too much expected of me. However I wanted to be a better father. I had hardly seen my own father after he came back from working in the Auxiliary Fire Service in London from roughly 1940-1946. And I wanted to be a more emotionally intimate Dad.

That's why I wanted to make amends in my second chance of being a father. Not so much enjoying the special delights of getting to know my grandkids, although that was occasionally joyful and fulfilling, but I really wanted to keep more intricate and deep contact with my own kids while they matured into adults and encountered some of the similar pleasures and dilemmas I met with in my first chance as a father.

After my first wife and myself divorced in the early 1970s, it wasn't very easy to keep close to all three of them. I remember taking Peter to Kendal Youth Hostel for a few weekends of walking in the Lake District, and I kept sending cards to Kate my youngest. However it was Melany with whom I managed to preserve a continuing, close relationship through the next 45 years. I can remember the glum, frozen silences of the other two in the back of the car as I collected them from Bretton Hall car park to spend part of a holiday or a weekend with Bren, my new partner, and myself. But Melany was different. She went on telling me stories about her life during the week and she didn't pay any attention to Peter and Kate.

That emerging closeness with Mel has continued to the present day. What is so nurturing about the second chance of fathering is how she shares, at 48, her work and domestic problems with Bren and me. A few weeks ago she came down by herself for the weekend. She wanted to talk to us about a work problem. She was getting fed up, as a research scientist at Edinburgh University, in having to constantly find the funding for her part-time post . She said she wanted to apply, for the first time in her life, for a full-time post in the Blood Transfusion Service in the city.

On the Saturday morning, she came into our bedroom and flung herself down at the foot of the bed, telling us everything about the work changes that she yearned for. We responded by offering to support her letter of application to the Blood Transfusion Service. Tentatively, Mel wrote a first draft and then she shared it with us. It wasn't very good. She hadn't any ideas about the conventions and genre expectations she was writing her letter within. She didn't know how to introduce herself or to show why she was particularly interested in the job. And more crucially she left out all the scientific details of her present work. Also she missed out her special people skills that helped her to communicate with the other people in her research lab.

We helped her as much as we could do, with a few jokes and gentle advice. She sent us a final draft on the Monday morning and we reciprocated by sending her our own written suggestions. Mel was very down-hearted when she didn't get the job. We tried to support her in taking the first steps towards a different kind of job possibility. Later, I felt strongly connected with her present realities in Edinburgh. She was a long way from us but our links seemed to be growing as we all aged.

TOO LATE TO BE A FATHER?

Our two children were adopted in the early 1970s when my infertility was discovered, after a decade of marriage and intense but childless coupledom. I think that our babies did have quite a lot of my attention. In their earliest years, I was so pleased they were with us, so magically it seemed. I was enthralled by their beauty and development, and in both cases, in comparison with stories from other parents, what 'good' infants they were. I remember changing nappies, taking turns with bottles, and generally sharing if not equally, because I was teaching at the university and Di took a few years off her school teaching career. Our life did revolve round the new arrivals, and the playgroups, friends and social circles associated with babydom. It was a relatively quiet time at the university. The dramas and reforming impulses of the late 1960s fading, my thesis completed, teaching in social history, apart from feminist challenges. more settled.

Still even at this stage I know I forsook them too often. I remember long hours of researching and writing that could have been theirs. I remember, a bit later, holidays of the three of them without me, and also holidays where though physically present, I wasn't very available except as an occasional playmate and constant photographical recorder of their doings. As Di said to me later, about our marriage, there was 'always something else' (by implication she meant, more important than me/us). These absences lengthened as my commitment to a new academic department intensified after 1975, and still more after 1979, when the project itself was under intense pressures. It was only in the late 1980s, that I fully realised how bad this situation was for myself, and those I loved. Curiously, it was a new relationship, with someone who taught me to be more reflexive about these things, that prompted the effort to change.

This involved backing down from university responsibilities and then taking early retirement, being part--time till 1993. All plans were defeated by Di's sudden death in 1992. The children had 'left home', I was preoccupied with grieving and looking after my mother, and trying to create a new and viable way to live, sans job, sans partner and sans children at home. In some ways this was my worst desertion, not registering how much my children needed me after the death of their mother. I think in part I was caught up in the myth of early adult 'independence', something their mother and I had shared.

For long time, my self-narrative of parenting has been almost completely negative: a story of failure and a practice of reparation, trying to be a better father and grandparent, the second time round. Two recent events have however punctured this 'bad father' narrative. The first, watching my son as a father: a dextrous multitasking and loving performance if even there was one, and he an academic too! The second, an important discussion with my daughter while we were gardening together – pruning red currants and carting compost! – who spoke her mind about the paralysing effect on herself that my own prolonged grieving and guilt and silence have produced. She has made me realise that the problem today isn't so much being a bad parent, as the grief and guilt itself that has stopped me remembering and sharing the positive parts (and in a more measured way the difficulties) in a more open and loving way

A FATHER STORY BECOMING MORE GENTLE

An important relationship developed between myself and my father towards the end of his life. He knew he was not long for this world. I sensed it so we were more gentle with each other for those last two of his years.

This did not stop him wanting to have one last attempt at getting me to convert back to Roman Catholicism.

There was one specific afternoon when he cornered me on a visit without the children and my partner. We spoke in a way that the cultural roots of my religious upbringing were more exposed. He opened with the usual guilt tripping gambit:

"You know you used to be more religious than me at one point you used to give me pointers about being open to caring for the people of Africa when you raised money for Oxfam"

I replied "But I have moved into a more critical understanding of the world. Now I cannot rely just on the trappings of beautiful hymns and charitable provision for the suffering poor."

He replied "But I don't want you and your children to die and go to hell. Surely you should at least baptise them so they do not suffer."

I replied "But you know we don't believe in heaven and hell; life just all comes to an end when we die."

He replied "I and your mother have to try to convince you otherwise. I want to be able to face god when he confronts me at the gates of heaven."

It ended when I told him that this kind of pressure could not work.

We parted on the understanding that he had done his duty and I would follow my own ways in the world. I think that mutual respect helped him to accept our differences and certainly gave me strength to continue to love him at the same time care about the future development of my understanding of relationships and political convictions.

Friendships I have today reflect that tolerance of diverse choices people make in their changing lives.

I have grown more proud of my father's achievements over the past 28 years since his death, Reading his World War 2 memoirs and learning more about the history of the struggles for the independence of the Polish nation has grounded my sense of self in that dual heritage of being a second generation immigrant.

The study of my father and mother's culture alongside my evolving Britishness has made me feel more like a citizen of the world.

A World of Fathers

The oldest father he knew was his grandfather, with the same name as his own father. His father was usually rather distant from his father, and mother, keeping them at arm's length, even though they lived just around the corner on the next street. His father was cautious in at least not seeking much social contact, as if it was all a bit of nuisance – women's work. He wondered why this was. Later he learnt that his father was severely beaten as a boy by both his father and mother, with a strap or what was at hand.

There was always a reticence, a barrier, between his father and his own father, his grandfather. The gap was similar to the gap between his father and himself, but more so, and with a tinge of fear and long resentment. His father was still a boy to his father, and was easily and regularly referred to as "Young Freddie", even when 60.

So the mystery was: how was it that his grandfather seemed so gentle and non-confrontational to him as a boy? Was it possible this was the same man?

One day when he, his grandfather, seemed very old, when he had cancer, when he discovered he loved to drink chilled water from the fridge, he had "the conversation" with him. It was in the brown back living room, where the range was always alight, burning hot, He must have been 10-11 by then. He feels 10-11. The words he, his grandfather, spoke were "Whatever you do, always be true to yourself." He felt pleasure in having such a direct and clear piece of advice from his grandfather. He knew that he doubted very much if his grandfather had said anything similar to his siblings – his sister would not have been spoke to in that way, and his brother was too young. He was blessed by the message. In some ways, that was that. There was no more to be said, he could die now.

But of course that was not the end of it ... his own father lived another twenty years. He never got so close as that <u>conversation</u>; he once broke down in tears on the phone when apologising for behaving badly on a recent visit. It may have been after the time he, his father, told him off for being so soft on his son, so that he would not grow up to be a real boy. He, his father, did come close on another occasion when he was about 18-19 when he started jostling and play wrestling on the floor behind the sofa for a small ball or something or other, and then somehow got over-excited and started frothing at the mouth. But that wasn't a very comfortable closeness! And then earlier was when he asked his father to test his revision for Biology at about 13-14 and he, his father, said "I didn't realise you knew so much", that is, about the sex and reproduction of rabbits or when he told him not to masturbate as that was a way of losing what he called "self-respect".

But now he is about the same age as when his father died. When he kissed him on the mouth when dead, it felt like the first time, at least since being a tiny toddler.

It was about the same time as his father died that he realised more fully the political thinness, the mystification and the actual patriarchal power and status of fathers and fatherhood – that he wished to be dropped, bit by bit into <u>the ocean</u>. His own grandfatherhood came as a surprise. He could not see himself at all as a grandfather until the very last week before the birth, then he became both very worried and very excited. It also brought a possibility of being a little less patriarchal.

How Slowly the Heart Reveals Itself ...

I've two stories of fathering. The first involves my step-son who I lived with for about eight years until he left home for work as a musician and DJ aged 16. We'd had an amiable but not intimate relationship in his younger years perhaps because during that time his mother and I lived in a group household with a shifting population of other adults. Our connection would become closer when the three of us went on holidays once or twice a year and I remember many of these trips fondly. However, as he grew older we spent less time together and I felt a developing distance between us.

Then when my step-son was about 14 or 15 I suggested pretty much out of the blue that we go on a bicycle trip together, just for the day. He wasn't especially keen but agreed and off we went up into the hills surrounding the city where we lived. It was a beautiful day and we found ourselves flying along through small villages and settlements and along country lanes, sometimes racing each other up and down the twisting roads. I struggled to keep up with him and it was pretty clear that he was enjoying his new-found sense of superiority as a cyclist.

Before we knew it we were more than 50 km away from home and it was beginning to get dark. I thought we might be able to catch a train back but by the time we got to the only nearby station it was too late. So we found a phone booth (no mobiles in those days) and let his mother know we would be staying out overnight and be back the next day.

We pedaled on through the last bit of daylight till we got to a town down the coast where we could rent a room for the night. We were both pretty tired by then so after pizza and a bit of TV we turned in. The next day we cycled back as far as a suburban rail station and travelled the last 25 km or so by train. I think the round trip must have been at least 100 km, much more than I'd thought when we'd set out but it was the sense of just taking off like that, the unplanned nature of the trip that delighted us both and re-established, for me anyway but I think also for my stepson, that sense of connection.

My second story of fathering concerns my own father. For as long as I can remember, I had believed that my father was a rather remote, not particularly loving parent. I had two younger brothers and it had always seemed to me that he was much more demonstratively affectionate towards them than to me. I had been a somewhat sickly and bookish child and early on my mother had formed a very close and protective relationship with me which seemed to somehow exclude my father. I was aware of this dynamic but somehow was never able to change or challenge it.

As the years went by I came to accept this picture of my father as being somehow removed from me and to believe that neither of us was aware of or able access the other's inner life. Then one day I had a moment of startling insight which challenged this whole picture. It involved a favourite photograph of mine which shows me, aged about five I think, standing on a river bank with my grandmother, my father's mother. I had always been especially close to this grandmother and treasure this picture which shows us fishing, me with a small rod in my hands dangling my line in the water and frowning in concentration, she holding a crude stick and a bit of string and smiling on.

And then I realised that this picture which I so love must have been taken by my father. He was always the great photographer in our family and he must have known about my feelings for his mother, feelings which I later learned he deeply shared. So there it was, this portrait of me, me his first-born child who he must have cared for dearly to have framed so tenderly. How slowly the heart reveals itself especially between men!

CHAPTER 17

Work

Zbyszek Luczynski

INTRODUCTION

Our stories about work highlight how we have struggled with integrating the work ethic into our lives. We show how we have internalised work as the instrument of being useful to society. Work is often confused with employment, but work is also domestic and other forms of work, as the first story makes clear.

The next story illustrates the stranglehold of employed work felt by the author pushing him back to work whilst still on sick leave following the behaviour of an oppressive line manager. He describes the effect of his struggle to maintain his integrity in his work within the local state whilst his management try to bend that work to fit into their neoliberal and cuts plans. Whilst on gardening leave for overstepping their boundaries, he began to appreciate the positives of reduced stress that came without a work defined life. He enjoys making time to develop his "creative juices." However, once back at work after a period of appreciating his experience, making a change to bring a balance between home and work, he began to revert to "the warrior both at work and in political activism." He ends with retirement from paid work being a chance to pursue both creative and political interests.

The third story tells us "Work was going to be me – what I would in time … BECOME." This is a sentiment echoed across all the stories we wrote on this theme. He traces his career which began with leaving school early at 15 years; he took on physically tiring jobs such as meat porter, plasterer's mate, and a stint in a supermarket, and he joined the Army for a while. Later he ended up in teaching which though physically draining "helped to build up my belief in myself and my general sense of self-worth." His experience in the typing pool at the college where he taught, staffed by women he reflects was a useful period on the way to becoming the "critically masculinity aware man that I am today." It demonstrated to other men and me "a degree of self-assuredness, which, by contrast ... they clearly lacked."

Having retired twice, the writer of 'Retirement' finds retirement projects unpaid and voluntary just as hard work that he contemplates a "third retirement from activist campaigning" to a less stressful lifestyle. "Masculinity has been defined historically as a relation to a job – as a vocation or as "bringing home the bacon." But this he says ignores "the subjective appeal or commitment to what they are meant to achieve, so doing good in the wider world perhaps." This reflects the secularisation of his earlier religious impulse to improve the world in the present not in the afterlife. As a non-Christian left winger, he is nevertheless still out to outdo his father and his private school masters, but also himself. He ends with a plea to "bring together the passion to know and explain ..., the complex desires of love and friendship which sometimes seem to embrace everyone and everything ... and the excitement of action which if sustained might just achieve some organic transition ..."

For the author of the last story in this section, "work is pleasurable ... – what makes me me", "work at work is pleasurable and exhaustion, feeling wanted, wanted too much", but home is also work, leading onto a detailed description of removing dust at home.

In conclusion, our stories have covered the contradictory feelings that work has developed in each of our lives. How we have defined ourselves sought dignity as well as rewards through it. We are a group of middle class men made up of teachers academics, community workers privileged to have had fulfilling jobs. We have been involved in political activism and at the same time developed in the group a supportive profeminist masculinity which is reflected in the contradictory relationships with work which are expressed in these stories.

***

On the Subject of Domesticity

When I was young I avoided all household tasks like the plague. Somehow they had become associated with a dull, tedious and apparently meaningless world that belonged to adults – especially my parents. Domesticity seemed to 'bring you down' even though at another level I fantasised about a better life with a better house which was bigger and more luxurious but which was also clean, tidy, warm, comfortable etc., completely failing to appreciate the reality that such things actually depended on functioning levels of tedious domesticity being applied to them.

The first big change happened when I went into the army. There I was expected – on pain of severe punishment – to wash and iron clothes meticulously, make my bed, keep my bed space and room spotlessly clean and tidy, and so on. It is true that I did gain a great deal of independent self-respect and personal pride from this, even though the actual standards required were ridiculously stringent and exacting, often obsessively so.

After I left, age 21, I shared a flat with friends for a while before eventually going off to college. At this point I did my share, still with a degree of personal pride, and also set about learning to cook – which also implied shopping, planning, washing up etc. Mostly I was OK at looking after myself with only the usual occasional lapses (e.g. where the washing up was left until the next day, and the like).

The next big change came about when I married and had my first son – which came at more or less the same time. Then it became a matter of personal pride that I shouldn't need or expect a woman to take on primary domestic responsibility for me or my son. At one level I probably did 'more than my share', especially since she was not good with nappies and sick and such like, which are a significant part of the package when it comes to young babies. I also had/have a meticulous streak which was put to good effect at this time. At another level, what I was not good at was getting up in the middle of the night. I have never coped well with lack of sleep, but I also tried my best to make up for any lapses here in other ways (actually I *did* get up in the middle of the night – not as much as I should have – but I just didn't cope with it very well).

Since then I have come to regard myself as domestically very competent – often more so than many women that I meet. It rankles me sometimes that, while I certainly do my bit around the house in more-or-less equal share, when it comes to the more traditionally 'male/masculine' matters of maintaining the car, re-wiring a plug and so on – anything 'technical' or what men often refer to as 'practical' – then I am expected somehow just know all about it and get on with doing that as well.

I am alright with this up to a point. I do take a certain pleasure, for example, in knowing that I can re-fit a kitchen, glaze a window or mend a kettle, and I accept my partner's inability to do such things, but at the same time I often feel typecast as typically 'male/masculine' by this and by her never making the attempt to learn or take responsibility for some of these things. Then again, she does almost all the gardening.

Now that she is retired as well we have a much more balanced division of labour.

Disappearing in Part

It was a pretty piss poor situation to be in when I was suspended for as I saw it doing my job of empowering the community groups with which I was working.

I disappeared in part.

I hid from neighbours and colleagues, ashamed, waiting for that sword of Damocles to fall; that which would darken my reputation stemming the sustenance of my family supporting wages.

No wonder I lost my confidence, libido, my cocksure body was wounded. "Senescent through stress" as my reflexologist reassured me as she worked on healing my body and mind in those first few weeks before I was able to move on to defend and fight back through the union in preparation for the disciplinary hearing.

I knew my boss had been gunning for me because I did not conform to her dictatorial management style of micromanagement. She sought to mould me and fellow team members into corporate manipulators ditching any role in enabling the voice of the community. She had no respect for my experience-based wisdom.

How could we resolve our polarised positions whilst retaining some dignity?

After a long three months of being on gardening leave while investigations were carried out, I started to appreciate the positives in a less work defined life style.

I was making time for getting in touch with my creative juices, jazzing it up, going to gigs, reading groups, and really appreciating my partner and sons. I spent most of the summer listening to my sons, hearing their changing views as I changed from being their protector to being their friend. I was supporting their independence and separation. That time gave me the chance to re-evaluate who I was as well as oversee improvements to our new home.

Once the disciplinary hearing was over the warmth of welcome I received going back to work confirmed this new approach and allowed me to be gentler in relationships during the working day.

I was able to share my responsibilities with co-workers acting less critically, focusing energy, even going to part-time working in the last two years.

I moved towards the retiring phase of ageing horizons, setting more realistic goals I thought at the time.

However once back to the grind and seeing the opportunities for political activism once part-time, I again reverted to being the purist-seeking warrior both at work and in political activism.

I ended the last year of work with a stressed related breakdown with six months sick leave to recover back to work where again I resumed my struggles with the dismantling of 38 years of community work for the Council resisting the neoliberal "everything out to tender" approach, which was being adopted across the board.

An angry old man still struggling against the systems which hold us in check against creative change and service for the good of the people, which now in retirement I have much more time to pursue.

Working Hard at Being a Man

Like so many of the other subjects that I have written about in this project, that of work seems to get jumbled up with the rest of my life in a way that makes it hard to separate out.

Taking it in its formal sense, as 'Work', i.e. in the vein of employment, it has been a rich and varied part of my life and one which has reflected back to me the changes that I have undertaken in my time. When I left school, age fifteen and with a handful of qualifications that no-one had ever heard of, let alone recognised, work was going to be ME – what I would in time (hopefully) BECOME. This notion of *becoming* was a hugely important part of my fantasy life because my self-esteem was about as low as it could be. But I was so lacking in confidence I just took a job in the local supermarket where the hours were long and the pay was rock bottom and where I was sexually abused by the women staff as a kind of workplace ritual or rite of passage.

A series of low-paid jobs followed, some better than others, some even with 'prospects' but I was unable to settle and very unhappy at home with a tyrannical father. So when I was eighteen I threw it all in and joined the army. My career in the army was short-lived, less than three years, but it gave me the beginnings of a sense of independence that I so badly needed and after another couple of years working and travelling around I finally enrolled at college and eventually became a teacher.

This was the hardest work I have ever done. Physical work, such as being a meat porter or a plasterers' labourer, was tiring in one way. It taxed my body but it left me personally intact. Teaching, on the other hand, drained me even while it gradually helped to build up my belief in myself and my general sense of self-worth. So while I grew in stature I was also heading for a breakdown at that point in my life where assorted pressures, work and domestic life, blew my lid like pressure cooker. Actually, it was more of a collapse than an explosion – I no longer had the energy for such a reaction.

What I understand now is that all of this was being worked out on what were separate stages in a grand 'theatre of masculinity'. This long, drawn-out process of 'becoming something' or 'making something of oneself' (phrases which were banded about almost constantly in my working class background) was about becoming a particular kind of *man,* one who could tick all the boxes on some kind of masculinity check-sheet. Starting work at fifteen, then, was as much about my first steps in leaving (or discarding) the femininity of the domestic sphere for the great, masculine 'real world' out there. And so it was – until I drove myself into the ground.

Once brief interlude in all of this must have been a precursor to the more critically masculinity-aware man that I am today, though I couldn't have known this at the time, and it now says a great deal about me as a personality. I was about twenty two and had about seven years of this masculinity-driven work experience under my belt. But I was already rebelling, even though I didn't understand why. I had been thrown out of the army for being a conscientious objector and for generally refusing to integrate into the narrow-minded brutishness which made up so much of the culture of army life. Now I was working in an office – driven by a different kind of masculinity admittedly, but also tempered by the presence of so many women. Cutting a long(ish) story short, and during a period when work in my department was slack and staffing short elsewhere, I offered to help out for a few weeks in the typing pool as a Dictaphone typist. This was a skill that I had picked up in the army and I was more than proficient in this role.

I remember feeling hugely proud of myself that I could do this and that I could surprise people out of their complacency about gender expectations and their expectations of me. The other women in the all-female pool subjected me to their ribald humour for a while, but it was short-lived and afterwards we soon just got on with the job in hand. In fact we enjoyed one another's company. Male colleagues, however, who just happened to make up all of the actual letter-*writers*, were much more sustained in their reactions and, apart from some of the more senior managers, kept up the raucous behaviour, the jibes and the comments, the corny puns, the 'Sweetie'-this and the 'Darling'-that – as well as the occasional touchings-up, almost for the duration. And the more they did it the more pathetic I knew they were.

Ironically this was a huge boost to my confidence. In short, it demonstrated to others and to me a degree of self-assuredness which, by contrast, they clearly lacked. Could this be read, in some oblique way, as being another victory for masculinity, then? In one way I think it was but, if so, I think it was for a better kind of masculinity.

'RETIREMENT'

Which is defined as:

1. 'removal or withdrawal from service, office, or business;
2. 'withdrawal into privacy or seclusion;
3. 'the act of going away or retreating'

I have 'retired' several times in my life in the first dictionary sense, nearly always accompanied by the fear I am retreating. . 'Running away' might express it better, because running away is always also running towards something else.

The first time was in 1989 at the end of a difficult decade fighting for an extended intellectual-political experiment and against (as it turned out) the neo-liberalisation and over-management of the universities. I was exhausted and also feeling I had sacrificed family and partner to the effort of keeping a little of this project alive. I wanted to spend more time with them and I owed them this, or more. I taught for three more years part-time, but in this time my father died, my mother came to live with us and then, in 1992, my partner of over 30 years died suddenly of a heart attack and our two children 'left home' for university. I spent a year without a job, probably the only time in my life when home-making and house-keeping became the most important thing. During this time I did also save my mother's life by getting her quickly to hospital. Perhaps it was also the nearest I will ever get to 'withdrawal into privacy and seclusion'. But we will see!

The second time I retired was in 2004 at the statutory age of 65, having spent almost a decade helping to build up postgraduate education in another – even more neo-liberalised – university. I had been invited into an ambitious Humanities Faculty mainly as a published researcher but got involved, again, with postgraduate supervision and support. On third-time, then half-time pay, I was soon doing as much there as many senior fulltime colleagues.

This odd pattern of non-retirement was repeated in 2004. I retired in the sense of leaving the institution - left paid 'service' that was rapidly becoming a 'business'. Always frustrated by the limits of the (real) politics of teaching and research, I went a bit mad in joining anti-war movements in two cities and being active locally, regionally and nationally in one of them. I found myself a new unpaid job as a movement organiser, also researching and writing more political pieces. Though I am more careful about domestic and personal relationships than before (though partner, housemate and friends might not agree) retirement in this second phase was more like doing what I always wanted to do. It is only recently, as I approach a 75th birthday, that the thought of retiring again comes frequently to mind, prompted in part by the wishes of my partner, partly by the apparently inexorable increase of public obligations.

How to explain this repeated pattern? I think it is more complex than a masculine attachment to work, or rather how can we unpack the components of such an attachment. Masculinity – across classes perhaps, has been defined historically as a relation to the job – as vocation or as 'bringing home the bacon'. But what about the subjective appeal of the activities themselves, or the commitment to what they are meant to achieve, so doing good in the wider world perhaps. I felt this way about teaching, learning, thinking critically and collective, more democratically organised intellectual work. Similarly peace campaigning promises an end to war, or at least puts you on the 'right' side in the very gendered struggles against violence, militarism and nuclear weapons. If we look to the planetary devastation, economic injustice and institutional deformation of the current phase of capital's development the actual value of opposing this has to be weighed before interpretation in terms of personal and unconscious motivation enters in. Getting a bit more personal, valorisation of work – I would say of practice – also relates, I am aware, to my young adult secularisation of a religious impulse to do good, an impulse which is all the more imperative if this world and this time, not an afterlife, is the only true theatre for improvement. Not quite unconsciously, I know my working is sometimes a 'payment' for a debt made up of the privileges I have been granted as the eldest son of a culturally quite undefended but socially aspirant middle class father. There is some curious cross identification involved in my life with social positions that are not my own, and which men like me have usually tried to dominate. Less consciously perhaps I am showing my father and those school masters at my private schools that as a non-Christian left-winger I can be as 'good' or better than they – but, angrily I think, not in the same way. Maybe this explains why I find it so difficult to say 'No', and why I do 'out-do' not only them, but also myself.

Anyway it is quite a tight knot that is tied here, ties me to 'doing too much' to the point even of exhaustion. What picks away at it always, loosening it in part, isn't even survival, but rather the desire and need to give more back to the friends, family and loved ones who in fact sustain me – though I do sometimes sustain them too. But I could not, will never, withdraw (in that sense of retire) while I remain capable of acting. This kind of connectedness with the world of people, creatures and materials is life to me. I do wish however to integrate the whole bundle better. How can we bring together the passion to know and explain (especially about power and culture), the complex desires of love and friendship which sometimes seem to embrace everyone and everything, needing its own expression, and the excitement of action which if sustained might just achieve some organic transition?

On Work, Ageing and Me

I. It is very difficult to isolate a specific memory of work, as work is always there, constant. And much of my work is so pleasurable that it is hard even to call it work – what makes me me. It is also alien to think of myself as retired or being fully retired, while at the same time being away from some of the more tedious aspects of paid work and the classism, sexism and racism there feels more pleasurable still.

But work is still physical labour, and biggest change in the long-term view is doing less housework. Now I do not live with children, and I live in a much smaller space than when I was younger.

So I come home from work one day from a demanding day's work when the children were teenagers. It has been meetings, demands from others, responsibilities. I am home later than expected and agreed, so I feel apprehensive, slightly sick, on approaching the house. To my great relief there is no food yet prepared. My back aches from the desk job. As a way of busying myself and keeping out of the way, I immediately start washing up the morning's breakfast things partly to clear a space for the preparing the food. I can stay in my own world a little longer. I am immediately told off for doing the washing up and told to sit down and rest from the exhausting day. I don't think I look very perky, and I don't try to hide it. I complain back that if I don't do such housework I am told off, and if I do I am also. Beyond that, I ignore this rebuke as I know I am making a falsely heroic gesture in doing this kitchen work, without love, to keep safely out of trouble. I am moving smoothly into martyr territory. Doing the washing up relaxes me, makes me feel slightly and spuriously virtuous, and clears the space, of the surfaces. Each washing to drain of each cup and plate carries the ambiguous, for me. Now the food can begin. It is a solemn process; home is work, work at work is pleasure and exhaustion, feeling wanted, wanted too much.

II. The flat *now* is generally fairly clean, by my standards at least; it is rather small; there are no teenagers now. Keeping the housework going is easy, and hoovering is not a high priority. I see some dust piles on the floor in the corner, and can't be bothered to get the hoover out, as that is a tricky, nuisance task that involves grappling with tubes, the machine and a cupboard full of items that are bound to spill out when disturbed. I kneel down with care and with my bare hands carefully brush and guide and shape the dust into small hills and then small mountains. It is dirty, dusty, work and I take care not to get the dust on my clothes or up my finger nails. It is also strangely pleasurable. It is small, aesthetic, functional, effective manual labour. I am told off for doing this as a human hoover, and that I should get the hoover out. But I actually like doing this so I reply minimally and continue doing it, making bigger ranges – then finally fully scooping as much as possible into a neat handful and taking it to the rubbish bin, which is actually a plastic bucket with a plastic bag inside it. I take care to deposit into the plastic bag what is now, in moving from the living room floor to the kitchen, reshaped in my hand into a sizeable dust ball. Dropping it in is not so easy as it wants to stick to my hand, and then on first go somehow evades the open mouth of the plastic bag and wafts to the floor. I recover it and replace it, this time more carefully, onto the opening and it floats happily inside, along with the mush of refuse. The task is done, although there are other possible and incipient piles and lines of dust lurking elsewhere, but they are safe for the time being. And I am safe too, knowing that there is undone cleaning that could be done, but which is not done, and so knowing too that such work is not too dominating, is instead resisted, so creating time for other things. The dust cleaning makes work into disposable art, and I remember to wash my hands afterwards.

CHAPTER 18

Sexuality and Relationships

Vic Blake

INTRODUCTION

When this topic was first suggested I wondered how the group would handle it. Thinking of how men so often talk about sex, as conquest or as something that you *do* to someone else – how might we, as older and more critically reflective men, respond to this exercise? In fact the stories themselves turned out to be varied and sensitive and included subjects which I have seldom heard other men talking about; masturbation and guilt, for example, cross-dressing, sexual fantasy, non-phallic or penetrative love making. Certainly they extended far beyond the narrow interpretation of (male) sex as being predominantly physical and penetrative.

One writer, for example, speaks from the start of his problems in defining sexuality at all, finding it difficult to extricate the idea from his deeply ambivalent feelings concerning the nature of his own gender. A difficult history of coming to terms with his fascination for women's clothes highlights not only his own personal identity issues but also confronts many of our fixed assumptions concerning the supposedly binary nature of gender. It also highlights what he sees as a prevailing lack of understanding and even hostility towards those so inclined.

Another of our members writes about sex but does so indirectly, reflecting more on his wonderings about the subject rather than the actual activity itself. Throughout he draws a distinction between actual sex and the world of his imaginings, which appear sometimes to be more exciting for him than the reality itself. This is in spite of the fact that often "... there is very little actual sex fantasised about in the fantasy", so that it becomes really difficult for him "... to identify what the sexual fantasies really consist of." Even where his fantasy does involve sex he then experiences a lack of interest and even disappointment when later meeting the object of that fantasy. Thus he draws attention to the complicated and so often disappointing interplay that exists between one's sexual fantasy life and actual reality.

For another member, no longer being controlled by the sexual urges of his youth becomes an extremely important issue, as is that of remaining in control at all in his sexual relationship with his partner. He now characterises this relationship as a 'non-phallic tenderness', relying more on "... affectionate, reciprocal sensualities than the narrow, unequal, obsessiveness of penetrative sex". He sees this as a very positive development in his life while all the while being at pains to emphasise the "... release and relief, with dignity, from the threat, fear and anxiety associated with penetrative sex" and from "... all that performance anxiety."

Another writer reflects, with a great deal of affection and just a tinge of guilt, upon his relationship with his now-deceased wife. He describes their living together as "... blissful and genuinely shared and this loving intimacy, with sex as central to it, was sustained through many changes and difficulties." Yet, what seemed like a very loving and sexually fulfilling relationship at the time now causes him doubt and he wonders whether he might have done more, might have been more considerate and responsive to her needs. "It is true", he says, that "... he didn't attend to, even discover, the fullness of her wants and needs, and this is a good reason for guilt and reparation, for trying better now there is a next time."

Sex for another of our members is talked about in terms of egalitarianism and responsibility. His earlier rebellions against his catholic faith lead him as a young man into sexual explorations in which the rigid principles of his religion are replaced by a fresh set of principles emerging out of his growing political and gender awakenings. These same principles have sustained his marriage through to fatherhood and beyond.

Another member writes a profoundly-moving story of an early life clouded by shame to do with his need to masturbate. After his mother discovers his girly magazines he is warned about the terrible consequences of his 'self-abuse' and of the likelihood of becoming unable "... to form "normal" sexual relationships later in life". Unable to resist his need to continue masturbating, however, he is riven with guilt and fear to the extent that, when the time comes for actual sexual relationships he finds that he is unable to function. He gets by in his subsequent relationships as best he can, still plagued by his 'shameful addiction' and seriously damaged by his fear and guilt, until he is eventually helped by his wife-to-be to begin to overcome this – and so begins his recovery.

Appropriately this section ends with a tale of changing sexuality: "want[ing] a sexual relationship that is much more other-centred, part of learning to put my partner's sensual skin pleasures first."

***

SEXUALITY, ALWAYS A COMPLICATED SUBJECT

The older I get the more blurry this idea becomes, rather like my own sexuality. I'm not even that certain anymore that the term sexuality has any validity, except for when we need to identify particular groups, presumably on the basis of their sexual preferences at any given point in time. Also I don't think that sexuality is only about sex. There is much more to it than that.

For the first half of my life I would have said that my sexuality was decidedly heterosexual in the narrow sense, with only fleeting flights of imagination, wondering purely out of curiosity what it might have been like if I were to have sex with another guy. My actual sexual attractions, then and now, have always been towards women. This much I can be clear about. From my thirties onwards, however, this fixedness and the imagined clarity gradually began to dissolve to the point where, now, I could no longer give a simple answer if questioned about my sexuality.

I don't remember exactly when it was that I first tried on women's underwear but I think I was probably in my twenties and it felt not only good, in a highly erotic sense, but also *right*. It was this that took me by surprise. The softness and the snugness of it was a complete life-changer that I hadn't bargained for when the thought first occurred to me. Now the jig saw puzzle of my sexuality was in pieces all over the floor although I struggled for years – decades - to preserve the fantasy that it was actually intact and that the picture of my sexuality was still quite clear in spite of my jumbled experience. I was in now in denial of something big which was increasingly to break through the facade that I had erected over the years.

Later on I found that I wanted to try on skirts and tops as well, the whole gamut of women's clothes, but it was only much later that I felt able to shop for occasional items, mostly ill-fitting and not *me* at all. It was always difficult and, having been in a series of heterosexual partnerships, it was almost always clandestine with all the guilt and shame that so often comes with this need. Yet, breaking through the guilt and shame, it always felt right at the time. There have been three occasions, however, when I have had sexual relationships with women while in women's clothes and they have been some of the most wonderful experiences of my life. On these occasions I felt like me, the whole *me*, not just this masculine, partial me. I did imagine the same thing with men but although, in my fantasy, this may have enhanced my sense of my femininity it was no more effective for that and, as I say, my actual preferences remain with women.

Later, during my time in therapy and as a member of various men's groups I slowly came to feel more comfortable with this side of my personality but it was only just a few years ago when I finally put the last piece of the jigsaw puzzle back in place. In some family correspondence that I came across between my aunt and her aunt I discovered that, as a young child, my mother had sold all my clothes at time when I was very ill in hospital. I already had uncomfortable later memories of being sent to school in my sister's hand-me-downs – and this would have been some years afterwards, but suddenly my constantly shifting gender identity made sense to me and I began at last to feel able to relax into it. Now I am perfectly happy just to go with the flow and to dress how the mood takes me at the time (always depending, of course, upon others).

This is not easy. We may have lived through a sexual revolution in which we can more easily be open about being gay or bi-sexual or trans-sexual, but to be a 'straight' guy who just wants to feel good in women's clothes still gets very negative reactions even among otherwise liberal-minded people. Fortunately my partner is reasonably OK with my dressing up but she clearly finds it difficult to talk about and accept fully. I have now begun to come out to various close friends but I don't think I will ever be in that situation where I can just dress as I please, when and wherever I please. I would love to but I just don't think we are ready for that yet.

I suppose, as a rider to all of this, I should explain that I don't go in for wigs or body-formers of any kind. I just love the clothes and the so-called feminine feelings which come with being able to wear them. I try to dress tastefully, rather than trying to look like some classic idea of a sexy woman with skimpy clothes, high heels and all that stuff. So I am not trying to pass as a woman, just simply to give full expression to that part of me that *feels* like a woman. In that way I am able to feel, for the first time in my life, fully rounded and complete as a person. What this has to say about actual *sexuality,* though, I am not certain.

WONDERING ABOUT SEX

For quite a long time he had wondered what it would be like to have sex with certain particular other people, especially particular women. These were usually women friends and acquaintances, including some people he doesn't know especially well.

One day at a work meeting a woman he didn't know made a special point of saying a special goodbye to him as he left the room before the end of the meeting. He had noticed her before and she certainly made it clear that she had noticed him. A few days later he got a handwritten note in a neat envelope, saying she was the woman who had said goodbye, and that she would like to meet. They did and she soon announced she would like to have a relationship. He asked "what kind of relationship?" She answered "a sexual relationship". They had sex a few times, he thinks it was three times, in different places, and it was very different to what he had experienced before, partly he thought because her body and vagina were tighter, and both enjoyed the sex immensely.

That was a long while ago. So now he sometimes wonders what a similar experience would be like now – what might be called fantasy, except that there is very little actual sex fantasised about in the fantasy. So it has become really difficult for him to identify what the sexual fantasies really consist of. It is thinking, imagining, he would really like to kiss a favourite a lot or perhaps fucking with her sitting on top of him. Or thinking of who out of several possibles he would fancy fucking most if he had to choose, a strange imperative, but with very little actual sexual content to the fantasy. He is, he feels almost, disappointed and disappointing in this situation. And then when he does happen to meet one of these fantasy women in the flesh he often doesn't really fancy them, or at least realise that he is no way *bothered* to consider this, doing this, at all.

There are, however, exceptions to this, especially when there has been at some point in real life some kind of spoken acknowledgement of love, attraction or special intimacy. One woman told him she had loved him and loved him. He kissed her on the cheek, she said "no lips", moved her breasts towards him, he touched one, and she said "I'm very good". He sometimes thinks of her differently after offering her breast, wondering what it would be like to have sex with her. That thought turns him on a bit, but rarely when he sees her face-to-face, though a bra strap or a smooth arm can do the trick.

Rather than being confessional on sex, such as describing the fuck in great vivid detail, this is non-confessional, non-sexual writing, from the vantage point of age and ageing. Sex as wondering about sex and not sex.

Towards a Non-phallic Tenderness and Intimacy between Ageing Husband and Wife

I hate the phrase,' sexual impotence' and I don't intend to use it again. I am now 74 and I want to turn my back on the controlling power of my sexual relations in my earlier years. I don't want to be in charge of who does what to whom, where and how it goes on.

In the present moment of time in 2014, I much prefer to use the more constructive phrase, 'A non-phallic tenderness' towards my wife. There's clearly more to affectionate, reciprocal sensualities than the narrow, unequal, obsessiveness of penetrative sex. For many ageing men (including myself) they are looking for some kind of release and relief, with dignity, from the threat, fear and anxiety associated with penetrative sex. In fact I suspect that some ageing men are contemptuous of Viagra and just want to get rid of all that performance anxiety when they discover they can't get it up anymore. Indeed, I don't want to waste my time worrying about my penile stiffness and hardness. There's more to sensual touching and communication than just that.

Of course, it's not as simple as that. There are also contradictory, past-focused elements occasionally breaking out as well. For example, the enduring persistence of masturbatory fantasies in ageing men's lives. In my imagination I sometimes re-visit past, sexual relations, filling in gaps and missed opportunities and encounters in my inventive, interior, reconstructions. I still half-cling to memories of intense, past performances usually improvised more daringly and positively. So these fantasies often mingle with the present warmth of sensual touching.

As men and women age, particularly in the lives of married couples who have been together for forty to fifty years, there are often changes and shifts in our sex lives. Sometimes there is more of a gentle, other-directed respect and tolerance shown towards the different needs and desires voiced by partners towards each other. Like in my relationship with my wife; cuddling, stroking, caressing, holding have replaced our earlier pattern of penetrative sex in our twenties, thirties and forties.

What used to be seen as the only, 'real' sex in my earlier life (penetrative sex) has been challenged in my 70s by sensual touching and being more affection and intimacy focused than orgasm-centred. This has become a part of learning to put my partner's sensual, skin pleasures first. For example, I sometimes massage my partner's back with circling hand movements. Her back is silky smooth and she asks me to massage her back to take away some of the pain in her lungs. I like to make sweeping, flowing hand movements across her top back and down into the valley of her backbone and sometimes flowing downwards along her spine to the hollow gathering ground at the bottom of her spine.

My partner repays me by twiddling my hair. She strokes my hair at the nape of my neck and sometimes combs my hair on the top of my scalp. There's almost a grooming tenderness in this sensual touching. Like in bed, especially in winter, we like to share our body heat in a curling up position. As I drift into sleep I like the fleeting pressure of touching, intertwining legs and brushing thighs with my partner.

Perhaps you can't separate out shared sensualities from the variety of sharing in a partnered life together. So perhaps sensual touching is a part of the intertwining contact and communication found in a more mature partnership involving mental, social, intellectual, practical activities. So, for example, sharing with my partner in August the discovery in a walled garden, of the creamy-white blossoms of a tall, columnar, Nymansay Eucryphia was an intense, sensual pleasure as well as an intellectual recognition.

LOVING SEX FOR EVER

One day in a crowded and forbidden place she pressed against his back, so that he felt her breasts, her belly, her hips, her breath. For many days after, he choked on his desire for her and could only take her in, absorbed, in silence, watching her strong, soft arms, that were bare in the summer, and drawn in to happiness and amusement by the energy with which she spoke and moved, her emphasis, her vehemence. When he finally asked her out and they kissed in the car, the rest came quickly, risks taken in the heat of it, in circumstances hardly easy. Later they danced together, in a way that others found quite scandalous, remarking on it prudishly.

So it was after adventures of many kinds, often driven by desire, the wedding didn't match how they actually were together. White dress, families assembled, icing on the cake and the familiar binding words of religion sweetened the saltiness somehow. Yet living together was blissful and genuinely shared and this loving intimacy, with sex as central to it, was sustained through many changes and difficulties: shared parenting, persistent inequalities, many conflicts and angry words - that is until she died. Somehow even his heaping of sharp things on their marriage bed didn't break the sex-led bond until this too material ending. After, when he mourned her, he missed her physical, breathing person: the feeling of stroking her back, not just naked but with her eager self so very close to her skin, her desire for him, his arousal and their accomplishment. It was then too, however, that he really came to see what she had done and been, especially for him and the children.

Held within a different kind of loving – gentler, rounder, more reasonable and many-sided – he looked back in guilt and wondered what this first relationship had been for him. Was it a well-sustained lust for her? No, now he thinks, it was much more than that, sex-love perhaps, but it is true he didn't attend to, even discover, the fullness of her wants and needs, and this is a good reason for guilt and reparation, for trying better now there is a next time. He has experienced other ways and combinations of sex and love: loving friendship, love without sex, love without much sex, love in the hope of sex, sex without love, sex over fantasies and representations, and love-sex adapted to an ageing body and preoccupied lives. He is surprised how much he craves for sexual intimacy and pleasure as an old man. He is surprised how much this 'sex' (which is a gift but not in general a given) continues to mean something quite specific, of the past and now lost for ever: the responsiveness of a woman to his desire and the same woman's desire which kindles his, a quickness just like hers. Does this aching absence mean that they are still in fact together?

HOW I STARTED AND HOPE TO CONTINUE

I started young on the road to discovering those pleasures on your own, hide bound by guilt of the Catholic faith. Those teenage gropings; going nearly all the way coming on the outside as we all seemed to agree was OK.

Then contraception was what we rebelled on; us progressive teenage catholic boys, jacking in that old fashioned guilt trip in the late sixties.

Sex was what pushed me out of the faith and into the seventies with a number of mutually lustful relationships alongside a growing political awareness of the socialist feminist variety which suited the sexual liberation.

Sex became passionate love and spread into caring respect and steady girlfriends who were feminist equal and giving in the relationship and in bed.

Long term fatherhood affected that sexual drive in a good way. Responsible sex led from cap to vasectomy without any loss of libido; though pain had been shared for the relief of worrying about contraception.

So sexuality and love swim together in my life. Slowing down as I age the process of caring with respect, gives sex its fillip and excitement.

Still exploring ways of seduction play within our busy lives remains that fabulous feeling where exchanging our interests' ideas warmth and affection.

This has sustained our relationship through loss of parents, difficulties of parenthood, and the changes ageing brings.

Our timing has to be right. Sometimes unexpected surprises lurk round the corner especially on holidays and relaxed weekend breaks.

I find keeping separate networks and interests and lots of good yoga help keep the spark of sex and love alive and long may that remain the case.

Masturbation

I got off to a bad start with sex. Around the time I stared high school aged 13, puberty and the rush of sexual urges completely overwhelmed me and I became a furious masturbator. Of course I know now that this was not at all unusual and that most of my friends were almost certainly pleasuring themselves as often as possible too. But at the time, no one I knew ever talked about it except in very derogatory terms. There was no sex education at school and my only source of information was derived from a booklet my mother gave me when she discovered a stash of *Playboy* and *Penthouse* magazines under my mattress. This rather old-fashioned publication warned of the numerous dangers of "self-abuse" which included fatigue, nervousness, and, if carried on for too long or too frequently, an inability to form "normal" sexual relationships later in life.

The result was I came to regard my masturbation as like a shameful addiction. I wanted to stop but couldn't and after a time I began to develop unpleasant symptoms after each masturbatory episode like headaches, trembling and a general feeling of being unwell. This went on throughout my teen years and although I did manage to function reasonably well socially I tended to be rather withdrawn.

When I started dating I was concerned that my years of secret masturbation were going to stop me from having sexual relations. In fact, this is exactly what happened at the beginning. Whenever my partner touched my penis or whenever I tried to insert my penis into my girlfriend's vagina I would lose my erection. To my partner I explained this away as me being afraid of an unwanted pregnancy but really I was convinced that this was my masturbatory payback. I just had so much misinformed baggage around sex that the normal performance anxieties a young man feels the first few times got hugely amplified.

Eventually, I found I could have penetrative sex but for quite a long while, probably until my late 20s early 30s the feelings of anxiety around partner sex remained. I never told any of my girlfriends about my masturbatory experiences, nor anyone else for that matter, and although I had learned that my early ideas about this were wildly mistaken, the rotten physical feelings I experienced after masturbation persisted.

There was no breakthrough moment in my process of sexual maturation. I talked about my problem with the woman I later married and she helped me work through a lot of things including my very narrow ideas about what sex is. I had some assistance from psychotherapists too at one point. Nowadays, I can have a wank and feel no sense of shame about it at all though I do feel a mild guilt that I still get off on what is essentially an objectification of young women's bodies. Also, the negative physical feelings continue though much reduced.

My Changing Sexuality

I suppose my fear of shame and humiliation has kept me from admitting my sexual failure. That fear probably comes from what the adolescent peer group did to me between my ages of 12-16 after being sent to a single-sex, state boarding school after the death of my mother.

I remember that peer group as a gang of wolves, always staring at you, always sniffing out any suggestion of softness or hurt and savagely pouncing on 'weakness'. I wanted to avoid laughter and ridicule being hurled at me so I boasted, desperately tried to fit in and invented or elaborated success stories with girls.

But at 70 I don't need to go on being regulated by my fear of ridicule. Even though I live in a hyper-sexualised culture in the U.K. in 2010 and am occasionally turned on by women's cleavages and bare midriffs, I've discovered what a mutually trusting, senior, male peer group feels like and it doesn't have any connection with that 1950s one.

So here goes; I can't get it up any longer. I can't maintain a firm, erect penis. I want to publicly share my farewell to penetrative sex, to heterosexual dreams, to being too orgasm-focused. This has created a barrier to relating to my partner in a different way.

Now I want a sexual relationship that is much more other-centred, part of learning to put my partner's sensual skin pleasures first. However I'm still in transition, perhaps I always will be, moving away from penetrative sex to the affection-led delight of holding, cuddling, caressing and touching.

I've been struggling over the last 10 years to simply BE within this reciprocal, slow touching and caressing. Sometimes the masturbatory fantasy of past conquest and performance get in the way. In my imagination I sometimes re-visit past relations and sites of fucking on cliffs, in the heather on Mull one balmy Easter, in hotel beds that still make me cling on to the intensity of past performances. But then I remind myself of my present reality of loss, of my inability to do penetrative sex.

Perhaps my sexual changes, not sexual failure, have opened up new spaces, within which I can learn more about bringing intimacy and sensual touching closer together. Perhaps I don't need to be so heterosexually driven into performance sex in my head so that I can play more mischievously with circling my fingers around the hollow dell at the bottom of my partner's back?

CHAPTER 19

Ending the Group

AM I AGEING? AM I CHANGING?

Coming to the meeting today was a little downbeat. The community centre was being used as a polling station; the woman in charge of the hall was upbeat, and welcoming, offering warmth and cups as surprises. The room was drab, blue industrial carpet, dull pink walls, a solitary table, even an interwar fireplace.

We gathered slowly, two could not come, one would come later in the afternoon, and two were getting on half an hour late. We three started slowly, the others joined. The meeting was less joyous, more functional and focused than usual. I paid attention, oddly used my laptop for the first time at the meetings, and tried to listen. So this is where the last meeting is to be, in a side room of a community centre used on a polling day.

The problems of editing the book, now becoming "the e-book", were efficiently resolved, whilst all the time wondering is this the last meeting, and also whilst worrying about the politics of work elsewhere. The *most active* and the *most passive* moment(s).

These memory work meetings have carried me over the last ten years or less. They have cradled and cradle me as I age, and change in ageing. Since the first meeting I have experienced direct ageism, perhaps for the first time; people seem sometimes confused by my activity. I should be **slowing**, slowing down. With them, that is, the meetings, and the men there, I have watched and felt my ageing and ageing body with curiosity and comfort, imaging the time of being *really old*.

(Now) I am in an old people's home, I am 89, my glasses have gone missing, I am pissed off. It is pretty caring here, and the puddings are tasty!

The first meeting used the theme "A time when you were conscious of your age". Now, fifteen meetings later, I am in a time when I am conscious of my age all the time. I am grateful for both these precious experiences and, to *you* who made them.

REFLECTIONS ON MY TIME IN THE GROUP

Reading back over my written work leaves me with mixed feelings. On the one hand there are stories there that move me, even now, to read; on the other hand there seem to be recurring themes which slightly disturb me. Sometimes the moving and the disturbing are the same.

I never consciously thought through any of my stories – or even what I would write about, before writing and always put it out of my mind until the point when I actually came to pick up my pen on the day. Sometimes this left me feeling disappointed after the event: that I hadn't mentioned this or that; or that I had chosen this particular set of experiences rather than that, or that I seemed to be revisiting certain recurring themes without realising it. Sometimes I felt very embarrassed.

What is clear is that I always went into the meetings very much 'men-and-masculinity-aware' – or at least that's how it felt. Thus, my treatment of each topic seems to be not only self-reflexive but self-analytic – and always particularly masculinity-conscious from the start. This suggests that, at this level at least, much of my writing *had* actually been thought through without my realising it - not so much the actual events themselves, but the ways that I selected and approached each event, the details within and the font of ideas that I tapped into in order to do this.

It is clear now that two themes come through more than any other: those of my early childhood and those to do with being bullied and feeling vulnerable. The latter, I think, is more important to me than I had realised at the time.

My early family life says a lot about the effects of poverty, including a poverty of outlook. I refer to my parents' naïve inability to prepare us adequately for the social world that we were entering. In fact they kept us as children for as long as they possibly could, even after we had left home. My father was profoundly damaged emotionally and (privately) a terrible and humiliating bully. All this left me with the enduring feeling of never having qualified as a 'proper' (i.e. adequately 'masculine') boy, feelings which were intensified by the taunts, the jeering and the bullying of other boys (I am reminded again of being sent to school in my sister's 'girls'' jeans with the zip up the side).

It is not that I didn't have friends so much that I always felt myself to be at risk of being overwhelmed by others, something that happened regularly and which gnawed my confidence away. 'Birds', I was later told, 'love to peck at ripe fruit' – and they certainly did. So I have always been (and remain) extremely sensitive: an acute observer of the moods of others; very awkwardly gendered and, most significantly perhaps, a seasoned believer that masculinity was something 'out there', external to me, that had to be learned and practised if one was to get by. Much later in life it became transformed into a subject in its own right, one that could be observed, analysed and better understood, thus (at last) achieving a kind of eccentric and detached mastery over it. A typically 'masculine' solution? Maybe it's not for me to say?

I have learned (painfully) from various encounters in the group that the momentum that sometimes builds up in me when travelling unthinkingly and too hastily from the depths of my unconscious despair to the heights of my (often considerable) enthusiasm, can come across as an attempt on my own part to overwhelm and even intimidate others. I wish it wasn't so. This is very much a reflection of what I always felt others did to me so I know I must be much more careful about this.

But I have also learned that good men – such as those in this group, who can open up so candidly and share and talk about their experiences and their feelings – are truly worth their weight in gold. This is revealing, for me, of a different kind of strength, the strength that can be found in frankness when coupled with genuine kindness, and the confidence that can come in time from learning to be candid and honest with oneself as well as others.

BEING "M" AND SAYING GOODBYE

This is a memory of the future. It was the last time he was able to come to the group. The previous time had just been too much, even getting to and getting on the train and the plane had been a major difficulty, getting off was even worse. And then there was the exorbitant cost, with these new even higher green taxes! But it was such a relief that unusually everyone was able to be there, by some fluke even Ray was visiting the UK and was able to come.

The beginning was full of matter of fact statements of worsening health problems, incontinence laced with tears of sadness and joy. Two of the partners had further health problems, sex was totally off the agenda, some of the old "communication" difficulties had not been resolved. Children had their own crises.

They discussed at length, for over an hour, whether they should spend time, "waste time", writing on what seemed likely to be his last visit to the group. In the end it was agreed that the topic should be "Being a man travelling/in transit". As often the topic could be interpreted in several different ways. He thought before writing that he would simply focus on the practicalities and the experience of travelling from there to here. In the event he found himself writing about <u>not knowing</u> what a man is, <u>not knowing</u> what being a man is, and <u>not knowing</u> the being called a man. He wrote about the first time he had realised that it was possible to simultaneously acknowledge being a man, and yet at the same time the possibility of not being a man, how he had written snippets of a novel about waking up one day and finding he wasn't a man anymore AND about a strange idea that it was not necessary to have people defined as men.

He looked around and was pleased it was a comfortable room with bright sofas and easy chairs, a soft carpet, spring brightness through the windows, and the low hum of traffic, just like the group itself.

After the writing, they <u>read out</u> their stories in the usual way. The theme of "In transit" brought up many different memories, some about loss, approaching death, saying goodbye, fathers, mothers, lovers, political change, resistance, and being bloody awkward, and so on.

After the stories, they analysed, or rather half-analysed, them. The archive had worked! It was already half-analysed. From now he would have to contribute to making sense – or not – of the memories without the warm comfort and physically together support of the men (or not?) in the group.

Sadly, it was now time to end and leave.

He thanked them all individually, joined in a collective hug, kissed them all, and put his coat on ready to go.

As they all moved towards the door to go, the door eased open itself, and in shuffled the other David (who had only come to the group twice), followed just behind by another ex-member of the group whose name he couldn't even remember (and who had come only once). "Sit down", they said in perfect unison, we need to begin again.

CHAPTER 20

Reflections: Opening Out on Ageing, Politics and Men

Vic Blake and David Jackson

As our Memory Work group moves into its final stages in late 2014, those of us who remain are starting to reflect on what has passed during its thirteen year history. Perhaps some of us are wondering what, if anything, we have achieved working together as ageing men now that we have all reached our late 60s/70s. Have the combined processes of talking, writing, reading, commenting and critiquing really helped us to think and behave differently as men in our personal relations and particularly in our gender relations? Has any of this made any difference?

It is true that as we reflect on and try to understand our pasts as males more clearly and more critically, the dynamic interactions between our individual life histories and the wider shifts in gender and sexual politics over the last 50 to 60 years come into sharper focus. And as we look back, individually and collectively, we are increasingly reminded that time is running out, even more so after the recent, sudden and deeply saddening death of one of our group. Perhaps inevitably, then, our sense of our own physical and emotional vulnerabilities has become increasingly important to us so that health concerns have become a more pressing feature of our discussions. As one of the group wrote,

> It's true that with medication things are much better now and I have had no accidents for a year or more. Yet my body is no longer the one I was in my forties. It is ageing. I am ageing, which is more difficult to realise.

Another member of the group has recently been struggling to cope with hearing aid problems, especially concerning telephone use and the build-up of wax in his ears, respiratory problems and chest infections, skin cancer and skin graft operations and blurred vision. These physical and emotional struggles have made this group member much more aware of his own limitations and boundaries, in particular in relation to his participation in the memory work group – so much so that in March 2014 he sent an email around the group which read:

> First I want to acknowledge that I can't keep on doing a 10-4 commitment to this group. Instead I'm trying to forge new, realistic limits for myself, and I hope for others in this group. Now I can manage the morning session (say, 3-4 hours) but I need to rest and sleep in the afternoon.

Others have had to cope variously with the traumatic effects of breakdown, prostate cancer, chronic pain and chest infections and more, as well as with the emotional, health and physical needs of loved-ones. This has also brought issues to do with self-caring and caring for others increasingly to the fore.

The work of the group has therefore developed so as to take account of these issues. Our work has been an attempt to produce to a greater or lesser extent an anti-ageist and anti-sexist space, but one which has also been nurturing and caring in a way that is unusual in the dominant forms of men's relations with others. Indeed this is a sentiment that we think our recently-lost member would very much have wanted to express and emphasise.

SETTING OUR WORK INTO A BACKGROUND OF GENDER AND SEXUAL POLITICS

In the 1950s and early 1960s, the UK operated under an extremely polarised, binary system of gender relations as it settled down again after the shifts and disruptions of the Second World War (Segal, 1990). This was, generally-speaking, typified by a rigid segregation of male wage-workers operating exclusively in the public sphere (although many working class women continued to work in factories), and female, unpaid, domestic workers in the private sphere. The legacies of that gendered, binary system still partly inform the changing meanings of gender and sexual relations in the UK today. Its traces can be clearly seen in the essentialist framework (Stoller, 2005) surrounding the gendered division of labour to be found in family care. An ideology of separate spheres is still clearly discernible where men are seen primarily as breadwinners outside the house and where women take on the bulk of family caregiving inside the family home (Hanlon, 2009).

Underpinning this male breadwinner/female caregiver division of labour one can still discern the legacy of the nineteenth century, gendered assumption that men and women are 'naturally' suited to their different and unequal spheres

(Thompson, 2005; Kimmel, 1997). This gave rise to the distorted belief that it was 'natural' for women to be caregivers and 'unnatural' and possibly 'deviant' (Thompson, 2005) for men to be caregivers. This supposedly 'natural' and essentialised divide between men's and women's work became more sharply questioned within Second Wave feminism in the UK from the late 1960s and early 1970s onwards. With the gendered and sexual disruptions of gay liberation, feminism, and the queering of gender relations came a wider destabilising of British men's conventional social status and positioning. Some men's traditional centre stage positions as main breadwinners, providers and heads of family households were in the process of being undermined. The rise of male unemployment, de-industrialisation and other changes in occupational structures, along with feminist challenges particularly around domestic violence and sexual abuse, were beginning to destabilise the habitual ways of being a man. Many, but not all, men were resistant to this and some began to react positively and to embrace change. One of our members writes, for example, of his experiences as a young man when he offered to help out in the typing pool for a month as a Dictaphone typist:

> I remember feeling hugely proud of myself that I could do this and that I could surprise people out of their complacency about gender expectations and their expectations of me. The other women in the all-female pool subjected me to their ribald humour for a while, but it was short-lived and afterwards we soon just got on with the job in hand. In fact we enjoyed one another's company. Male colleagues, however, who just happened to make up all of the actual letter-*writers*, were much more sustained in their reactions and, apart from some of the more senior managers, kept up the raucous behaviour, the jibes and the comments, the corny puns, the 'Sweetie'-this and the 'Darling'-that – as well as the occasional touchings-up, almost for the duration. And the more they did it the more pathetic I knew they were.

Key transitions in gender relations and sexual politics, such as Second Wave feminism and the Stonewall riot in gay politics, affected members of our group in various ways, even if not always consciously, and have directly or indirectly influenced many of our stories. Collectively, sometimes individually, these stories tell a story of struggle and endeavour, of a desire for change and of the difficult hurdles which continue to stand in the way.

MISCONCEPTIONS ABOUT AGEING MEN

The inevitable fact of our ageing requires that we address a number of misunderstandings about ageing men. Stagnant representations and media stereotypes of ageing men as miserable or 'grumpy old men', 'dirty, old men', 'boring, old farts', and so on, do no justice at all to older men generally, and they are certainly not borne out by the energy and vitality of the various representations of ageing men that are to be found in our stories.

Older men aren't worn-out, passive, static subjects. Although from a distance their lives may seem to be hardly moving, they are in fact characterised by rapid shifts and changes in their bodies and their personal circumstances and forcing, through adaptation, the need for ambivalent and newly-emerging selves. Frequent life events, such as severe illness, breakdown, hospitalisation, loss of job security and status, or the infirmity or death of a spouse, force adjustments in later life. Alongside these uneven processes of ageing and bodily adaptations go changes in the meanings and experiences of masculinity. Only when we conceive of ageing men as people in constant motion and movement do we begin to appreciate more fully the subjectivities of ageing men and begin to catch further glimpses of the surprising richness of their complex and contradictory lives.

Our inevitable ageing processes frequently provoke a confrontation with social change. The loss of physical function already referred to can destabilise masculine identities and so may stir up a critical re-assessment of who and what we are as men in a shifting and sometimes bewildering world. The collapse of former social power and status, economic productivity, bodily strength, sexual potency that ageing men encounter in old age weakens some ageing men's attachments to patriarchal relations (Silver, 2003). Admittedly, other ageing men cling on to old, defensive routines and identities and sometimes refuse to acknowledge their increasing fallibility and fragility. However, these changes and losses can also begin to open emancipatory possibilities for other men in moving beyond obsessive concerns with work success, ambition, competitive individualism and an over-emphasis on selfish sexualities as a means of sustaining their belief in their masculinity. It has also been suggested that some ageing men can develop a critical, self-reflexiveness regarding how power operates in gender relations (Meadows and Davidson, 2006). From this innovatory perspective on old age a tentative movement can sometimes be discerned, in some ageing men, towards an "ageing men's anti-patriarchal standpoint" (Calasanti and Slevin, 2006).

Similarly, the memory work group has experienced many different shifts and contradictions in its own varied processes of change. Change has never been linear or hierarchical but erratic and fragmentary and the possibilities it opens up are not given or set in stone. So these processes of change are more about a zigzagging disorder than any fantasy of a coherent 'onwards-and-upwards' (or downwards) progression. However, as we see it, the group has gone through four main processes of change; these are not discrete but which overlap with each other and come into play variously, either concurrently or at different times. These are:

- Awakening to gendered difference
- Developing an awareness of gender equality and respect
- Understanding the past and imagining the future differently
- Critical exposure and political change

AWAKENING TO GENDERED DIFFERENCES

Our personal, often fumbling awakenings to gender-awareness are re-visited throughout the stories of the group, in seemingly 'safe' accounts relating, for example, to clothes or hair or food, as well as in more 'difficult' areas such as those relating to sex or violence or power. Here one of our stories speaks of the beginnings of these processes of change and of our movements through an extended, often contradictory, process of personal re-positioning and reconstruction and of later political change:

> One evening in the early seventies when I was twenty-four I was watching "Top of the Pops" with some friends, when I said "That Tony Blackburn – he's just like an old woman."
>
> Then CRASH! I received a slap on the head from a female friend. "Don't say things like that you sexist."
>
> I realised I wasn't as right on with women as I thought.
>
> That incident stays with me to this day as a turning point for me.
>
> That slap knocked some awareness into me that made me develop a self-awareness policeman inside me I still use today.

This story highlights a world of everyday, casual, and often unconscious sexism displayed by many men in the years before and during the seismic changes of

Second Wave feminism in the late 1960s and early 1970s in the UK. At twenty-four the writer is still learning about the frustrations and anger of women and about men's reluctance and resistance to change. We see how Jane's slap provokes the start of a gender uncertainty in the writer when he says: "I realised that I wasn't as right on with women as I thought." This was to be a critical "turning point in his life and marked the beginnings of a gendered re-framing of who he was. As he says, the slap helped him to develop a 'self-awareness policeman inside me that I still use today."

In this very different account a brush with a highly institutionalised expression of masculine power changes the writer forever:

> We were all billeted in a barracks, a kind of large dormitory hall with a screen door on the exit which we were warned not to let bang shut if we decided to leave the building after lights out. Anyway, I had an asthma attack on the second night we were there and decided I had to go outside to catch my breath. In my hurry to leave I let the screen door swing shut behind me and it closed with a loud bang which attracted the attention of a NCO who happened to be standing nearby. This fellow came over and after telling me off decided I needed to be taught a lesson. So he ordered me to jog double time around the camp perimeter.

When he tries to explain why he couldn't do this he is told, "to shut the fuck up" and his punishment is doubled to two circuits round the camp. He was very lucky, he says, not to have been hospitalised as a result. The life-changing extent of this experience becomes evident later on:

> I think I have deliberately avoided ever being put in such a position again in my life. I have also been very reluctant to exercise coercive power over others which I've mainly had to do as an employer or manager … . It seems to me this kind of power is a kind of weakness when you have to use force to get your way.

An unwitting moment of discrimination and a brutal exercise of physical power, one exercised by a man over women, the other by a man over another man; both writers speak of the diminishing effects of such practices, for victim and perpetrator, and both are determined to learn from this and to change for the better. Learning from past experience and leaving established gender assumptions behind is a common theme in these writings, but this is not always easy as not everyone has had change impressed upon them quite so dramatically as this.

DEVELOPING AN AWARENESS OF GENDER EQUALITY AND RESPECT

To begin with, many of our stories, and the incidents and experiences they contained, were remembered uncritically and often revealed a tacit acceptance of conventional masculinities and assumptions. As one group member puts it:

> I know that down the years this (memories and feelings of early subordination) has made it difficult for me to see my own power so that I have imagined myself to be power-less when in fact I may have been in a very powerful situation.

Such early personal blinkering to gender and age issues created for some a kind of collusion with taken for granted, patriarchal or ageist norms that might well have prevented a gendered and anti-ageist awareness from developing in our memory work. On the other hand, the fact that these particular stories are selected and written down in the first place, and the very context in which this happens, suggests some prior level of awareness of or concern with at least some of these issues.

Still, one cannot afford to ignore the fact that alternative readings of these stories are always possible and can show them to be much more complex and multi-layered than at first appears – or indeed than the writer intends. Thus one writer warns us about too much complacency in these matters, considering what a feminist perspective might have made of our memory work:

> One feminist reading of these stories might conclude that they show how unconscious many men are of the power which they themselves exercise, especially in relationships with women, unconscious too of the systemic nature of male privilege.

But, then, the stories themselves are only one part of the process of memory work; what went on after reading and during the following discussion was always intensely critical of any lingering sexist or ageist assumptions and attitudes and of those institutional contexts and cultural currents which continue to perpetuate these.

DEVELOPING AN AWARENESS OF GENDER EQUALITY AND RESPECT FOR WOMEN

Thus the memory-writing process, combined with the critical discussion which accompanied it, helped us to cast a more critical eye over our pasts and urged us to challenge for ourselves our taken-for-granted assumptions concerning our unconsciously-gendered life stories. Accordingly, one member, writing on domesticity, begins with the ignorance and selfishness of his youth and then goes on to show how those early tendencies and crude insights became disrupted and overturned during a lifetime:

> When I was young I avoided all household tasks like the plague. Somehow they had become associated with a dull, tedious and apparently meaningless world that belonged to adults – especially my parents. Domesticity seemed to 'bring you down' even though at another level I fantasised about a better life with a better house which was bigger and more luxurious but which was also clean, tidy, warm, comfortable etc., completely failing to appreciate the reality that such things actually depended on functioning levels of tedious domesticity being applied to them.

Ironically, it was when he was in the army that these assumptions first began to change:

> There I was expected – on pain of severe punishment – to wash and iron clothes meticulously, make my bed, keep my bed space and room spotlessly clean and tidy, and so on.

Thereafter he speaks of needing to look after himself, when he went to college for example, but the most significant transition comes after he gets married and when he is also looking after his first son. Until then he had been concerned with his own individual responses to domestic labour in terms of 'personal pride' and 'independent self-respect' but in his newly married state he begins to become more other-directed and more gender-aware, conscious of the need for a more equal partnership. What his partner was doing for him and his son was something he felt unable to ignore, commenting that;

> ... it became a matter of personal pride that I shouldn't need or expect a woman to take on primary domestic responsibility for me or my son.

The possibility, however, – that this may have been in part a control mechanism or a masculine defence against the feelings of vulnerability that can accompany dependency, was not lost on the group. On the other hand, the writer expresses some frustration about being typecast as 'typically masculine' by women who may themselves be less-than-adaptable when it comes to sharing in 'more typically male' domestic activity:

> I am alright with this up to a point. I do take a certain pleasure, for example, in knowing that I can re-fit a kitchen, glaze a window or mend a kettle, and I accept my partner's inability to do such things, but sometimes I feel typecast as typically 'male/masculine' by this and by her never making the attempt to learn or take responsibility for some of these things.

This writer senses that personal change is a complex, difficult and multi-layered process – and one which is not only down to him alone. Changing gender attitudes is a process which has significant implications for us as men – of course it has. But it often has very significant implications for others as well. For example, friends and loved ones of either sex may cling on to their own personal investments in the gender order and so may not always find these changes so easy to take on board. This would seem to suggest that, at the end of the day, we may need to be our own judge as to whether we have changed and, if so, whether that change has occurred for the better. And this presupposes that we have grown sufficiently in confidence to be able to make that judgement.

UNDERSTANDING THE PAST AND IMAGINING THE FUTURE DIFFERENTLY

Bob Pease (2000, p. 75) observes that "Remembering is not only an attempt 'to understand the past better but to understand it differently'". Some of the group found that as they changed over the thirteen years of meetings that their viewpoints also shifted. As a result they weren't just recalling the past more clearly but they were remembering it through a different lens or prism. An example of this critical movement is one of our group's reflections on parenting and fathering:

> I am struck by the way that my own stories progress in terms of reflection and thoughtfulness. I wrote an early story about my relation with my father ... which now seems quite naïve and too simple by half, a bit self-justificatory perhaps and not altogether fair to my parents, especially **** [his father].

Much later the same writer is moved to write a second story about fathering in which he observes:

> For long time, my self-narrative of parenting has been almost completely negative: a story of failure and a practice of reparation, trying to be a better father and grandparent, the second time round. Two recent events have however punctured this 'bad father' narrative. The first, watching my son as a father: a dextrous multitasking and loving performance if even there was one, and he an academic too! The second, an important discussion with my daughter while we were gardening together – pruning red currants and carting compost! – who spoke her mind about the paralysing effect on herself that my own prolonged grieving and guilt and silence have produced. She has made me realise that the problem today isn't so much being a bad parent, as the grief and guilt itself that has stopped me remembering and sharing the positive parts (and in a more measured way the difficulties) in a more open and loving way.

Others, too, have sought to reconsider/re-evaluate their past through writing later stores (see the 'Peeing' section, for example).

All cultures have their dominant key narratives that direct (often unfairly) its members' cultural positions and viewpoints vis-à-vis one another. One example in the above second story on fathering draws our attention to the residual power in our culture of a prevailing 'bad father' narrative which commonly surfaces, for example, in warnings to children such as, 'Wait till your father gets home!' – even while fathering attitudes and practices are changing for the better.

In this story, the writer begins to recognise the inappropriateness of his earlier representations of himself and his own father. Although his selection of memories still point to a story of some family neglect ("... there was 'always something else'"), he is now able to weigh up his memories more accurately and to do greater justice to himself. So he now perceives that, "our babies did have quite a lot of my attention", and he can now permit himself to recognise that he shared some of the domestic labour around baby-work like 'changing nappies, taking turns with bottles.'

From this fresh standpoint, assisted by memory work processes, the writer is able to see that his preoccupation with grief after the sudden death of his wife had paralysed him in his relations with his daughter and "had stopped me remembering and sharing the positive parts ... in a more open and loving way." Having questioned the 'bad father' narrative and watching his son's "dextrous multitasking and loving performance" as a young father he is able now to recall earlier events in a different mode, moving away from his earlier critical self-narrative of parenting that had been "almost completely negative; a story of failure and a practice of reparation."

Another writer, however, finds this process of moving on from past mistakes to be far more difficult:

> Naïve and unworldly, I didn't know where to begin and so made a real hash of it while desperately wanting to learn from [his father's] mistakes and be a kind and loving – truly fulfilling father to my own children. Instead, and in spite of myself, I became angry, selfish, domineering and even heavy-handed, just like him. *'The bee stings and then dies itself,'* I wrote many years later in a poem.

This writer does talk of changing, of being more reflexive and less hard on himself, but it is clear from this that the process of change is never complete. We are, and to some extent we remain, our past. We can only become more than that by learning how to forge a different and better future for ourselves, and others.

CRITICAL EXPOSURE AND POLITICAL CHANGE

So is political change the object of memory work? In part, maybe it is and one member of our group offers the following thoughts on what this means for him:

> I don't see memory work as primarily about reflecting on one's own life; that is one of millions. I remain much more interested in changing men generally rather than seeing the memory group as a question of individual therapeutic change. This is a political position – the search for the loss of ego towards for the great struggle, or if you prefer the Great Struggle.

I think all of us would agree with this emphasis on wider political change as opposed to a more narrow concern with purely individual or 'therapeutic' change. But if we believe in the mantra of the personal being the political – and especially if we consider the personal as being only really meaningful within the context of one's relationships, then clearly there is a case to be argued. But memory work can also make an important contribution to the furtherance of wider political change for men and for women, as well as for ourselves as ageing men, so how might it do this?

By its nature, memory work has the potential to increase the possibility for individual agency and for change as we critically reflect upon our own past experiences and learn to re-evaluate these in the light of the experiences of the group and with the help and support of the group. In some cases, almost inevitably, previously 'undigested' material will be re-visited and re-appraised, helping us to come to terms with some of its troubling effects and to change direction. As we have seen, some of the writing on 'fathering' shows this quite clearly. But the final example shows that sometimes an acknowledgement and acceptance of what happened in the past is all that is possible, creating the potential for a different kind of 'moving on'.

In the kind of work that we do, then, there are some things which come to light which are *not* so easy to re-evaluate, and which are not so easily tempered by the balanced or more nuanced view. Certain fathering (and presumably mothering) practices, for example, may not be so easily re-interpreted as being 'good enough' so that in memory work, as in therapy (although they are different), we at times find ourselves confronting issues which are *not right,* either within ourselves or within others. Violence and abuse are obvious examples; the writer who was persistently sexually abused by older female colleagues at work being one case in point. Another writes of a trip to the theatre when:

> the lights down and some way into the spectacle, he took my hand and drew it down his penis.

These are not just personal issues because they speak of behaviour which is unacceptable *per se* and of an urgent need for change – attitude change, yes, but also wider political change which goes way beyond the purely personal and involves us all. When issues such as violence and sexual abuse become institutionalised within our social structures and are embedded in existing cultures of masculinity, they become a palpable and disturbing presence for all of us and create an urgent need for meaningful political change.

So, although the process of change begins for us with making visible to ourselves and others how we became the men that we are, it is through our deepening understanding of ageing processes and of masculinities that we can also can become aware of how to *un*-make and/or move on from the past and from those emotional investments and practices that encouraged our clumsy and sometimes damaging commitment to dominant masculine identities in the first place. If we can learn to understand how it is and why it was that we actively bound ourselves into a particular, masculine culture and society, then real change becomes possible, not just for ourselves but for others with whom we come into contact. When *we* change, others have to deal with the implications of this. But this process necessarily involves degrees of intimacy, self-examination and critical self-exposure that most men (arguably) would find daunting to say the very least:

> There seem to be rules about this kind of stuff, rules that have dark origins that are dangerous to explore.

And, from an early story ...

> I am resisting adding this, but dammit I trust you. As a youngish teenager I found a woman's swimsuit that my mother never wore. I put it on occasionally when I was at home alone. Once I did it when my sister was there and went to show her. As I remember it there was no hint of condemnation from her. I look back on it as an important moment of trust between us.

Where does this take us? Trying to effect change purely at the political level raises the risk of this becoming disingenuous and hypocritical if this is not equally borne out in our personal lives. If real and meaningful change in our gender attitudes, beliefs and practices is to come about, then we have to be able to practice what we preach, to be able to show irrefutably that it can be done, that it works and that it evidences a better way forward for others. We do still, of course, have to continue to struggle for change at the macro level – at the political, structural, economic and ideological levels, but we have to do much more than this. The personal and the political are inseparable and so have to go hand in hand.

So it is not overly simplistic to suggest that, if only men could learn to trust one another more, then there might be less conflict in the world. We know from our own experience that simply learning to trust one another as *men* - let alone being prepared to publically reveal one's most intimate inner secrets to a listening circle of those other men – was at first a frightening prospect for some of our group. After all, this is not what *men* do and we all knew only too well the potential and considerable risks involved for us in doing so. And yet somehow we managed this. The change over time in the nature, the intimacy and the depth – and the tenderness of some of our stories testifies not only to the very real presence of this fear early on, but also to the extent to which the group's members learned to face up to it, to overcome it and to trust one another. In doing so I believe we really have become changed and better men.

Something which, perhaps, testifies to this—but which might easily be glossed over as insignificant by some is the extent to which we were able *at all*, as a group of up to ten men, to meet in the way that we did for an entire day at a time; men are hardly best known for their spontaneous, amiable and selfless sense of cooperation. Yet, in contrast, we found ourselves able not only to work through our agenda productively but also to do so in a climate of critical support, without any kind of hierarchical structure and without competition or conflict entering into the equation - or at least not to any appreciable degree. In this setting a deepening trust and intimacy, as two sides of the same coin, were able to grow.

In the account below, written in the later days of the group, one of our members writes movingly of a time when he was overcome by feelings of guilt and shame. Like so many boys of his age his early teenage years found him puzzled and overwhelmed by sexual urges and he became, as he puts it, 'a furious masturbator'. Later, when his mother finds a stash of girly magazines under his mattress, she gives him a booklet which warns him:

> ... of the numerous dangers of "self-abuse" which included fatigue, nervousness, and, if carried on for too long or too frequently, an inability to form "normal" sexual relationships later in life.

In a culture of profound guilt and shame about masturbation, his discovery by his mother must have felt shameful enough. Unable to talk about it he was left in the dark, so this new and frightening cloud of mis-information became a damaging self-fulfilling prophecy in its own right. His quite normal adolescent feelings and coping mechanisms now began to feel like some 'shameful addiction', something which he couldn't kick but which now made him withdrawn, frightened and ill:

> I wanted to stop but couldn't and after a time I began to develop unpleasant symptoms after each masturbatory episode like headaches, trembling and a general feeling of being unwell. This went on throughout my teen years and although I did manage to function reasonably well socially I tended to be rather withdrawn.

He becomes so fearful that this is going to damage his future sexual relationships that when he finally does find a sexual partner this is exactly what happens and he is unable to sustain an erection when touched or trying to engage in penetrative sex – his 'masturbatory payback', as he guiltily describes it. Fortunately, however, he finds someone who is understanding enough to enable him to talk about it and to help him through this.

The collective process of critical exposure, then, is not (and perhaps *should not* be) confined to personal criticism in the negative sense. It would, after all, be impossible for trust to grow in any such a narrowly judgmental environment. Instead our criticism, *while always needing to seek its mark*, has had to be effected within a climate of mutual warmth, care and support, qualities which are not always so readily evident among men. So, while always remaining critical, this process has also helped us in coming to terms more caringly with *ourselves* and our often deeply uncomfortable personal histories, as well as in our relationships with other men and women. In this supportive climate one member is able to write for the first time of his experiences of dressing in women's clothing and of the long-term difficulties involved in coming to terms with this. The social taboos relating to transvestism (a term which is almost entirely reserved for males) are still considerable and damaging and are yet to be adequately addressed in the arena of sexual and gender politics.

Similarly, the process of ageing brings with it its own very intimate issues to do with sexuality that are very often extremely difficult for men to have to have to come to terms with. Does the eventual failure of the phallus, for example, the apparent epicentre of our maleness, therefore spell the end of us as 'Men', as is so widely presumed? Seemingly not! Linn Sandberg (2011) speaks of couples' capacity for transcending this life change and for intimacy and love to continue and flourish in other, sometimes new ways. Another of our writers makes similar observations from his own experience:

> I hate the phrase,' sexual impotence' and I don't intend to use it again. I am now 74 and I want to turn my back on the controlling power of my sexual relations in my earlier years. I don't want to be in charge of who does what to whom, where and how it goes on.

He speaks instead of a new 'non-phallic tenderness' towards his wife, where mutual stroking and a more sensitive awareness of each other's bodies and needs now takes precedence over the more narrow phallic-centred sexuality of his years. Does he miss all that? Perhaps, but at another level it seems not:

> I suspect that some ageing men are contemptuous of Viagra and just want to get rid of all that performance anxiety when they discover they can't get it up anymore. Indeed, I don't want to waste my time worrying about my penile stiffness and hardness.

This raises some profound questions about us as men. Lynne Segal (2013) is but one who writes of how men's relationships (with women) tend to be dominated by their phallic preoccupations. As a group of ageing men, and as we all come closer to the eventuality of this so-called 'loss of sexual function', do we then cease, somehow, to be 'proper men'? Is this the final and decisive act of castration, the ultimate vindication of a lifetime of Oedipal anxiety, the sum of all our fears all wrapped up in the inevitable consequence of growing older?

If memory work has changed us as men, and if it has helped us in certain ways to be 'better', more rounded men, then that change and the potential for growth continues for sure as we grow older. Perhaps, with the benefit of extended experience, and/or (for whatever reason) a lessening dependence upon phallic-based ideas of masculinity in order to sustain our belief in ourselves, then change for older men can become a very positive and enriching experience. Whatever the reader may make of the actual contents of this volume, these thirteen years of collective memory work, of intimacy, trust, tenderness and support from other like-minded men have helped – beyond words – in making this into an attainable reality.

REFERENCES

Calasanti, Toni M. and Slevin, Kathleen F. (2006) *Age Matters: Realigning Feminist Thinking*, New York: Routledge.

Hanlon, Niall (2009) Caregiving masculinities: an exploratory analysis, in Kathleen Lynch, John Baker and Maureen Lyons (eds.) *Affective Equality: Love, Care and Injustice*, Basingstoke: Palgrave Macmillan, pp. 189-198.

Kimmel, D. C. (1979) Life-history interviews of aging, gay men, *International Journal of Aging and Human Development*, 10(3): 239-248.

Meadows, Robert and Davidson, Kate (eds.) (2006) *Maintaining Manliness in Later Life: Hegemonic Masculinities and Emphasised Femininities*, New York: Routledge.

Pease, Bob (2000) *Recreating Men: Postmodern Masculinity Politics*, London: Sage.

Sandberg, Linn (2011) *Getting Intimate: A Feminist Analysis of Old Age, Masculinity and Sexuality*, Linköping: Linköping University Electronic Press.

Segal, Lynne (1990) *Slow Motion: Changing Masculinities, Changing Men*, London: Virago.
Segal, Lynne (2013) *Out of Time: The Pleasures and Perils of Ageing*, London: Verso.
Silver, Catherine (2003) Gendered identities in old age: Towards (de)-gendering?, *Journal of Aging Studies*, 17: 379-397.
Stoller, Eleanor Palo (2005) Theoretical perspectives on caregiving men, in Betty J. Kramer and Edward H. Thompson (eds.) *Men as Caregivers*, New York: Prometheus, pp. 49-64.
Thompson, Edward H. (2005) What's unique about men's caregiving?, in Betty J. Kramer and Edward H. Thompson (eds.) *Men as Caregivers*, New York: Prometheus, pp. 3-19.

www.ingramcontent.com/pod-product-compliance
Lightning Source LLC
Chambersburg PA
CBHW021943290426
44108CB00012B/945